Language Contact and the Germanic Langua

History, archaeology, and human evolutionary genetics provide us with an increasingly detailed view of the origins and development of the peoples that live in northwestern Europe. This book aims to restore the key position of historical linguistics in this debate by treating the history of the Germanic languages as a history of its speakers. It focuses on the role that language contact has played in creating the Germanic languages, between the first millennium BC and the crucially important early medieval period. Chapters on the origins of English, German, Dutch, and the Germanic language family as a whole illustrate how the history of the sounds of these languages provide a key that unlocks the secret of their genesis: speakers of Latin, Celtic, and Balto-Finnic switched to speaking Germanic and in the process introduced a 'foreign accent' that caught on and spread at the expense of types of Germanic that were not affected by foreign influence. The book is aimed at linguists, historians, archaeologists, and anyone who is interested in what languages can tell us about the origins of their speakers.

Peter Schrijver is professor of Celtic languages and culture at the University of Utrecht. He is a historical linguist working on ancient and medieval languages in Europe. His publications include *Studies in British Celtic Historical Phonology* and *Celtic Influence in Old English*.

Routledge Studies in Linguistics

Language Contact and the Origins of the Germanic Languages

Peter Schrijver

LONDON AND NEW YORK

First published 2014 by Routledge

2 Park Square, Milton Park, Abingdon, Oxon OX14 4RN
711 Third Avenue, New York, NY 10017, USA

*Routledge is an imprint of the Taylor & Francis Group,
an informa business*

First issued in paperback 2016

Library of Congress Cataloging-in-Publication Data

Schrijver, Peter.
Language contact and the origins of the Germanic languages / Peter
    Schrijver.
      pages cm. — (Routledge Studies in Linguistics ; 13)
    Includes bibliographical references and index.
  1. Languages in contact.   2. Germanic languages—Etymology.
3. Germanic languages—Grammar, Comparative.   4. Germanic
languages—Grammar, Historical.   I. Title.
    PD582.S37 2013
    430—dc23
    2013017509

ISBN: 978-0-415-35548-3 (hbk)
ISBN: 978-1-138-24537-2 (pbk)

Typeset in Sabon
by Apex CoVantage, LLC

Contents

Preface

This book is written for anyone who wants to know more about the earliest history of one of the most successful language families in the world, both in terms of numbers of speakers and in terms of the ideas expressed by those speakers during the last 1300 years: Germanic. The idea behind this book is that the English, Dutch, and German languages, and indeed the Germanic family as a whole, are founded on the input of people who did not originally speak Germanic but switched to it in the course of time. Additionally, I hope to show how studying language can contribute to our knowledge of the history of its speakers, and in this sense the book is intended not only for an audience of linguists but also for historians and archaeologists. Readers are not required to have any previous knowledge of linguistics, for all important concepts and the methodology of language reconstruction will be explained to them. This does not mean, however, that this book is an easy read throughout. Although I have aimed at maximum clarity, complex matters – and there are some to be found here – cannot be made simpler than they are, although they can be presented more simply than they usually are. It is my hope that anyone with genuine interest in language history and a little bit of time on their hands can understand everything I have written.

I have not striven to present the current consensus on language contact and the rise of the Germanic languages, first of all because there is none and, secondly, because presenting consensus in historical linguistics is a dreary and sterile business. Instead, I have concentrated on full and coherent argumentation regarding the theme of the book, so that readers who agree or disagree with what I write will be able to understand and formulate why. This effort entails that the book is not at all comprehensive: many ideas that over the years have been expressed in print about the origins of the Germanic languages are left unmentioned, not necessarily because I find them incorrect, but because they are not germane to the issues raised in the book.

This book has been long in the making, and I have done my utmost to test the patience of some of my colleagues and of the publisher. There are various reasons for the delay, apart from my inveterate optimism in planning ahead and the fact that academic life itself has a habit of interfering with work. In spite of the crushing weight of published scholarship on the history of the Germanic languages, where an article published in 1870 is usually as relevant as one published last year, there is actually very little accumulated knowledge on which to fall back if one wishes to find out about the role that language contact has played in the early history of the Germanic languages. Another reason for the delay is the vastness and complex nature of the linguistic material involved. Anyone who has tried to master the historical phonologies of Old English or Dutch will know what I am talking about, and the reader will get a bitter taste of it in the chapter about Dutch. By definition, language contact involves more than one language, and in the case of early Germanic, the contact languages lie outside Germanic. Hence, one may spend the best part of one's life studying Germanic philology and not be able to write one sensible word about the theme of this book. Latin, the earliest stages of the Romance languages, Irish, British Celtic, Finnish, and Saami are the contact languages that will make an appearance in this book, and more than a glancing acquaintance with all of them was required in order to assess their contribution to Germanic.

A major advantage of a long gestation period is that it has given me the opportunity to try out, in various talks and in specialist publications, some of the ideas that will be presented here (see in particular Schrijver 2002, 2009, 2011a). All reactions, which varied from matter-of-fact criticism to mild enthusiasm and roaring silence, have been taken on board to the best of my abilities.

My thanks are due to Lisette Gabriëls, who read the manuscript before publication and suggested many improvements, and to Willem Vermeer, who has been my mentor and subsequently my partner in crime in ancient language contact studies.

I. Introduction

1. WHAT THIS BOOK IS AND IS NOT ABOUT

In recent decades, a wealth of scholarly literature about language contact has seen the light of day. Ever since Uriel Weinreich (1953) not only made the study of language contact respectable again but also restored it to a position of central importance in the linguistic enterprise in general, it has become clear that language contact is one of the most important triggers for language change. From among the vast literature on that subject, I wish to mention in particular Thomason and Kaufman (1988) and Thomason (2001), which are influential and eminently accessible general surveys.

This book aims to find out the extent to which language contact has been involved in the emergence of the individual Germanic languages and of the Germanic language family as a whole. Pride of place is given to the origins of English (chapter II), German (chapter III), and Dutch (chapter IV), while the origin of the Germanic family itself as well as the earliest histories of its East, West, and North Germanic branches are the subject of chapter V. Since it is relevant to the origins of English, the origin of Irish is discussed at length in chapter II, section 8.

Since the main interest of the book lies with fundamental structural changes caused by contact, I shall have next to nothing to say about the borrowing of words. Loanwords usually form a thin varnish and do not affect grammar to any noticeable extent, and so it is with the Germanic languages, however packed they may be with loanwords from many sources. Language contact causes structural changes if it affects the sound system (phonology and phonetics) and syntax. For practical reasons, this book is almost completely about sound change rather than syntactic change. That has to do with the time frame it covers and with the nature of the available source material. Because of the emphasis on origins, the chosen time frame is between the first millennium BC (chapter V) and the period spanning late Antiquity and the earliest Middle Ages (approximately the first to eighth centuries AD; chapters II, III, and IV). In this period, contemporary written sources dealing with the languages involved are very scanty, if not altogether absent. Therefore, much of the argument will revolve around reconstructed stages of Germanic languages. This is not necessarily a great disadvantage because the state of the art in the linguistic reconstruction of the Germanic languages is so evolved that there is a wealth of information available, and the methodology used for reconstructing language, the so-called comparative method, is one of the most robust methodologies available to science (see I.3). But this emphasis on reconstruction, and consequently our dependence on the comparative method, does allow a much firmer grasp on the sound systems than on syntax. While the comparative method enables us to reconstruct sound changes (I.3) and the chronological order in which those changes operated (II.4.2), there is no reliable method for reconstructing syntactic changes (II.4.1), let alone putting those changes in a chronological order. For that reason, this book will largely ignore syntactic change and concentrate on sound change through contact.

Although the theme of the book is evidently linguistic, dealing with language contact inevitably entails dealing with communities of speakers of different languages that interact with one another. Since I shall have a lot to say about communities shifting from one language to another, the question arises who those communities were and why they shifted to a new language. Language shift is always the result of strong political or socio-economic pressure, and this is where linguistics and history meet. It is the specific aim of this book to explain how linguistics can contribute to our knowledge of history. I contend that language is one of the most important sources for the history of the 'Dark Ages', the period spanning late Antiquity and the early medieval period.

Since using language to reconstruct history is by no means straightforward, I have been as explicit as possible in explaining the lines of linguistic thought that underpin the conclusions of the book. I have tried to avoid the use of linguistic jargon, and since I do not assume that the reader has any previous knowledge of linguistics, I have explained all concepts and terminology that are necessary in order to follow the line of thought.

2. LANGUAGE CONTACT AND LANGUAGE CHANGE

I follow Thomason and Kaufman (1988) in differentiating between two ways in which languages in contact may influence one another: change through borrowing and change through shift. The difference is best explained from the point of view of a speaker. Let us use the example of someone who speaks English as his mother tongue and is exposed to Welsh because he lives in a community in which Welsh is widely spoken. He might easily adopt Welsh language features in his English, such as words for notions that do not have an English equivalent, e.g. *Eisteddfod*, the name of the most famous Welsh cultural festival. Once he starts doing this, he is changing his

English through borrowing. He has set foot on a slippery slope, which theoretically may lead him to borrow ever more words from Welsh, including words for notions for which English does have an equivalent, and ultimately even for basic vocabulary items, such as words for body parts, the sun and moon, water and fire, and basic verbs of the type 'do, make, go'. In cases of intensive borrowing relations, our English speaker may also adopt structural features, such as pronunciation (think of the characteristically Welsh intonation patterns) and items of Welsh syntax. Essentially, our English speaker is a fully competent speaker of English, who borrows from Welsh irrespective of whether he is almost completely ignorant of Welsh or a fluent speaker of that language. What he does is change English (his own English, that is) by borrowing from Welsh.

Now suppose that our English speaker starts learning Welsh, in the hope of becoming part of the local Welsh community. He experiences what every learner of a second language is faced with: English will interfere with the Welsh he is trying to learn. Whereas Welsh words will be acquired relatively easily, it is much more difficult to adopt a perfect Welsh pronunciation and perfect Welsh syntax. As a result, even a relatively successful learner of Welsh will betray himself as a non-native, in particular because of his English accent and his imperfect ability to master the rules of Welsh syntax. The variety of Welsh that he speaks has arisen as a result of change through shift, that is, because the speaker has shifted from a language he speaks fluently (in this case English) to a language he knows imperfectly (Welsh). His way of not quite mastering Welsh is called *imperfect learning*.

So, by and large, borrowing betrays itself by the introduction of loanwords, to which borrowing of sound structure and syntax may or may not be added, while change through shift betrays itself through the introduction of sound structure and syntax, to which borrowing of words may or may not be added. Borrowing and change through shift are useful concepts that discipline our thinking about language contact, but the model to which those concepts belong is just that: a model. Reality is often more complex. What is actually borrowing may look like shift. Thomason (2001: 11, 80–81) points out that speakers of Montana Salish, in the northwestern United States, for cultural reasons refuse to adopt English loanwords; if English influence on Montana Salish were to betray itself (all speakers are bilingual), it would be through borrowing of sound structure or syntax, not through borrowing of words. So the contact situation would look like change through shift (i.e. speakers changing Montana Salish by shifting from English to Montana Salish) rather than borrowing (i.e. speakers changing Montana Salish by borrowing features from English). That would be an inaccurate account of the real situation, in which speakers of Montana Salish are in the process of shifting to English.

Another complication is that what looks like borrowing may actually be shift. In bilingual Welsh-English communities, the local variety of English often betrays the influence of Welsh intonational patterns: an English stressed syllable adopts low tone, while the immediately following syllable adopts high tone. The phenomenon arose when speakers of Welsh learned English but stuck to Welsh intonation (change through shift). But a native monoglot speaker of English who lives in a bilingual Welsh-English community and is confronted with English spoken with a Welsh accent on a daily basis may well import a Welsh intonational pattern into his own English (change through borrowing). Hence a feature that arose through shift can spread through borrowing.

In view of such complications, my use of the terms *change though shift* and *borrowing* comes with a health warning. In this book, *change through shift* always means that the change started as a result of people who spoke language A becoming bilingual in A and B, and then shifting to language B, in the process introducing elements of A into B. Subsequently, the change that entered B from A may (and usually does) spread through B by borrowing. Nevertheless, I shall take pains to find out which of the two terms (*change through shift* or *borrowing*) is appropriate for the individual cases of change through contact that are discussed throughout the book.

3. LANGUAGE CONTACT IN DEEP TIME

While the literature on language change through contact is vast, it is also one-sided in that it focuses on the collection and analysis of examples for which there is little doubt that a contact situation is involved. Thus, it is possible to study speakers of Scots Gaelic shifting to English, German immigrants in the United States speaking English, or an ancient text in Greek written by an Egyptian in the first century AD. What has been studied much less is how, in the absence of extralinguistic evidence for contact, a contact situation can be reconstructed on the evidence of linguistic data alone. This will be one of the main preoccupations in the following chapters. When we are dealing with linguistic changes that happened long ago, precise information about language contact situations that may be implicated in the changes is usually absent. For instance, we might want to assume that during the early medieval period a Celtic-speaking population in England switched to speaking Anglo-Saxon. In the process, the Celtic from which people switched vanished, which would make it very difficult to determine how the original Celtic might have influenced Anglo-Saxon, for all that is left of the original Celtic is a so-called substratum in Anglo-Saxon: presumedly Celtic features that survived in the speech of Celts who switched to Anglo-Saxon and that then spread in the Anglo-Saxon community to a lesser or greater extent. What we are assuming is that a vanished substratum influenced Anglo-Saxon, and we assume that it did only because we think we can prise apart the substratum from the Anglo-Saxon in which it has nested itself. Before we know it, we are involved in a circular argument.

As an antidote against substratomania, Thomason and Kaufman (1988: 111–112) write:

> In order to be able to make educated guesses in this area [i.e. interference through language shift], we must be able to identify a substratum language or language group (some of) whose speakers shifted to the target language [i.e. the language to which people switched] at the relevant time period; we must have information about its structure; and we must have information about the structure of the target language before the shift. These methodological prerequisites have frequently been ignored by substratum enthusiasts. . . . It is possible, for instance, that Celtic languages of the British Isles owe their un-Indo-European-like system of initial-consonant lenition, and other features too, to a pre-Indo-European substratum; but since we have no information about what language(s) the pre-Indo-European inhabitants spoke, we cannot establish such a cause for these changes (even if we were to agree that an external explanation is needed).

These so-called methodological prerequisites are brought into position in order to chase serious linguists away from exploring language shift in deep time. That is because the impossible is demanded: Thomason and Kaufman convict a murderer only if they have seen him commit the murder. That stance is perhaps understandable in the case of linguists who are not used to the subtlety of the detective work that goes into language reconstruction, but I was surprised to find that an eminent Indo-Europeanist and Celticist recently embraced this point of view, too (McCone 2005: 406). It is precisely the job of historical linguists to unearth the subtle and indirect clues that point to contact situations in deep time, as I hope to show.

4. THE COMPARATIVE METHOD

All of historical linguistics, including this book, would be reduced to a very learned form of informed speculation if it were not for the comparative method, which has been with us since 1878, when Hermann Osthoff and Karl Brugmann published their famous Neogrammarian manifesto in the preface to volume 1 of their *Morphologische Untersuchungen auf dem Gebiete der indogermanischen Sprachen*. This was the most important of a number of breakthroughs in the nineteenth century which secured historical linguistics a place at the forefront of science. Typical of the status of historical linguistics was that it provided inspiration for Darwin's theory of evolution.[1] The backbone of the comparative method is how it deals with sound change, as any good textbook on historical linguistics explains in detail.[2] The present book prides itself on not requiring any previous knowledge about linguistics on the part of the reader, so an explanation is in order. In fact, since every educated human being should be aware of the method and hardly anyone actually is (and this includes not a few professional linguists), it would be irresponsible of me not to explain it, however briefly. Let me do so by giving a practical example.

Welsh and Breton are closely related languages that belong to the Celtic branch of the Indo-European language family. Both languages enter the written record in patchy sources from the end of the first millennium AD, which multiply considerably during the later medieval period. Being related means that Welsh and Breton stem from a common ancestor, Proto-British, which was spoken approximately during the sixth century AD in western Britain. Apart from a few names in Latin sources, no texts in Proto-British survive, so we have no direct access to that long-lost language. Yet historical linguists feel confident that they would be able to keep up a simple conversation with a sixth-century Proto-Brit, not by bombarding him or her with thirteenth-century Welsh or fifteenth-century Breton in the idle hope that a basic rapport might be struck up in this way, but by actually speaking a reconstructed variant of sixth-century Proto-British. How is this done?

Consider the following list of words in Medieval Welsh and Medieval Breton. Since we shall concentrate on the vowel sounds, note that Welsh *aw* is pronounced as [au] (as in English *house*), and Breton *eu* is pronounced as [ø] (as in French *feu* 'fire'). In all words, stress is on the first syllable.

	Medieval Welsh	Medieval Breton	meaning
1.	*brawd*	*breuzr*	'brother'
2.	*mawr*	*meur*	'big'
3.	*diawg* (2 syllables)	*dieg* (2 syllables)	'lazy'
4.	*marchawg*	*marcheg*	'horseman'
5.	*ofer*	*euver*	'vain'
6.	*bore* (2 syllables)	*beure*	'morning'
7.	*brodyr*	*breuder*	'brothers'
8.	*trindawd*	*trinded*	'trinity'
9.	*llawn*	*leun*	'full'

All Welsh words look similar to their Breton counterparts, and their meanings are more or less the same. Hence it is not too hard to believe that the Welsh and Breton words are cognates; that is, they derive from the same ancestral, Proto-British forms. What we shall do now is to figure out how the Proto-British forms were pronounced.

The **first step** is to align each individual phoneme (i.e. each sound, keeping things simple) of a Welsh cognate word with its counterpart in the Breton cognate word:

	Welsh		Breton
1	*b*	~	*b*
	r	~	*r*
	aw	~	*eu*
	d	~	*z*
	Ø	~	*r*
2	*m*	~	*m*
	aw	~	*eu*
	r	~	*r*
	etc.		

Wherever a Welsh sound corresponds to the same sound in Breton, as in the case of *b* and *r* in the word for 'brother' and *m* and *r* in the word for 'big', things are simple: the words for 'brother' and 'big' in ancestral Proto-British will have had the same sounds in the same positions in the word. But wherever Welsh and Breton have different sounds, it is unclear what to reconstruct:

	Welsh		Breton	Proto-British reconstruction
1	*b*	~	*b*	**b*
	r	~	*r*	**r*
	aw	~	*eu*	**?*
	d	~	*z*	**?*
	Ø	~	*r*	**?*
2	*m*	~	*m*	**m*
	aw	~	*eu*	**?*
	r	~	*r*	**r*

Reconstructed forms, whether they be individual phonemes or whole words, are conventionally written with a star in front of them, in order to indicate their hypothetical nature. What we shall now do is to follow a procedure that will enable us to fill in the question marks involving the Welsh vowels *aw* and *o*. The same procedure would allow us to fill in the other question marks, but following that through would lead us too far astray.

So we wish to find out which Proto-British sounds are hiding underneath Welsh *aw* and *o*. The **second step** in the procedure is to establish so-called regular correspondences. In the cognate pair 1, *brawd ~ breuzr*, we observe that where Welsh has *aw*, Breton has *eu*. This correspondence recurs in 2, *mawr ~ meur*, and in 9, *llawn ~ leun*. We have found that the correspondence Welsh *aw ~* Breton *eu* is not limited to a single word but is recurrent: there is a regular correspondence between Welsh *aw* and Breton *eu*. It is typical of related languages that cognate words are made up of phonemes that correspond regularly to one another.

So we have found a regular correspondence Welsh *aw ~* Breton *eu*, which occurs in words 1, 2, and 9. But Breton *eu* is involved in another regular correspondence as well, that is, with Welsh *o*: see words 5, 6, and 7. A third regular correspondence, between Welsh *aw* and Breton *e*, can be found in words 3, 4, and 8:

> regular correspondence a: Welsh *aw ~* Breton *eu*
> regular correspondence b: Welsh *o ~* Breton *eu*
> regular correspondence c: Welsh *aw ~* Breton *e*

If the word list were extended to include more words containing Welsh *aw* and Breton *eu*, more examples for each regular correspondence would be found, confirming the recurrence of the patterns involved.

We are now ready to take the **third step**, which concerns establishing the number of phonemes in Proto-British that gave rise to the Welsh and Breton vowels. Although only two different Welsh (*aw*, *o*) and two different Breton (*eu*, *e*) phonemes (sounds) are involved in the three regular correspondences, the number of phonemes that may be reconstructed for Proto-British is maximally three, not two. That is because the number of regular correspondences rather than the number of different sounds involved in them equals the maximum number of Proto-British phonemes:

> regular correspondence a: Welsh *aw ~* Breton *eu* < Proto-British *X
> regular correspondence b: Welsh *o ~* Breton *eu* < Proto-British *Y
> regular correspondence c: Welsh *aw ~* Breton *e* < Proto-British *Z

X, Y, and Z are cover symbols for whatever sounds are hiding behind them. The symbol < is a shorthand for 'develops from' (its counterpart > means 'develops into').

A crucial aspect of the comparative method is that the maximum number of three phonemes in Proto-British can be reduced to two or one if they show a so-called complementary distribution. If, say, correspondence a, *aw ~ eu*, always occurs in a sound context in which correspondence b, *o ~ eu*, never occurs, a and b are said to be in complementary distribution. The consequence is that a and b go back to just one rather than two sounds in

Proto-British. It so happens that all three regular correspondences are in complementary distribution:

a. Welsh *aw* ~ Breton *eu*:	only in words consisting of one stressed syllable (*brawd, mawr, llawn*)
b. Welsh *o* ~ Breton *eu*:	only in the first (stressed) syllable of words that have more than one syllable (*ofer, bore, brodyr*)
c. Welsh *aw* ~ Breton *e*:	only in the second (unstressed) syllable of words that have more than one syllable (*diawg, marchawg, trindawd*)

Consequently, the three regular correspondences can be reconstructed as one Proto-British phoneme (rather than three phonemes), which we shall call *X.

The **fourth step** is to turn our findings so far into so-called sound laws: rules that govern the development of a phoneme on its way from the protolanguage to the daughter languages. Sound laws are formulated in such a way that they do not allow exceptions. Formulating the sound laws that govern the development of *X in Welsh and Breton is easy now that the complementary distributions have been found:

Proto-British *X	> Medieval Welsh *aw* in final syllables (e.g. *brawd, marchawg*)
	> Medieval Welsh *o* in non-final syllables (e.g. *ofer, brodyr*)
Proto-British *X	> Medieval Breton *eu* in initial syllables (e.g. *meur, beure*)
	> Medieval Breton *e* in non-initial syllables (e.g. *dieg, trinded*)

It can easily be seen that this formulation of the sound laws involving *X completely accounts for the developments of *X in Welsh and Breton (at least as far as can be judged on the basis of the word list). If Welsh words were to turn up that have *aw* in a non-final syllable, or Breton words with *eu* in a non-initial syllable, they violate the sound laws. In that case the sound laws need to be refined until they account for the exceptions as well, or the exceptions have to be explained in a different way (as loanwords or new formations, for instance).[3]

The **fifth and final step** is filling in *X with phonetic content. This is the least exact step in the procedure, for it is based on educated guesses. Deciding what *X may have sounded like is possible by studying the phonetics of its children, i.e. Welsh *aw* and *o* and Breton *eu* and *e*. What all four have in common is that they are vowels (to be more exact, *aw* is a combination of two vowels, together forming one syllable, a so-called diphthong). So *X probably was a vowel. Three out of four of its offspring are simple vowels (*o*, *eu* = [ø], *e*) rather than diphthongs (*aw*), so *X probably was not a diphthong. Three out of four of its offspring are produced with lip rounding (the *w* in Welsh *aw*, the *o*, and Breton *eu* [ø], so it is reasonable to assume that *X was a rounded vowel. Vowels can be close (produced with the mouth almost closed, as in the case of [u]), open (produced with the mouth relatively wide open, as in the case of [a]), or mid (in-between, as in [o]). Three out of four children of *X are mid, so *X is bound to have been a mid vowel. So *X probably was something like a rounded mid vowel, i.e. a sound like [o] or [ø]. This best guess can be further refined on the basis of other considerations. The oldest sources of British Celtic are names in Latin texts, which cover the period between the first century AD and the end of the first millennium. Around 600 *X was spelled as <o> (Welsh *mawr*, Breton *meur* 'big' appears in names as <mor>, for instance); earlier it was spelled <a>. The latter agrees with the way in which *X was pronounced in the closest cognate languages of British Celtic, viz. Irish *á* [aː] and Gaulish *a* (exact pronunciation unclear). Currently, the best guess as to the nature of *X is [ɔ], that is, an open-to-mid rounded back vowel (back means the vowel is pronounced with the tongue slightly retracted), approximately as in British English *dog* [dɔg].

This five-step procedure can be performed for all individual sounds in all of the Welsh and Breton words cited earlier, and indeed for all sounds that make up the entire lexicon and grammar of Welsh and Breton. In this way, the lexicon and most of the grammar of Proto-British can be reconstructed. Since British Celtic is closely related to Irish, the common ancestor of those two can be reconstructed as well, and so on, until we reach Proto-Celtic, the common ancestor of all Celtic languages; Proto-Italo-Celtic, which is the common ancestor of Celtic and the Italic language family (whose best-known member is Latin, itself the ancestor of the Romance language family); and finally Proto-Indo-European, the common ancestor of all Indo-European languages.

The power of the comparative method is based on the fact that sounds in languages change in such a way that their behaviour can be captured by rules which ideally allow no exceptions (sound laws). Its most powerful effect is that it enables us to reconstruct protolanguages, even though those protolanguages may look nothing like their descendants. We have seen one simple example of this effect: based on the Welsh sounds *aw* and *o* and the Breton sounds *eu* and *e* we were able to reconstruct one single phoneme in Proto-British (not two, as are attested in Welsh or Breton), and we were able to ascribe a probable sound value [ɔ] to that sound, which differs phonetically from all of its offspring in Breton and Welsh (*eu*, *e*, *aw*, *o*). This effect becomes more noticeable when deeper reconstructions are made. For instance, we can be certain that the Proto-Celtic form from which Welsh *pump* 'five' and Irish *cúig* 'five' are descended was *$k^w enk^w e$*, even though not one single sound of *$k^w enk^w e$* survives unchanged in its descendants. Similarly, and at a deeper level, English *I* [aɪ] and Russian *ja* 'I' can be reconstructed with equal confidence as Proto-Indo-European *egĤom* (where *ǵ* sounds like *egg*y*olk* and the *H* is a consonant whose exact phonetic value has not been determined apart from the fact that it was a fricative produced at the back of the mouth). The comparative method is the backbone of all linguistic reconstructions (starred forms), which appear abundantly in this book.

II. The Rise of English

1. LANGUAGES COMPETING FOR SPEAKERS: ENGLISH AS A KILLER LANGUAGE

It is common for languages with expanding populations of speakers to grow at the expense of other languages. The better a language manages to increase the number of its speakers, the more aggressively it behaves towards competing languages. If we were to trace back the pedigrees of all monolingual speakers of English in the modern world, we would find that the majority stem from ancestors that one or two centuries ago spoke a different language. That is especially true for areas in which English is a newcomer, such as North America, Australia, and New Zealand, where it ousted the languages of immigrants from other parts of the world than England. Those languages, such as Norwegian, Dutch, German, Russian, and Italian, survive in good health today in their old homelands. The hundreds of native languages of North America and Australia have fared much worse, however, and many of them are on the brink of extinction, if not already beyond. English is one of a handful of particularly successful killer languages in the modern world, together with Spanish and Portuguese in Latin America, and Russian and Chinese within their respective state boundaries. The scale on which those killers operate nowadays may be unprecedented, but there is nothing new about languages expanding at the cost of others. It is simply a condition of survival that is as old as linguistic diversity itself.

Although in this book I shall continue to speak about language competition and killer languages, there are three ways in which the imagery is potentially misleading. Firstly, a language, defined as a chain of mutually comprehensible neighbouring dialects, is not the basic unit at which the competition takes place, although it is the unit on which this book focuses. Within a language, dialects (language varieties spoken in a particular area) and sociolects (varieties spoken by a particular layer of society) compete in the same way: think of the loss of dialectal variety over the last century in most European countries as a result of the spread of one or a few varieties. On the most elementary level, the tiniest difference between the speech of two speakers engaging with one another is subject to the same type of pressure, as one of the speakers may choose to conceal or highlight that difference in order to avoid or create social distance.

That brings us to the second possible confusion to which the imagery may give rise: it is not so much languages that compete with one another as people, who, consciously or unconsciously, instrumentalize language as one of the means to express social relations. In no way is the English language intrinsically fitter than the languages it replaces. It is the behaviour of its speakers that is responsible for the rate at which a language spreads or contracts. English spread across Ireland from the sixteenth century onwards not because English is a better language than the native Celtic language Irish that it replaced but because it was the language of the political, economic, and social elite as well as of colonist farmers who immigrated from Britain. Since a good command of English became a condition for upward social mobility, the Irish-speaking population felt pressure to become bilingual Irish-English speakers. When in the nineteenth century the Great Famine hit the rural poor in particular, many of whom happened to be Irish speakers, and Irish became stigmatized as the language of the destitute as well as the backward, the stage was set for a large-scale switch from Irish-English bilingualism to English monolingualism, and Irish political independence and the active promotion of Irish fluency through the school system and civil service have managed to achieve very little in their efforts to turn the tide.

Language hitches a ride on the back of human history. The mechanisms responsible for a language's spread or contraction are as complex as the factors determining the course of history itself. Any ploy between the extremes of genocide and the successful flogging of undubbed television programmes is capable of promoting one language at the expense of another. A language may spread because its speakers decide to slaughter all male speakers of another language, take their land, and enslave female speakers, for reasons that have nothing to do with language. Or a language may spread because people wish to master that language as one way of becoming part of a society that offers its speakers the opportunity to climb the social ladder more effectively. Perhaps surprisingly, the historical linguist has a hard time telling such extremes apart on the basis of linguistic evidence alone. The expansion of a language is usually just a concomitant effect of particular socio-political or economic changes. Consequently, saying that languages rather than speakers compete is a metaphor. But since this is a book about linguistics and early European history, it is also a useful abstraction, because when we say about Ireland, for instance, that English is outcompeting Irish, that statement subsumes all possible historical scenarios responsible for the fact and allows me to postpone, sometimes indefinitely, answering the question of what exactly went on in Ireland between 1600 and the present day. The deeper we delve down into history and prehistory, the murkier will be the historical record and the greater the need for the abstraction.

The third possible misconception to which talk about competing languages may give rise is that whenever languages meet, there will inevitably be competition between them. Such is not the case. Bilingualism and even multilingualism are the norm in many parts of the world up to the present day. For instance, many people living in the northeastern Caucasus are at least bilingual and more often tri- or quadrilingual. They would often speak Russian and the East Caucasian language Avar, which is the lingua franca of Dagestan, as well as one or more local languages of East Caucasian, Turkish, or Iranian extraction. This situation has been relatively stable for centuries, apart from Russian, which is a nineteenth-century newcomer in the area. Each language has its own particular niche in which it is used, and people switch from one language to the other accordingly. High-ranking officers and civil servants in the Austro-Hungarian Empire before 1918 would be fluent in German, Hungarian, and one or more Slavic languages, such as Croat, Slovenian, or Czech. In those settings, multilingualism is a matter of survival. For many people living in Wales, western Scotland, the Finnmark, Frisia, Brittany, the Lausitz, Graubünden, South Tyrol, or the Basque Country, to mention just a few European examples, bilingualism has been a fact of everyday life for generations. So languages can coexist relatively peacefully within a single community and even within the confines of a single skull. Why, then, highlight languages struggling with one another? Firstly, because this happens to be a book about people shifting from one language to another. Such shifts inevitably go through stages at which people are bilingual, but those stages may not last more than one or two generations. Therefore, the focus here is on unstable bilingualism that results in shift. And, secondly, the nature of the material discussed in this book involves looking at language within a span of a couple of centuries. That wide a time frame increases the chances that what at one point was stable bilingualism will become destabilized and give way to language shift.

English's history as a killer language has a respectable pedigree in Britain, too. It has made heavy inroads into Scots Gaelic and Welsh. It finished off Manx on the Isle of Man at the beginning of the twentieth century and Cornish about a century before that. Scots Gaelic, Welsh, Manx, and Cornish are all Celtic languages. Before the modern period, the rise of English likewise matched the decline of Celtic languages. English also managed to swallow up languages that were introduced into Britain by erstwhile conquerors. One of them is the French dialect of Anglo-Norman that was introduced as an upper-class language from the eleventh century onwards. Danish in the east and Norse in the northwest of England and in Scotland were imported in the period of Scandinavian expansion between the late eighth and eleventh centuries, and they, too, ultimately fell victim to English, sometimes within a generation or two, sometimes after many centuries.

2. THE ANGLO-SAXON SETTLEMENTS

The origin of English is famously tied up with an extinction event, as Anglo-Saxon settlers moving from their homelands in present-day northern Germany and Denmark brought along the dialects ancestral to English and gradually destroyed the fabric of Roman British society in a colonization movement that started after 400.

> In the archaeological view . . . the sequence of the transition from Roman Britain to Anglo-Saxon England is remarkably clear and comprehensible. Within the latest levels of Roman-period sites of virtually all types, including villas, villages, towns, forts, cemeteries and temples, a new, intrusive Germanic material element is often found. . . . This phase is the beginning of a subsequently unbroken sequence of Germanic cultural presence, soon a dominance, in Britain. It is a phase of radically different character, sequentially unconnected, to earlier isolated finds of Germanic character in Britain. . . . Thus this phase is rationally to be identified as the inception of the Anglo-Saxon Period. From this point onwards the new Germanic sites regularly outlive the earlier Roman sites, on which any late intrusive Germanic element is always ephemeral. There is no known case of any continuing, hybrid Romano-Germanic site emerging from this meeting of cultures.[1]

When by the seventh century the dust begins to settle, Anglo-Saxon kingdoms cover most of England and southern Scotland. The written record is dominated by Latin—the language of the Church and of learning rather than everyday speech—and by Old English. The latter is an array of dialects that presumably directly continue the dialects imported by the Anglo-Saxon settlers in the preceding centuries. They replace the British Celtic language, which was widespread before 400 but in the course of the medieval period managed to survive only at the western and northern fringes of Britain, in Cornwall, Wales, and Cumbria, although initially some pockets probably still remained elsewhere, e.g., in Devon, Dorset, and the Fens and in the former northern British kingdoms between Strathclyde and Edinburgh.

Latin must have been spoken widely in late Roman Britain as well, probably not so much the Classical, literary variety based on the works of Caesar and Cicero, which early post-Roman British authors like Gildas and St Patrick strove to write, after it had become the language of the Church, but rather the grammatically much simplified Late Spoken Latin that flourished throughout the Roman Empire from Libya to Hadrian's Wall and that is ancestral to all modern Romance languages. Its fate in Britain between 500 and 700 is not clear, but it is reasonable to think that a form of Spoken Latin survived well into this period (see section II.5.2).

At a conservative estimate, the population of Britain on the eve of the Anglo-Saxon migrations amounted to two to four million[2]—that is, two to four million speakers of Celtic and/or Late Spoken Latin. We know that the number of speakers of those languages shrank dramatically in the course of the medieval period, withdrawing as they did to Wales, Cornwall, and, across the Channel, Brittany, where they survived as the medieval written languages Welsh, Cornish, and Breton, respectively. Spoken Latin became extinct in Britain. But where did the people who spoke those languages go? Many possible scenarios have been entertained: they fell prey to genocide, inflicted either by the sword or by gradual starvation; they mass-migrated to areas beyond the immediate grasp of the invaders; or they were enslaved to become a vast underclass of mainly agricultural labourers. They may even have thrown in their lot with the new powers so successfully that they became as Anglo-Saxon as the Anglo-Saxons themselves, both culturally and linguistically. Circumstances may have varied from one period to the next and from one place to the next, so that multiple scenarios may have come about. What all these scenarios have in common is that they are quite drastic: they are geared to explain the almost unimaginable: how, in the course of just a few centuries, what began with a few boatloads of Anglo-Saxon mercenaries managed to transform a land populated by millions into a linguistically and culturally Anglo-Saxon society.

3. THE VANISHING OF THE CELTS AS SEEN BY LINGUISTS

To a large extent, it is linguistics that is responsible for thinking in terms of drastic scenarios. If a large Celtic-speaking indigenous population shifted to speaking the language of the Anglo-Saxon conquerors, linguists would expect to find certain traces of that shift, which in this particular case they do not. In order to understand the role of linguistics in the debate about Anglo-Saxon settlement, we need to introduce a few general concepts.

3.1. Absent Traces of Language Shift: Sound System and Syntax

When people adopt a second language, they find it difficult to acquire it so perfectly as to be indistinguishable from native speakers of that second language. That is because their first language provides a matrix into which the second language tends to be squeezed. The phenomenon is well known to anyone who has tried to learn a foreign language. Native speakers of English have difficulty pronouncing, say, German and French *r*-sounds because they tend to substitute the standard German and standard French uvular trill [ʀ] by their native standard English alveolar approximant [ɹ]. The converse holds for native speakers of French and German. Such interference by one's first language is especially prominent in the sound system, as this simple example illustrates, and also in syntax. English has a fairly rigid Subject-Verb-Object

(SVO) word order, whereas its close cognates Dutch and German have a different but also fairly rigid rule that stipulates that the verb must come in second position in the clause, except in subclauses, where the verb is placed towards the end of the subclause. Contrast the following pairs:

	English (SVO)	German (verb second in main clauses; verb final in subclauses)
1.	Yesterday John saw a frog.	Gestern sah Johann einen Frosch.[3]
2.	John saw a frog yesterday.	Johann sah gestern einen Frosch.
3.	I presume that John saw a frog yesterday.	Ich nehme an, dass Johann gestern einen Frosch sah.

Speakers of English learning German will quite naturally, that is, unless they are corrected, attempt to get away with applying their native SVO word order to German, which produces problematic German sentences such as:

1a. *Gestern Johann sah einen Frosch.
2a. ?Johann sah einen Frosch gestern.
3a. *Ich nehme an, dass Johann sah einen Frosch gestern.

(Here, * indicates forms and clauses that are unacceptable to native speakers of German. ? indicates that the clause is barely acceptable.)

German speakers learning English will initially tend to apply the German verb-second rule to English, with similarly incorrect results. As the English rule of verb placement is simpler than the German rule, Germans will more quickly master the English rule than English native speakers will master the German rule.

Since vocabulary is generally more easily acquired than a foreign sound system or syntax, second-language learners as a rule will not import their native vocabulary into a second language, unless the latter has been learned very imperfectly. The exception is specialized vocabulary, which the learner is unlikely to have come across in the second language (such as names of economically and culturally unimportant animals and plants), vocabulary for which the second language has no appropriate counterpart (e.g. exotic fruits and vegetables), and names. As a rule, learners do not introduce elements of the morphology of their first language into their second language either: for instance, English native speakers learning German are unlikely to attach the English third person singular present tense marker -s (as in *talks*, *sits*, *goes*) rather than its German counterpart -t to German verb stems (*sprichs*, *sitzs*, and *gehs* do not occur in the speech of second-language learners), again unless German is learnt very imperfectly.

What start out as problems facing the language learner can be perpetuated to become a regular feature of a language. Fully bilingual speakers of English and Dutch, for example, may speak a variety of English with perceptible interference from Dutch. If communities of such speakers exist, this variety may become the norm, which is then transmitted to new generations learning English. When the community in time becomes monolingual in English, the language that is responsible for the interference, in this case Dutch, survives exclusively in the form of the interference features in English. This happened and is still happening in South Africa, where speakers of Afrikaans, a language that has split off from Dutch, have been shifting to English over the generations. In the standard pronunciation of South African English, the voiceless plosives /p t k/ appear with Afrikaans-Dutch phonetics: in word-initial position, they lack the aspiration which is so typical of other varieties of English ([pʰ tʰ kʰ]) but which is absent in Afrikaans and in most varieties of Dutch ([p t k]). This pronunciation has become the norm, spreading across English-speaking communities in South Africa, so that nowadays even speakers whose ancestors never spoke Afrikaans do not aspirate their *p*, *t*, and *k*. So we can say that today there is an Afrikaans (Dutch) substratum in South African English, which historically reflects the fact that the present population of speakers of South African English is partly made up of former speakers of Afrikaans (Dutch), whose variety of English has become so influential that it has spread across the English-speaking community. The reason why that variety has become so influential has nothing to do with linguistics but rather with the social, economic, and political position of its speakers. This is an important point: second-language acquisition predictably leads to the rise of varieties of the second language which show interference by a speaker's first language. But on the basis of linguistic argumentation it is not predictable whether those varieties will become community languages that are transmitted to children within the community, nor whether such community languages will spread beyond their place of origin, nor whether they will eventually succeed in becoming a standard language entering the written record. Every step along that way is determined by the vagaries of history. Since this book deals with language contact over long stretches of time, it is important to be constantly aware that most language varieties that show interference from another language will have perished at some stage of this long and uncertain road and will never appear in the ancient written or modern spoken record.

If, however, millions of speakers of British Celtic had shifted to the language of the initially much less numerous Anglo-Saxon colonists, presumably because that was the language of a new economic and political elite, Old English should at least show some traces of interference from British Celtic, particularly in its sound system and its syntax. But not a single British Celtic feature has been convincingly identified in Old English phonology or syntax. This apparently complete disappearance of the British Celts calls for an explanation.

3.2. Rarity of British Celtic Loanwords and Place Names

Although on theoretical grounds we would not expect to find a lot of British Celtic lexical items in Old English (see II.3.1), the number we do find is surprisingly small. A recent survey by Richard Coates retains just ten loanwords as probable: *cumb* 'valley', *luh* 'sea, pool', *torr* 'outcrop, peak', *binn* 'manger', *brocc* 'badger', *trem* 'pace', *trum* 'strong', *wered* 'sweet drink', *stor* 'incense, medicinal wax', and *dēor* 'brave'.[4] Much of the surprise at this small number derives from the idea that Roman Britain showed greater cultural and material complexity than the Anglo-Saxon homelands in northern Germany and Denmark, so that one would expect that the Anglo-Saxons upon arrival in Britain encountered many concepts for which they did not have words, which would have induced them to borrow words from British Celtic. Such borrowings are not to be found, however, with the possible marginal exception of *stor*. However, the premiss of a complex Romano-British society may not be correct. By the middle of the fifth century, Roman British culture had all but collapsed: town life hardly functioned at all, coins were no longer produced, and even pottery production seems to have ceased. Materially, therefore, the difference between Anglo-Saxons and Britons may well have been very small indeed.

Place-name specialists stress that although British Celtic toponyms do survive in England, they constitute a tiny minority. Oliver Padel recently (2007) contrasted the situations in Cornwall and Devon. Devon was conquered by Saxons by the early eighth century; Cornwall came under Saxon rule in the course of the ninth and tenth centuries. While British Celtic disappeared at some point in time in Devon, it continued to flourish in Cornwall, where it developed into a late medieval literary language which died out as late as the nineteenth century. Cornwall is littered with Celtic place names, whereas Old English place names are very rare. Devon shows the converse distribution: there are hardly any place names of Celtic origin. In this respect, Cornwall is clearly the exception, while the situation in Devon is typical for the whole of England. Padel convincingly argues that Saxon rule over Cornwall took the shape of elite dominance: ultimate political and economic control passed from a Cornish to a Saxon ruling class, and by and large the population was allowed to live and work where and how it had done before. Saxon immigration was limited. Elite dominance cannot, however, explain the extreme rarity of Celtic place names in Devon and, by extension, in the rest of England. A model that is capable of explaining that state of affairs is the North American one, as Padel explains, 'whereby a major replacement of population, language and place-names occurred over a large area in a comparatively short space of time' through a massive colonization event that went hand in hand with acculturation, deportation, and killing of the natives.[5] As agricultural land in England was redistributed among Anglo-Saxon settlers, the farmsteads, villages, and most landscape features acquired Anglo-Saxon names.

A highly specific linguistic feature which points to harsh treatment of British natives in Anglo-Saxon society is the fate of the early Germanic word *walhaz* in Old English. In the West Germanic ancestor of Old English, *walhaz* meant 'foreigner', more specifically 'Roman', and even more specifically 'person of Celtic or Romance speech'. The perspective here is that of a Germanic-speaking neighbour of the Western Roman Empire, living in what are now the Low Countries and Germany. To him, his Roman neighbours would be culturally and linguistically clearly distinguishable from himself, being citizens of the Roman Empire and speaking either Latin or Celtic or both. On the Continent, *walhaz* survived into the later West Germanic languages as a term of reference to persons and areas of Romance speech. Old High German *walh* 'person of Romance speech/origin' and Dutch *Waal* 'Walloon' testify to that meaning. Place names containing the element *walhaz* denote pockets in the Germanic-speaking world where Romance was spoken (e.g. *Walchensee* in Bavaria, Germany, and *Waalwijk* in North Brabant, Netherlands). A *walnut* (German *Walnuss*, Dutch *walnoot*) is etymologically a nut from France. In Old English, *walhaz* developed into *wealh*. This retained the inherited meaning 'a foreigner, more particularly a pre-Anglo-Saxon inhabitant of Britain who spoke Celtic or Latin or both', but it is indicative of the social position of the British natives that in the West Saxon dialect of Old English it acquired the new meaning '(British) slave'. The old feminine derivative of *walhaz*, Old English *wīln* < *wīelen* < *wealh-īn-*, even exclusively means 'a female slave' and is likewise concentrated in the Saxon south of England.[6]

3.3. The Celts as Suppressed Masses: Celtic Influence on Middle English

The linguistic evidence presented here—the extreme dearth of British Celtic loanwords in Old English, the absence of British Celtic features in the Old English sound system and syntax, and the rarity of British Celtic place names in England—conspires to render the idea that the Anglo-Saxons freely absorbed millions of British natives into their society quite untenable. There is a familiar loophole, however: all we know about Old English is based on written sources. Since writing during the Old English period was firmly the province of the ecclesiastical and political elite, written sources reflect the language of the elite. If social differences between the Anglo-Saxon elite and the British natives were kept large enough, that might ensure that hardly a trickle of the natives' language managed to enter the elite's language. Exterminating or expelling the natives is the most drastic form of enlarging a social difference, but enslaving them, as indeed happened, although on what scale is unclear, may well have produced a similar enough effect. So would a system of apartheid laws which systematically favoured Anglo-Saxons over the native British and which over the generations would have had the effect of dispossessing the natives. Such laws were indeed promulgated, as the late seventh-century Wessex Laws of Ine demonstrate, although it is not clear whether the situation in Wessex may be extrapolated to the whole of England.[7]

There is a body of linguistic evidence that indeed shows that British natives of low social status must have been present in some numbers in Anglo-Saxon England. In the course of the Old English period, the literary language, which started out as a patchwork of dialectal varieties of local significance, became increasingly influenced by the standard developed in the West Saxon area, which had its centre in the south. This standard withstood the politically traumatic period of Norse settlement, which stretched intermittently from the ninth to the eleventh century and affected most of the east and north of the island. It did not survive, however, the imposition of Norman rule in 1066. This underlines the idea that Old English writing was an occupation of the elite: when the elite is replaced, so is its written standard, which after 1066 became Anglo-Norman (i.e. Old French). By the thirteenth century, the Middle English literary language had arisen. This was itself a patchwork of dialectal varieties, but by the end of the Middle Ages all those varieties shared a large number of innovations, whose overall effect was a dramatic simplification of the language and in some respects a marked convergence on the grammatical structure of the neighbouring Celtic languages. Here are a few examples:

(1) Loss of grammatical cases: Old English had four cases, Middle English none, apart from a vestigial genitive in -s which survives into Modern English; Welsh, Cornish, and Breton do not have grammatical cases.

(2) Development of an auxiliary verb *do* for emphatic purposes; this function survives in Modern English usages such as *I do like fishing*; in other contexts, *do* became a petrified auxiliary: *I don't like fishing, do I like fishing?, under no circumstances does he like fishing*. Breton, Welsh, and Cornish make extensive use of the auxiliary verb 'do' in constructions that subtly emphasize the verb (e.g. Welsh *pysgota a wnaf*, lit. 'fishing I-do').

(3) Development of the progressive, consisting of the verb 'to be' and a verbal noun in -*ing* (*I am fishing*) rather than a participle (the present participle in -*ande* was replaced by the verbal noun suffix -*ing* in the course of the Middle English period). Breton, Welsh, and Cornish have a progressive consisting of the verb 'to be' + a preposition (which is no longer recognizable as such) + a verbal noun (e.g. Welsh *rydw i yn pysgota*, lit. 'I am *yn* fishing').

In recent years, a lot has been written about these and similar phenomena.[8] The weight of the evidence in favour of Middle English convergence towards British Celtic is such that it cannot reasonably be denied anymore. The simplest explanation for this convergence is that Celtic substratum features arose in Old English varieties spoken by former British Celts. Those varieties were spoken by people of such low social standing at the time that they got the chance to influence the elite varieties only after the collapse of Old English literature and society, which occurred by the Middle English period. Interestingly, the Middle English innovations that constitute the convergence start their spread in areas that lie on the western (examples 2 and 3) and northern fringes (example 1) rather than in the southeastern and eastern heartlands of Anglo-Saxon colonization. It is in the southwest and the north that the Anglo-Saxon conquest penetrated latest, after about 600, and there British Celtic speech must have been in good health longest. Those parts stand the best chances of having given rise to Celticized varieties of Old English which for centuries remained substandard and therefore did not enter the Old English written record. After the socio-political upheaval in the wake of the Norman conquest, new written standards were created, which gave the Celticized varieties a new lease of life.

There is one potential spanner that has been thrown in the works of this elegant scenario: most of the phenomena ascribed to Celtic influence surfacing in Middle English are also attested in some form or other in the other West Germanic languages. Dutch, for instance, lost its case system, but it did so later, at the end of the medieval period; it has auxiliary 'do', albeit in substandard speech (*ik doe even de bloemen in het water zetten* 'I'll just put the flowers in the water', word for word 'I do just the flowers in the water put'); and it has a progressive consisting of 'to be' + a preposition + a verbal noun (*ik ben aan het vissen*, 'I am fishing', word for word 'I am at the fishing'). If English got these from British Celtic, how did they end up in Dutch (as well as in German)? Did Dutch have its own Celtic substratum, which was in relevant respects identical to fifth- to eighth-century British Celtic? Or did those Celtic features enter West Germanic before the fifth century, when the ancestors of the Anglo-Saxons were still living on the Continent next to Celtic neighbours, only to be transported to England by the Anglo-Saxon settlers as a substandard variety, where those features were reinforced, perhaps, through renewed contact with Celtic speakers hundreds of years later? We shall have cause to return to this matter later on (section II.10), so we shall ignore it for the moment.

4. THE RECONSTRUCTION OF BRITISH CELTIC

As we have seen, Middle English Celticisms are Celtic features of Middle English grammar that surface in the written record many centuries after they had arisen in varieties of Old English spoken by British natives. The pattern of their surfacing in Middle English indicates that these Celticized Old English varieties probably emanated from communities in the southwest and north of England rather than from the southeast. Apparently, therefore, British

justified in pushing back the origin of this 'do'-construction to the common ancestor of British Celtic (as defined by Welsh, Cornish, and Breton) and Irish, whatever that means in terms of absolute chronology. But what cannot be determined is whether that common ancestor made frequent use of this construction (in which case Irish innovated by decreasing its frequency) or whether it was rare (in which case British Celtic innovated by increasing its frequency).

4.2. Reconstructing the British Celtic Sound System: Relative and Absolute Chronology of Sound Laws

In principle, the reconstruction of the western British sound system (as of any sound system) is conducted in a similar fashion but with much greater resolution than can be achieved with syntax. The history of a sound system can be described with great accuracy in the form of sound laws, which, it should be remembered, do not allow exceptions. It is possible to rank sound laws in an ordered sequence. In order to understand this procedure, consider the following example, which involves three well-established sound laws that occurred in the prehistories of Welsh, Cornish, and Breton and consequently may be projected back to their common ancestor:

(a) *nd, *mb, *ng > *nn, *mm, *ŋŋ, respectively

   e.g. Proto-British *kambos 'crooked' > Middle Welsh *camm*

(b) *u > *o and *i > *e if the following syllable is word-final and contains *a or *ā (so-called *a*-affection)

   e.g. Proto-British *brunnā 'breast' > Middle Welsh *bronn*

(c) *o > *u and *e > *i immediately before a nasal (*n, *m) followed by a plosive (*p, *t, *k, *b, *d, *g)

   e.g. Proto-British *pempe 'five' > *pimpe > Middle Welsh *pymp*

(d) final syllables are lost (so-called apocope)

   e.g. all of the examples above

It should become clear from just looking at these rules that what happens to words fed into the rules is affected not only by the way the rules are formulated but also by the order in which they operate, for this determines the results. The input of rule (a), *nd, *mb, *ng, conditions rule (c), but the output of rule (a), *nn, *mm, *ŋŋ, does not. So the order in which we put (a) and (c) determines what happens to the vowel in words containing an original sound sequence, say, *emb: if the order is first (a) and then (c), *emb comes out as *emm*; if the order is first (c) and then (a), *emb comes out as *imm*. Similarly, the output of rule (b), *o and *e, may or may not be an input for rule (c), depending on how we order rules (b) and (c) with respect to one another. And, finally, rule (b) is conditioned by the input of rule (d). Feeding concrete words into the rules and observing their conduct should clarify the issues at hand. Assume the existence of two words, *sondos* 'this (masculine)' and *sondā* 'this (feminine)'. Both have been reconstructed for the common ancestor of British Celtic, Irish, and another branch of Celtic, Gaulish, for reasons that go beyond present purposes, so let us just accept that these are forms that go back deep into the prehistory of Celtic. When they surface in ninth-century Old Welsh, *sondos* has become *hunn* and *sondā* has become *honn*. One other sound law in addition to the four above has affected the Welsh forms: initial *s-* has become *h-*, but that does not interfere with any of the four rules, so we shall ignore it here. The riddle that needs to be solved is: which sequence of sound laws turns *sondos* and *sondā* into the observed Old Welsh outputs *hunn* and *honn*, respectively? A sequence that does just that potentially describes what really happened, while a sequence that does not is incorrect. Let us try four possible sequences:

I	*sondos*	*sondā*
(a) *nd, *mb, *ng > *nn, *mm, *ŋŋ, respectively	*sonnos	*sonnā
(b) *u > *o and *i > *e before *a or *ā in the word-final syllable	=	=
(c) *o > *u and *e > *i immediately before nasal (*n, *m) plus plosive (*p, *t, *k, *b, *d, *g)	=	=
(d) final syllables are lost (apocope)	*sonn	*sonn
(e) adding the development *s > *h yields Old Welsh	**honn	**honn

Since this sequence yields the incorrect output for *sondos* (> Old Welsh has *hunn*, not **honn), it is incorrect, so we must try another sequence.

II	*sondos*	*sondā*
(b) *u > *o and *i > *e before *a or *ā in the word-final syllable	=	=
(c) *o > *u and *e > *i immediately before nasal (*n, *m) plus plosive (*p, *t, *k, *b, *d, *g)	*sundos	*sundā
(a) *nd, *mb, *ng > *nn, *mm, *ŋŋ, respectively	*sunnos	*sunnā
(d) final syllables are lost (apocope)	*sunn	*sunn
(e) adding the development *s > *h yields Old Welsh	*hunn	**hunn

This sequence performs just as badly because the output of *sondā* is incorrect (> *honn*, not **hunn). So we must try yet another sequence.

III		*sondos*	*sondā*
(c) *o > *u and *e > *i immediately before nasal (*n, *m) plus plosive (*p, *t, *k, *b, *d, *g)		*sundos*	*sundā*
(b) *u > *o and *i > *e before *a or *ā in the word-final Syllable		=	*sondā*
(a) *nd, *mb, *ng > *nn, *mm, *ŋŋ, respectively		*sunnos*	*sonnā*
(d) final syllables are lost (apocope)		*sunn*	*sonn*
(e) adding the development *s > *h yields Old Welsh		*hunn*	*honn*

Sequence III produces the attested Old Welsh forms correctly. But so does one other sequence.

IV		*sondos*	*sondā*
(c) *o > *u and *e > *i immediately before nasal (*n, *m) plus plosive (*p, *t, *k, *b, *d, *g)		*sundos*	*sundā*
(b) *u > *o and *i > *e before *a or *ā in the word-final syllable		=	*sondā*
(d) final syllables are lost (apocope)		*sund*	*sond*
(a) *nd, *mb, *ng > *nn, *mm, *ŋŋ, respectively		*sunn*	*sonn*
(e) adding the development *s > *h yields Old Welsh		*hunn*	*honn*

As long as rule (c) precedes (b), and rule (b) precedes (a), the input yields the attested Old Welsh output. Additionally, rule (d) must follow (b); otherwise, its conditioning *ā is lost too early, but (d) cannot be ordered with respect to (a). Sequences III and IV are the only ones that will produce the attested results, so they are both correct (of course, only one of them actually happened, but we cannot decide which one on the basis of the material adduced so far). All other sequences produce results that are not attested and are therefore incorrect: we can be sure that none of those actually happened.

Such an ordered sequence of sound laws is called a relative chronology. Relative chronologies can be extended by incorporating more sound laws and more inputs and outputs. Ideally, a relative chronology can be produced of all sound laws that occurred between, say, Modern Welsh and its ultimate ancestor, Proto-Indo-European, thus spanning a period of approximately 6000 years. By contrast, it is impossible to construct relative chronologies of syntactic or morphological changes, unless one is so lucky as to be able to link them up indirectly with sound laws. This explains why historical phonology, the study of sound change over time, is the most powerful tool for getting a handle on the linguistic past: sound change can be fitted into rules that do not allow exceptions, and those rules can be put into a relative chronology.

In the case of British Celtic, reasonably successful attempts have been made to turn the relative chronology of sound laws into an absolute chronology, in other words, into a chronological order that puts absolute dates on the occurrence of each sound law. This is not at all a straightforward exercise, nor are its results foolproof in the way in which a relative chronology is. Establishing an absolute chronology is impossible on the basis of purely linguistic arguments. The minimum requirements are:

(1) the presence of a corpus of linguistic forms (words, names) that are fossilized at various points within the relative chronology
(2) absolute dates that can be attached to these fossils.

British Celtic fossilized forms come in two basic shapes: names in ancient inscriptions and toponyms.

There is a corpus of Latin inscriptions spanning the period of c. 400 to 1200 which contain British Celtic names. The important point is that the inscriptions can be given an approximate absolute date based on epigraphic criteria (the shape of the letters changes over time). Most names consist of ordinary nouns whose etymology is usually well known, so there is control over the input and the output.[13] For instance, a British Celtic name (in the Latin genitive singular -*ī*) VENDESETLI occurs in an inscription dated to the fifth or sixth century on palaeographical grounds (CIIC 390; observe the wide margin, which reflects the disagreement among specialists in epigraphy). Etymologically, it consists of a first member *windo-* 'fair' and a second member *saitlo-* 'life (span)', which together form the male personal name, in Proto-Celtic form, *Windo-saitlos* 'having a fair life'. This ends up as the Middle Welsh name *Gwynnhoedl* /gwənnhoedl/. The same name turns up in another inscription as VENNISETLI, dated to the fifth to early sixth century (CIIC 376). Although the approximate absolute dates of the inscriptions in which VENDESETLI and VENNISETLI occur are the same, it is clear that the different forms of the name imply different stages in the relative chronology. The innovative stage in the relative chronology can now be given an absolute date: the spelling -NN- in VENNISETLI indicates that the inscription postdates one of the sound laws we saw earlier (a. *nd*, *mb*, *ng* > *nn*, *mm*, *ŋŋ*, respectively). We may conclude that that sound law had taken place by the early sixth century at the latest. How much earlier the rule occurred cannot be established with accuracy, however. One might think that VENDESETLI predates the sound law, which consequently cannot have happened earlier than the fifth century, but since orthography as a rule is conservative and does not immediately adopt sound changes that have just occurred in the spoken language, it would even be possible to say that the sound law happened in the fourth century, at least on the basis of the evidence presented here, which is admittedly patchy. In languages with a strong orthographic tradition, such as Latin or almost all modern European languages, orthography may even lag many centuries behind the spoken forms (the spelling *ea* in English *great*, for instance, is a more than thousand-year-old relic of Old English orthography).

So VENNISETLI is a fossil of a particular stage in the development of Proto-Celtic **windo-* 'fair' + **saitlo-* 'lifetime' to the Welsh name *Gwynn-hoedl* that had been reached by the early sixth century. It therefore puts an absolute date, in this case before the early sixth century, to the sound law **nd, *mb, *ng > *nn, *mm, *ŋŋ*.

The second type of datable fossil is British Celtic toponyms in Anglo-Saxon territory. This is one of the main foci of Kenneth Jackson's influential book *Language and History in Early Britain*. After outlining the numerous pitfalls that the method entails, Jackson states (pp. 196–197): 'As a general rule it is obvious that the [Anglo-Saxon] invaders must have taken over a given [British Celtic] name when they first came into contact with the place and needed a name for it; hence, if we can fix roughly about the time when they reached that particular area we can give an approximate date for the loan, and base our linguistic deductions on this.' He adds two cautionary remarks: names of important towns (e.g. London, York) and major water-ways (e.g. Thames, Severn) may well have been known to the Anglo-Saxons and consequently borrowed by them well before they conquered the areas involved, so that the Anglo-Saxon name fossilizes a form that dates from before the conquest. Furthermore, Jackson states, British Celtic language enclaves may have persisted in Anglo-Saxon territory for generations, during which time the Celtic language kept evolving and, as a result, so did the form of place names; if such evolved place names were then taken over into Anglo-Saxon speech, they fossilized at a later date than the date of conquest of the area. Sticking to examples of the sound law **nd, *mb, *ng > *nn, *mm, *ŋŋ*, we can cite preserved inputs in e.g. *London* < Romano-British *Londonium*. But since this is a major town, its name is bound to have been known to Anglo-Saxons well before they conquered the area towards the end of the fifth century. Since, therefore, the English name *London* may have been borrowed into Anglo-Saxon much earlier than the fifth century, it can hardly be used to date the transition of **nd* to **nn* in British Celtic. Another example, one that is much less likely to have been known to the Anglo-Saxons before they conquered the place, is the Roman fort of *Anderitum* (Pevensey, Sussex) > Old English *Andred*, which according to the *Anglo-Saxon Chronicle* was taken by the Anglo-Saxons in 477: apparently the sound law **nd > *nn* had not yet occurred in the British Celtic spoken around the place *Anderitum* by about 477. The output of the same sound law is attested in the manor name *Croome* (Worcestershire) < Old English *Cromme*, besides *Crombe* < British Celtic **Krumbā*, lit. 'crooked', which is situated in a more westerly area that was not occupied by the Anglo-Saxons until the sixth century.

A third method for the absolute dating of sound laws makes use of Latin loanwords. Generally speaking, the influx of Latin loanwords into British Celtic started in the course of the first century AD, when most of Britain became part of the Roman Empire. At that point in time, Latin words were adopted into British Celtic and then treated as if they were British Celtic. Once adopted, such loanwords would undergo any sound change that subsequently occurred in British Celtic. So we can state that any British Celtic sound law which affected Latin loanwords can be dated to the late first century AD at the earliest, although here too uncertainty lurks: one must allow for the fact that contact between British Celtic and Latin could have stretched as far back as Caesar's expedition to Britain around the middle of the first century BC.

Let us take an example. Latin *commendō* 'I commit for preservation, entrust' was borrowed into British Celtic and ended up as Middle Welsh *kymynn* /kəminn/ 'bequeaths, commits'. Along the way, *commendō* participated in two of the sound laws that were discussed earlier, $*e > *i$ before *nd* (*kommind-*) and $*nd > *nn$ (*komminn-*), both of which as a result can be dated probably after the middle of the first century. In light of the more precise dating for $*nd > *nn$ that was arrived at earlier (between the fourth and early sixth centuries), this is not very helpful, but it illustrates the method. A higher resolution cannot be attained, however, for Latin loanwords continued to be adopted at least as long as Roman rule lasted, into the early fifth century, and through the Latin of the Church well after that date. A special position is occupied by Latin loanwords connected with Christianity, which probably date from the later third century at the earliest, when Christianity became more widespread (e.g. Welsh *carawys* /karauis/ 'Lent' < Latin *quadragēsima*).

Dating sound laws by an absolute chronology is essentially based on reasonable assumptions rather than on the iron-clad logic that establishes the relative chronologies of sound laws (as well as the sound laws themselves). Reasonable assumptions are just that: it is reasonable to assume that the Anglo-Saxons borrowed a place name when they occupied the territory in which the place was situated, but it is also possible that they borrowed the name earlier or later. Dating inscriptions on the basis of epigraphy is to some extent subjective: authorities may and often do disagree on dates within a certain margin. Yet reasonable assumptions are all we have in those fields, and they are better than unreasonable ones. It is, of course, possible that reasonable assumptions are incorrect, but the point is that the chances are relatively small. They can be made even smaller, for instance where an absolute date based on epigraphic evidence happens to coincide with an absolute date based on the evidence of Anglo-Saxon place names.

5. THE LINGUISTIC MAP OF PRE-ANGLO-SAXON ENGLAND

As there are sophisticated methods for its reconstruction, the common ancestor language of Welsh, Cornish, and Breton is so accessible that with a bit of practice we would be able to strike up a conversation with a second-century

British Celt in his native language and explain to him how his language had changed—quite dramatically as a matter of fact—by the end of the sixth century. But this confidence in our capabilities does not stretch beyond the British Celtic that was spoken in the west of Britain, since it is from there that the languages come on which our reconstruction depends (i.e. Wales, Cornwall, and, in the case of Breton, probably also Devon). In the absence of any knowledge about the peculiarities of the Celtic dialects that were spoken in, say, Kent, Essex, and East Anglia and around York, it has usually been assumed that changes in western British Celtic also affected those British Celtic dialects in the far east. This is another example of a reasonable assumption: it is a fact that Celtic was spoken from east to west Britain when the Romans established their rule and that under Roman rule the travel of people, products, and ideas from the southeast to other parts of the country would generally have been unimpeded, probably more so than ever before. Unimpeded traffic and contact of speakers tend to slow down processes of change that would lead to dialectal fragmentation, and also to encourage the development of a dialect continuum: a chain of dialects in which mutual understanding, from one village to the next, would be ensured. In such a continuum, linguistic innovations would gradually spread along traffic axes from the economic and political centres in the east towards the less densely populated west and north. The western areas in which Welsh, Breton, and Cornish arose would be the logical terminus of those linguistic innovations, so developments that would start in the east might arrive in the west a few generations later. Given the plausibility of this scenario, why cast doubt on the idea that the lost eastern British Celtic was essentially identical to western British Celtic?

Two recently advanced hypotheses have shaken the idea that western British Celtic may be used as a proxy for the language with which the Anglo-Saxons engaged in the east: the language of the east may well have been Late Spoken Latin rather than Celtic (II.5.1), and the little we know about eastern British Celtic points to it being closer to the Continental Celtic language of Gaul than to western British Celtic (II.5.2). Both issues require detailed attention.

5.1. Spoken Latin in Britain

Generally speaking, Latin successfully eliminated almost all other languages within the confines of the Western Roman Empire, the exceptions being three languages that survived in relatively remote areas: Albanian, probably in the higher reaches of the Balkans; Basque in the Pyrenees; and Celtic, which survived only in the extreme west and north of Britain, where Welsh, Cornish, and Breton originate. There is no a priori reason to think that Britain, being an island far away from Rome's centres of power, was so superficially Romanized that Latin would just be the language of the political and military elite. Most of Britain formed part of the Roman Empire for no less than 350 years. Culturally and economically, Britain's southeast saw the development of a Roman civil society, which included such features as towns, temples, rural villas as foci of agricultural activity, and a dense network of roads. Latin was the means of written expression for the elite, as hundreds of monumental inscriptions indicate, but also for the man in the street, who reported the loss or theft of petty objects to the goddess Minerva Sulis of Aquae Sulis (Bath) in written Latin. The Romanized British southeast is known as the 'Lowland Zone', which runs southeast of an approximate line that connects Dorchester, Bath, Gloucester, and Wroxeter and bends sharply eastwards towards Lincoln, then northwards past York until it hits Hadrian's Wall near Corbridge. By contrast, the 'Highland Zone', which largely consists of the moorlands, uplands, and rugged coastal areas of Devon and Cornwall, Wales, the Pennines, Yorkshire, and Cumbria, was culturally only superficially Romanized, with emphasis on the military.[14]

The general assumption, therefore, is that in the Lowland Zone, at least, Latin was probably more than a thin upper-class veneer over a largely Celtic-speaking society. There is a specifically linguistic reason, too. Western (i.e. Highland) British Celtic underwent a period of rapid and deep changes in its sound system and its morphology in the two centuries that followed the collapse of Roman rule in Britain. Most of these changes are strikingly similar to changes affecting Late Spoken Latin in western Europe during the same period. One might think that Celtic and Latin developed in tandem because Celtic with a Latin accent had high status: Latin, after all, was the official language of the politically and culturally powerful Roman Empire as well as of the Christian state religion, and speakers of Celtic may have wanted to sound as Latin as possible in order to be associated with that power. But it is almost certain that after the collapse of Roman power in Britain speakers of Latin had exceptionally low social status. That conclusion is arrived at by considering Latin loanwords in western (Highland) British Celtic. Virtually all of them—there are hundreds—date from the Roman period. The influx of loanwords almost completely came to a halt by the fifth and sixth centuries, precisely during the period when the sound system and the syntax of Highland British Celtic became Latinized. The Latinization of the British Celtic sound system but not of the lexicon strongly indicates that it resulted from low-status speakers of Latin rapidly shifting to high-status Celtic and in the process retaining a Latin accent but avoiding the use of Latin words. This is a reversal of the situation in previous centuries, when Celtic speakers shifted to Latin.

The surprising thing is that this low-status Celtic variety with a Latin accent became so successful in spreading itself that all surviving varieties of Highland British Celtic (Welsh, Cornish, and Breton) are packed with its Latinate features. How is that possible, if it was spoken by low-status speakers, who are not as a rule linguistic role models? Only if speakers of Latinate Celtic were so numerous that they would have swamped the speakers of other varieties of Celtic. This linguistic scenario evokes images of large numbers of destitute Latin-speaking refugees from the Lowland Zone entering the Highland Zone before the gradual advance of the Anglo-Saxon warrior-settlers in the fifth and sixth centuries. What is relevant to the present discussion of the linguistic map of pre-Anglo-Saxon Britain is that by the end of the Roman period the east was apparently home to a population of Latin speakers large enough to swamp the population of Celtic speakers in the west by the fifth and sixth centuries. How large is impossible to say: given that the Lowland Zone was more densely populated than the Highland Zone, a population large enough to outnumber the Highland Zone natives might still be a small proportion of the entire Lowland Zone population. Nor is it possible to say from which parts of the Lowland Zone these migrants originated. At the very least, Latin-Celtic bilingualism must have been widespread in the Lowland Zone; at the most, Latin may have almost completely displaced Celtic altogether (but we shall see that there are other considerations pointing to the survival of Celtic in the southeast: II.5.3 and II.5.4).[15]

The conclusion is that the Anglo-Saxons initially may have met with speakers of Latin rather than Celtic, which has obvious implications for an explanation of the absence of Celtic influence on Anglo-Saxon: maybe there was no Celtic influence because the Anglo-Saxons met hardly any speakers of Celtic because the latter had become speakers of Latin over the preceding centuries. This conclusion transforms the question about Celtic influence in Old English into a question about British Latin influence in Old English, which brings along its own complexities. The little that is known about the way in which Latin in Britain developed after the first century suggests that it did not differ substantially from the late Latin of Gaul, which ultimately became French (see section II.5.2 below).[16]

There is tentative evidence from place names that indicates that British Celtic had a different status from Latin in the Lowland Zone. Richard Coates has pointed out that a number of British Celtic words which survive as English place names have peculiar features. They tend to occur in simple names, such as *Creech* and *Crick* (Welsh *crug* 'barrow'), *Penn* (Welsh *penn* 'head, end'), *Ross* and *Roos* (Welsh *rhos* 'headland'), and *Avon* (Welsh *afon* 'river'). What they never do is form the second element of early English generic compounds of the type **Long-creech*, however, nor do they enter the Old English lexicon as loanwords. That suggests that these British Celtic terms were borrowed into Old English as names denoting specific landscape features rather than as ordinary nouns (Coates 2007: 181). Direct contact between British Celtic and Anglo-Saxon is not required to explain the presence of these British Celtic words in Old English: it is enough to assume that British Celtic donated the place names consisting of those terms to Latin, and Latin then donated them to Anglo-Saxon. By contrast, a number of Latin place-name elements do form generic compounds together with Old English terms and often enter the Old English lexicon. Examples are Old English *strǣt* 'street' (Latin *strāta*), *ceaster* 'fortification, town' (Latin *castrum*), *camp* 'open land' (Latin *campus*), **eccles* 'church' (Latin *ecclēsia*), and **funta* 'well' (Latin *fontāna*). The status of these terms in Old English suggests direct contact between Anglo-Saxon and Latin (Parsons 2011: 126–127). The place-name evidence therefore seems to indicate that at least in some parts of the Lowland Zone Anglo-Saxon was in direct contact with Latin and borrowed place names from Latin rather than from British Celtic.[17]

5.2. The Latin Inscriptions of Early Medieval Britain

So far, we have seen mostly indirect evidence pointing to the survival of spoken Latin in Britain during the early medieval period. But there is also a corpus of well over 300 Latin inscriptions from Britain that can be dated between about AD 500 and 1200.[18] They are known as the 'Early Christian' or 'Celtic' inscriptions of Britain, though it is not clear whether the people who produced them were all Christians (many of them certainly were) or speakers of Celtic (many names in the inscriptions are of Celtic origin). The inscriptions are found mainly in Wales and Cornwall; some are from southern Scotland, Man, Herefordshire, Somerset, Devon, and Dorset (where all four are from Wareham). The area forms a wide northern and western arch, which includes the Highland Zone as well as adjacent areas of the Lowland Zone, which Anglo-Saxon occupation did not reach until around AD 600.

5.2.1. Was Late Latin Spoken in Britain during the Early Middle Ages?

Although the language of the inscriptions clearly is Latin, it is not immediately evident that the inscriptions were carved or commissioned by people who spoke Latin. One consideration is that the use of Latin grammatical cases in the inscriptions does not conform to Classical Latin standards at all. Another reason to doubt whether the inscriptions were produced by Latin speakers is that they appear on gravestones and almost all show variations on a small number of standard phrases that do not presuppose more knowledge of Latin amongst the early medieval bereaved than does the appearance of R.I.P. (*requiescat in pace* 'may (s)he rest in peace') on modern gravestones. One formula consists of the name of the deceased, usually followed by his or her affiliation ('son of X', 'wife of Y'), which appears in the Latin genitive case. The genitive denotes possession, in this case of the grave:

1. CIIC 373/ECMW 171	SEVERINI FILI SEVERI
	'(grave) of Severinus, son of Severus'

By Classical Latin standards of grammar and spelling, this inscription is completely correct.

In another widespread formula, the name of the deceased appears in the nominative case, which denotes the subject of a clause, and is combined with *hic iacet/iacit* 'here lies':

| 2. CIIC 392/ECMW 77 | VERACIVS PBR HIC IACIT |
| | 'Veracius the priest lies here' |

PBR is an abbreviation of Latin *presbyter* 'priest'. The grammatical structure of this sentence is also correct by Classical standards.

In many inscriptions, however, the use of the Classical Latin grammatical cases is blatantly incorrect. An example:

| 3. CIIC 387/ECMW 95 | FIGVLINI FILI LOCVLITI HIC IACIT |
| | 'Figulinus son of Loculitus lies here' |

By Classical Latin standards, the subject of the clause, 'Figulinus, son', should be in the nominative (*Figulinus filius*) rather than in the genitive. One way of explaining this oddity goes as follows: 'The writer (as is often the case in this tradition) knows the Latin funerary formula *hic iacet*, but has no control over the Latin case system. From his familiarity with epitaphs written in the genitive throughout but without a verb [as in example 1] he made the incorrect deduction that *-i* endings were the norm for Latin even if there was a verb' (Adams 2007: 618).'[19] A similar confusion underlies the following text:

| 4. CIIC 334/54 | CATACVS HIC IACIT FILIVS TEGERNACVS |
| | 'Catacus lies here, the son of Tigernacus' |

In J. N. Adams' words again (2007: 618): 'The writer has failed to put the name of the father [*Tegernacus*] into the genitive but has used the nominative instead (. . .). Here we see a classic feature of imperfect learning: the writer knows a single case form and puts it to more syntactic uses than one.'[20]

| 5. CIIC 376/174 | VENNISETLI FILIVS ERCAGNI |
| | '(grave) of Vennisetlus, son of Ercagnus' |

In this example, *Vennisetli* is in the genitive, but *filius*, which should agree in case with *Vennisetli*, appears in the nominative instead of the genitive *fili*. Adams states (2007: 619): 'Some writers knew the nominative form of *filius*, but this knowledge was not accompanied by an ability to make the name and *filius* agree.' On the basis of texts such as these, Adams concludes: 'By the time when these inscriptions were written Latin was all but a dead language. Parallels . . . can be cited from the Roman period itself for the attempt to keep a dead language going for the writing of funerary inscriptions, because it was felt to be appropriate that a respected language should be used for epitaphs even after genuine knowledge of that language had been lost.' In a nutshell, the medieval Latin inscriptions of Britain offer no evidence for the survival of spoken Latin in Britain, but rather the opposite: they show that spoken Latin had died out amongst the writers who carved the inscriptions.

This is certainly a possibility, but it is useful to ask oneself how compelling the idea is. Let us compare a parallel situation in the history of the Irish language. Consider the following phrases in Irish, which illustrate some of the developments that occurred in the period straddling the boundary between Old Irish (600–900) and Middle Irish (900–1200):

Old Irish:	1. *Ailbe daltae Maíni* 'Ailbe, foster son of Maíne'

The two forms ending in *-e* are Old Irish nominatives, and the one in *-i* is a genitive. This phrase is formed correctly according to Old Irish grammar and spelling. The same phrase with the same meaning may appear in Middle Irish in a variety of spellings. I cite only three:

Middle Irish:	2. *Ailbe daltae Maíni* (= Old Irish)
	3. *Ailbi daltai Maíne*
	4. *Ailbi daltae Maíni*

An interpretation of these data along lines similar to Adams' reading of the British Latin evidence would run as follows. Some writers of Middle Irish still had a good enough grasp of the language to produce the phrase using the correct case forms, as in example 2. Others, apparently, were hopelessly confused, using the genitives *Ailbi* and *daltai* where nominatives would be correct, and the nominative *Maíne* instead of the expected genitive *Maíni* (example 3). Others again had lost their sense of grammatical agreement and aligned a genitive *Ailbi* with a nominative *daltae* (example 4). Such maltreatment of the grammatical cases must surely mean that to the scribes of 3 and 4 Irish was a dead language?

No, it does not. A correct assessment of the Middle Irish phenomena is possible if we know how the Irish language changed between the Old and Middle Irish periods. One of the key developments that characterize Middle Irish is that all Old Irish word-final unstressed vowels, including *-e* and *-i*,

The Rise of English   37

had become /ə/.[21] So the Old Irish phrase *Ailb*[e] *dalta*[e] *Main*[i] had come to be pronounced as *Ailb*[ə] *dalta*[ə] *Main*[ə]. This phonetic development obliterated the Old Irish difference between the nominative and the genitive of all three words. The loss of this difference does not conform to Old Irish standards but is in complete alignment with the rules of Middle Irish. In the absence of a normative Middle Irish spelling system, it did not matter whether a scribe wrote word-final *-e* or *-i* (or for that matter *-iu*, *-eo*, *-ea*) because that did not interfere with the language as it was spoken, for all were pronounced /ə/. In the same sense it would not matter whether we write English *beat* or *beet*, or *would* or *wood*, for both spellings of those pairs are pronounced identically.

If we apply this analogy to the Latin inscriptions of Britain, the 'confusion' between, say, the nominative *Tegernacus* and the genitive *Tegernaci* could be the result of a sound change in British Latin that obliterated the difference between *-us* and *-i* in final syllables, turning both into something like /ə/. This is just a possibility, and we have no reason to suppose that vowels in final syllables actually turned into /ə/ in British Latin. But the change is not implausible, given that the closely related Latin of France did turn the vowels of final syllables into /ə/ or zero during the early medieval period, and all Romance languages lost the Latin genitive case at a very early date. The point I am making is that the confusion of grammatical cases we observe in the medieval Latin inscriptions of Britain is closely comparable to the phenomenon observed in Middle Irish texts. If the latter is readily explainable as the result of a sound change occurring between Old and Middle Irish rather than the extinction of Irish, why, then, should we exclude the possibility that Latin in Britain simply changed from Classical to medieval British Latin rather than becoming extinct? It would be illogical to assume that a bad command of Classical Latin in the British inscriptions necessarily means that Latin in Britain had become extinct by the early medieval period, just as it is illogical to assume that a bad command of Old Irish amongst Middle Irish scribes necessarily implies that Irish had died out: the language had just moved on to a different phase of its development.

So in trying to answer the question whether Latin was still a living, spoken language amongst those who made the early medieval Latin inscriptions of Britain we are back to square one. Yet it is possible to make headway by studying the inscriptions more closely and by shifting the frame of reference from Classical Latin written standards to the standards of the Latin that was spoken in late Antiquity and the early medieval period. This is the language called Late Spoken Latin. Our knowledge of Late Spoken Latin comes from three sources:

- Violations of Classical Latin grammar and spelling in late Antique and early medieval Latin inscriptions: the rule of thumb is that if these inscriptions show grammatical forms and spellings in a correct Classical Latin form, that does not mean that Latin had stayed the same.

Such 'correct' grammatical forms and spellings just point to the fact that the author was well educated in the norms and practices of writing Classical Latin; only if he slipped up and deviated from the Classical norm do we obtain potentially valuable information: either he just made a stonemason's mistake (e.g. when he wrote *ihc* instead of *hic* 'here', swapping letters), which is uninformative, or he let on that the Latin he spoke was actually different from the Latin he wrote (e.g. when he wrote *cives* instead of *civis* 'citizen', betraying that in speech /i/ and /e/ in final syllables had merged into /ɪ/, which could be spelled as either <e> or <i>).

- Similar violations in Latin texts in early medieval manuscripts.
- Linguistic reconstructions based on our knowledge of the development of Romance languages such as French, Spanish, and Italian, to which Late Spoken Latin is ancestral.

Late Spoken Latin codifies many of the sweeping changes that affected Latin between the Classical period of the first century BC and the earliest manuscript attestations of French, Spanish, and Italian in the centuries around AD 1000. Let us begin by returning to inscription number 2:

2. CIIC 392/ECMW 77	VERACIVS PBR HIC IACIT
	'Veracius the priest lies here'

The grammar and spelling of this inscription conform to Classical Latin standards, with one exception, which is where things start to become interesting: Classical Latin 'lies' is not *iacit* (which exists but means 'throws') but *iacet*. In fact, almost all of the Celtic Latin inscriptions that contain the formula show *iacit* rather than *iacet*, so that this cannot be just a stonemason's mistake. One explanation for *iacit* is that the stonemason or the person who commissioned him simply did not know Latin well enough and therefore confused the two very similar verbs. Another, more interesting take on the matter is that the confusion of *iacit* and *iacet* would have made perfect sense to any speaker of Late Spoken Latin. In Classical Latin, *iacit* ['jakit] 'throws' and *iacet* ['jaket] 'lies' were pronounced differently, and this pronunciation difference is reflected in spelling. In Late Spoken Latin, however, both had merged as ['jātʃɪt], as a result of three sound changes:[22]

- [k] became [tʃ] before front vowels (i.e. vowels such as *e* and *i*, which are produced by moving the tongue forward from its neutral resting position).
- Short vowels became long vowels if they were both stressed and followed by a single consonant + a vowel, as is the case with *a* in *iacit* and *iacet*.

- In final unstressed syllables, the difference between the vowels [e] (< Classical Latin *ĕ*) and [ɪ] (< Classical Latin *ī*) disappeared: they merged into one single vowel, which was probably pronounced as [ɪ];[23] this affected the final syllables of Classical Latin *iacet* and *iacit*, which as a result became identical.

So in Late Spoken Latin, ['jātˤɪt] meant both 'throws' and 'lies'. But in view of the conservative nature of Latin orthography, which tended to adhere to Classical Latin norms of spelling throughout Antiquity and the medieval period, ['jātˤɪt] continued to be spelled as *iacet* if it meant 'lies' and as *iacit* if it meant 'throws'—unless, that is, a scribe slipped up, not because he wrote bad Latin (*iacet* and *iacit* are both appropriate spellings of what was pronounced as ['jātˤɪt]), but because he was insufficiently aware of the spelling conventions of Classical Latin. In this sense, the spelling of 'lies' as *iacit* instead of *iacet* is comparable to spelling English *meat* as *meet*.

Rather than just being a mistake, therefore, the spelling *iacit* for Classical Latin *iacet* 'lies', which occurs in this and many other Celtic Latin inscriptions, may well reflect developments in Late Spoken Latin because it agrees with what we know about that language. If so, the spelling *iacit* suggests the presence of speakers of Late Spoken Latin in western Britain around approximately 500. The corpus of inscriptions shows yet another variation in the formula *hic iacet* that points in the same direction:

---

6. CIIC 353/ECMW 127   TRENACATVS IC IACIT FILIVS MAGLAGNI

'here lies Trenacatus, son of Maglagnus'

Instead of *hic* 'here' the inscription reads *ic*.[24] This also shows interference of spoken Latin: the sound [h] was lost in Latin at an early stage, probably already by the first century BC, but the standardized orthography held on to writing *h* in words that used to have it, such as *hīc*. After the third century AD, *h* was frequently omitted in words that originally had it and added to words that originally did not, a liberty that persisted in early medieval manuscripts.[25] The spelling *ic* in our inscription betrays the influence of spoken Latin. The *Trenacatus* inscription, which is from Llanwenos, Wales, and dates from around AD 500, is interesting for other reasons, too. It forms part of a group of bilingual Latin-Irish inscriptions. The Irish part, which is written in the curious Irish Ogam script, contains only the name of the deceased in the Irish genitive singular: '(grave) of Trenacatas'. The name, with its -*a*- in the second syllable, is Irish rather than Latin or British Celtic. The inscription belongs to the trilingual environment of the Irish settlements in Wales, where Irish and British Celtic were spoken as well as, presumably, Latin.

So *ic* and *iacit* instead of *hic* and *iacet* indicate that Late Spoken Latin was used in western Britain in the fifth and sixth centuries. If this were all the evidence for spoken Latin in post-Roman Britain, the extent to which Latin was still spoken could have been very small: all it requires for the introduction of the *hic iacet* formula and its *ic iacit* variant is one or two trend-setting stonemasons who spoke a bit of Late Spoken Latin or imported the formula with its variations *ic* and *iacit* from, say, Gaul, as well as a large number of Welsh stonemasons copying their linguistic behaviour. But there is more to be gleaned from the inscriptions if we study non-formulaic words.

7. CIIC 391/ECMW 78	SENACVS PRSBR HIC IACIT CVM MULTITUDNEM FRATRUM
	'Senacus the priest lies here with a multitude of brethren'

The significant portion is *cum multitudnem fratrum* 'with a multitude of brethren', which in Classical Latin would have been *cum multitudine fratrum*. The first conspicuous feature is the loss of *-i-* in *multitud(i)nem*. This may be a simple mistake by a stonemason who forgot to carve the letter, but it is also possible that the vowel was lost in speech by a process called syncope: the rule in early medieval French is that in a word in which the stressed syllable was followed by two unstressed syllables, the first unstressed syllable was lost if it was followed by a single consonant (*multi'tudinem* > *multi'tudnem*, where ' denotes stress on the following vowel). It is impossible to decide which of the two explanations is correct.

The second issue is that in Classical Latin the preposition *cum* 'with' is followed by the ablative case (*multitudine*) rather than the accusative case (*multitudinem*). In all of Late Spoken Latin, word-final *-m* at the end of a word consisting of more than one syllable had invariably been lost in speech. So it was purely a matter of spelling whether *-m* was written or not, and a matter of education whether it was written in conformity with Classical Latin rules or not. Writing *cum multitudnem* with an *-m* does not conform to Classical standards, but it is an easy mistake to make for anyone speaking Late Spoken Latin: the use of an accusative *multitudnem* instead of an ablative *multitudine* is a typical trait of Late Spoken Latin, when the accusative had ousted the ablative as the case that was used after prepositions.[26]

Another case of an omitted word-final *-m* is SINGNO for Classical Latin *signum* 'sign' (CIIC 427b/ECMW 301). This shows two other features which are readily explained against a Late Spoken Latin background. The spelling <o> for <u> in the final syllable is common in late Antique and early medieval Latin texts,[27] and the spelling <ngn> reflects the spoken Latin development of *gn* to *ŋn*.[28]

Other developments seen in the British Latin inscriptions that make sense if they were inspired by Late Spoken Latin are the development of Classical Latin *ae* to *e* and the spelling of Classical Latin stressed long *ē* as <i>.[29]

All of those Late Spoken Latin developments are widespread in areas in which Latin developed into a Romance language, and particularly in Gaul, where Latin turned into French during the early medieval period. Being critical, one could still downplay the significance of those features in British Latin and say that they were imported by immigrant scribes from Gaul, along with the *hic iacet* formula, rather than reflecting native British Latin usage. But there is one feature for which that explanation is impossible: the loss of word-final -*s*. In Late Spoken Latin, loss of -*s* occurred in Italy and in the area in which Rumanian originated but not in western Europe, where -*s* was retained.[30] Omission of -*s* in later Latin inscriptions from Gaul is relatively rare and more likely to be scribal than phonetic.[31] In the British Latin inscriptions of the early medieval period, however, there are so many instances of the loss of -*s* that they are unlikely to be just scribal errors:

(1) -*o* instead of Classical Latin -*us*

CIIC 381/ECMW 87 ALIORTVS ELMETIACO 'Aliortus Elmetiacus'

CIIC 328/ECMW 44 [R]VGNIATO [FI]LI VENDONI '(?)rugniatus son of Vendon(i)us'

CIIC 394/ECMW 103 FVIT [C]ONSOBRINO MA[G]LI MAGISTRATI 'he was cousin (*consobrinus*) of Maglus the magistrate'

CIIC 325/ECMW 33 VASSO PAVLINI 'servant (*vassus*) of Paulinus'

CIIC 435/ ECMW 315 LATIO 'Lat(t)ius'?

(2) -*e* and -*i* instead of Classical Latin -*is*

CIIC 394/ECMW 103 VENEDOTIS CIVE 'Venedotian citizen' (Classical Latin *Venedotis civis*)

CIIC 402/ECMW 184 MVLIER BONA NOBILI 'good and noble (*nobilis*) wife'

CIIC 408/ECMW 229 PRONEPVS ETERNALI 'great-grandson of Eternalis' (Classical Latin *pronepos Aeternalis*)

CIIC 413/ECMW 272 CAELEXTI MONEDORIGI '(grave) of Caelestis, son of Monedorix' (Classical Latin *Caelestis Monedorigis*)

CIIC 435/ECMW 315 CLVTORIGI '(grave) of Clutorix' (Classical Latin *Clutorigis*)

CIIC 455/ECMW 403 CAMVLLORIGI '(grave) of Camulorix' (Classical Latin *Camulorigis*)

CIIC 515/Scot. 9 DVO FILII LIBERALI[32] 'two sons of Liberalis (*Liberalis*)'

The loss of word-final -*s* in early medieval British Latin would also explain the hypercorrect addition of -*s* in CIIC 393/ECMW 101 IN HOC CONGERIES LAPIDVM 'in this heap of stones' (Classical Latin *in hoc congerie lapidum*). The relevance of the loss of final -*s* to the question of the survival of Latin in Britain lies in the fact that this feature cannot possibly have been imported into Britain by incidental visitors from nearby areas in which Latin was spoken: in those areas (France, Spain, Portugal) word-final -*s* was preserved. In the Latinity of western Europe, loss of -*s* is characteristic of

British Latin and of British Latin alone, where it may have been caused by the influence of British Celtic. What better evidence for the survival of British Latin as a spoken language in the early medieval period?[33]

5.2.2. *The Collapse of the Classical Latin Case System in British Latin*

With this conclusion in mind, let us return to the issue of the confusion of the nominative in *-us* with the genitive in *-ī*. We have seen a number of sound changes that probably affected the Late Spoken Latin of Britain, most of them along with western European Late Spoken Latin. None would account for the confusion of *-us* and *-ī*, however: *-us* lost its *-s*, and *u* in final syllables merged with Latin *ō*, but there is no evidence in the corpus to suggest that *-u* was confused with *-ī* as a result of a sound change of final vowels to something like /ə/. So the possible parallel with Old and Middle Irish, which was explained earlier, breaks down. If it is not sound change that can be made responsible for the *-us*/*-ī* confusion, we need to explore the possibility that grammatical change is involved. In this context it is relevant to point out that a similar confusion of nominative and genitive can be observed in a different class of nouns, viz. the feminines ending in *-a*:

CIIC 320/ECMW 26 CVLIDOR[I?] IACIT ET ORVVITE MVLIERI SECUNDI [. . . ?][34]
    'Culidorus? / Culidorix? lies (here) and Orfita (his) second wife'
    (Classical Latin: *Culidorus? / Culidorix? iacet et Orfita mulier secunda*)

This is a possible example of a cross of the formula *nominative hic iacet* 'X lies here' and the formula *genitive* '(grave) of X'. ORVVITE is the genitive *Orfitae*, agreeing with the genitive *mulieri(s)* 'wife'. *Secundi* is usually taken to be the genitive of the name of the father of *Culidor-: Secundi [fili]* 'son of Secundus', but this is unlikely for two reasons. The normal order in these British inscriptions is **fili Secundi*, and placing this phrase so far away from *Culidor[i]* is curious. The possibility I have chosen is to take *secundi* as an alternative spelling of *secunde*,[35] which developed regularly from earlier *secundae*.[36] Another example of the spelling *-i* for what originally was *-ae* can be found in CIIC 419/ECMW 284:

FILIAE SALVIA[N]I HIC IACIT VE[.]MAIE VXSOR TIGIRNICI ET FILIE EIVS ONERATI [HIC IA]CIT RIGOHENE [ ]OCETI [ ]ACI
    'the daughter of Salvianus lies here, Ve[.]maia wife of Tigirnicus, and his (her?) honoured daughter [here? li]es, Rigohena . . .'

As in the preceding inscription, the two formulae were mixed: the subject of *hic iacit* is in the genitive instead of the nominative. The subject genitives are *filiae, Ve[.]maie = Ve[.]maiae* and *onerati = honoratae*, and

Rigohene = *Rigohenae*.[37] The same mixture of the formulae can be found in the following two inscriptions:

CIIC 401/ECMW 183 BROHOMAGLI IATTI IC IACIT ET VXOR EIVS CAVNE
    'Brohomaglus (son) of Iattus lies here and his wife Cauna'

Here the genitive *Caune* = *Caunae* replaces the nominative *Cauna*.

CIIC 451/ECMW 401 TVNCCETACE VXSOR DAARI HIC IACIT
    'Tuncetaca, wife of Darius, lies here'

The genitive *Tunccetace* = *Tuncetacae* replaces the nominative. Notice that in both inscriptions the word *uxor* = *uxsor* 'wife', which should agree in case with the genitives *Caunae* and *Tuncetacae*, is in the old nominative.

So just as the masculine genitive in -*i* (phonetically long *ī*) is used instead of the nominative in -*us*, the feminine genitive in -*ae* is used instead of the nominative in -*a*. In neither case do we have reason to believe that the confusion was the result of sound change. An unexpected source offers a clue towards what is going on: Welsh.

Welsh contains hundreds of Latin loanwords. Among them is the Latin personal name, ultimately of Greek origin, *Ambrosius*. This appears in Medieval Welsh in two very well-attested forms: *Emreis* and *Emrys*. A number of regular sound changes have been involved in turning the Latin source form into its Welsh descendants, but we shall focus on just one: the development of Latin -*o*- into Welsh -*ei*- and -*y*-. This development falls under the heading of so-called final *i*-affection, which means that the vowel *ī* or the consonant *j* in the final syllable of the word changes the vowel of the preceding syllable. The handbooks on the history of the Welsh language are unclear about the conditions under which final *i*-affection operating on *o* produced Welsh *ei* or *y*, but the basic rules are straightforward and come to light when we study a number of examples:

(A) *o > ei
    (1) Proto-British *korkjos > Middle Welsh *keirch* 'oats' (cognate with Old Irish *corcae* 'oats')
    (2) Latin *spolium* > Proto-British *spoljon > Middle Welsh *yspeil* 'booty'
    (3) Latin *solea* 'sole' or *solium* 'seat' > Proto-British *solja, *soljon > Middle Welsh *seil* 'foundation'
    (4) Latin *Lōndonium > Middle Welsh *Llundein*[38]

(B) *o > y
    (5) Proto-British masculine plurals that ended in *-ī turn *o in the preceding syllable into *y*: e.g. *corn* 'horn', plural *kyrn* <

Proto-British **kornī*; similarly, *llory* 'cudgel', plural *llyry*; also in Latin loanwords: *escob* 'bishop', plural *esgyb*; *abostol* 'apostle', plural *ebestyl*; *pont* 'bridge', plural *pynt*

(6) Latin *Salomō* > Proto-British **Salomī* > Middle Welsh *Selyf*
(7) Proto-British **Touto-rīgs* (lit. 'tribal king') > Middle Welsh *Tudyr*
(8) Proto-British **Maglo-kū* (lit. 'princely hound') > **Maglo-kī* > Middle Welsh *Meilyg*

On the basis of these forms, it seems that **o* regularly became *ei* if the final syllable contained **j* (1–4), while it became *y* before an **ī* (5–8). There are a number of possible counterexamples, but they are unconvincing: Latin *memoria* 'memory' > **memorjā* > Middle Welsh *myfyr* (not ***myfeir*) and *historia* 'history, story' > **istorjā* > Middle Welsh *ystyr* (not ***ysteir*) are irregular in any case because the syllable **-jā* never causes final *i*-affection.[39] Proto-Celtic **gdonjos* 'man, mortal' turns up as Middle Welsh *dyn*, but the intermediate stage may well have been **dunjos* in British Celtic before *i*-affection operated: the development of **o* to **u* before a nasal consonant is widespread in Welsh although the exact rules are difficult to pin down.[40] Hence **gdonjos* > **dunjos* > *dyn* illustrates the behaviour of **u* rather than **o* under *i*-affection.

The only words that continue to provide problems are the pair *Emreis* and *Emrys*. The general rule predicts that *Ambrosius* > **Ambrosjos* should regularly become *Emreis*. The alternative form *Emrys* presupposes a final syllable without **j* but with long **ī*. This does exist, not in British Celtic, but in the Latin inflected paradigm: the Latin vocative and the Latin genitive of *Ambrosius* are both *Ambrosī*, and this would yield Middle Welsh *Emrys*. Since prehistoric Welsh, like Late Spoken Latin, lost the system of nominal cases, it is in general unlikely that it would preserve two case forms of the same word. But *Ambrosius* is in one respect a special type of noun, for it is a personal name, and personal names in languages with a case system occur frequently in the vocative, which is the case used when addressing a person ('(hey) Ambrose!'). Because of that frequency and because of the widespread fact that personal names often have a formal beside an informal form (think of *Ted*, *Bob* beside *Edward*, *Robert*), it is not unlikely that *Emrys* reflects the petrified Latin vocative rather than the genitive. An exact parallel is the Scottish personal name *Hamish*, which goes back to the Scots Gaelic vocative *a Sheumais* (Anglo-Irish *Seamus* reflects the nominative of the same name). A similar example is the Middle Welsh name *Pyr*, which reflects the Latin vocative *Porī* rather than the nominative *Porius* (the latter would have become the unattested Middle Welsh form **Peir*).

The relevance of all this to the confusion of the nominative in *-us* and genitive in *-ī* in British Latin inscriptions can now be revealed. Latin *Ambrosius* and *Ambrosī* were both borrowed into Welsh, the latter not because it was a genitive but because it was a vocative; this vocative happens to have the same form as the genitive (exactly as in the case of Scots *Hamish*). If a grammatical case system breaks down, as it did in Late Spoken Latin and in contemporary British Celtic, confusion of the nominative (the case of the subject) and vocative (the case of the addressee) is psychologically a relatively small step because the addressee commonly refers to the same person as the subject of the clause, as it does in examples 2 and 3 although not in 4:

(1) *John helps me.* (*John* = subject = nominative)
(2) *John, help me!* (*John* = vocative = the same person as the subject = nominative)
(3) *John, can you help me?* (*John* = vocative = the same person as the subject *you* = nominative)
(4) *John, can I help you?* (*John* = vocative = the same person as the object = accusative)

The vocatives in sentences of type 2–3 show a functional similarity to the nominative in type 1, which is not shared by the genitive in any of its functions (usually possession). Hence if a case system breaks down, as it did in Late Spoken Latin, this functional similarity can easily lead to a merger of the nominative and vocative. This is especially relevant to the British Latin inscriptions: personal names and kinship terms form the bulk of the words attested, and vocatives are used particularly frequently in the case of personal names and kinship terms, like Latin *filius* 'son', vocative *filī*. So we can formulate the hypothesis that it is the vocative *filī* that bridged the functional gap between the nominative *filius* and the genitive *filī* and enabled speakers of Late Spoken Latin in Britain to use *filius* and *filī* interchangeably in nominative and genitive functions. The point of this hypothesis is that it provides a linguistically reasonable account for the confusion of the nominative *filius* and genitive *filī* in the corpus of inscriptions. Rather than demonstrating scribal incompetence, the confusion *filius/filī* is a natural development given what we know about the development of Late Spoken Latin in general.

All this accounts for the confusion of the nominative and vocative = genitive of nouns ending in *-ius*, such as *filius* and the personal names *Lovernius*, *Carausius*, and *Veracius*, which occur in the corpus. But how about the very frequent nouns ending in simple *-us*, such as *Catacus* and *Paulinus*, which originally had a vocative ending in *-e*, which was different from the genitive ending in *-ī*? And what about feminine nouns ending in *-a*, such as *Potentina* and *Avitoria*, whose vocative was *-a*, too, but whose genitive ended in *-ae*? In both categories of nouns, we find that the nominative and genitive were confused in the British Latin corpus, but in neither could the vocative have had a mediating role.

This is a good moment to bring various strands together and to gauge the extent to which the sound changes that affected the final syllables of Late

Spoken Latin in Britain can be made responsible for the collapse of the British Latin case system. We have already met a number of the sound changes involved:

(1) Word-final -*s* and -*m* were lost.
(2) Classical Latin *ŭ* and *ō* merged in final syllables; I write the product of the merger as *o*, while in the inscriptions it was spelled as <O, U>.
(3) In final syllables, Classical Latin *ae*, *ĕ*, and *ĭ* merged completely in all known varieties of Late Spoken Latin, and the interchange of *ae*, *e*, and *i* in the British inscriptions strongly suggests that the same merger affected British Latin; the product of the merger will be written as *ι* (pronounced like *i* in English *kin*); this was spelled as <E, I>.
(4) In a large number of Romance languages, Classical Latin -*ī* in final syllables affected vowels in the preceding syllable, according to language-specific rules. This suggests that for a while -*ī* remained distinct from -*ι*, which did not have those effects. In British Latin, the reflex of -*ī* was consistently spelled as <I>, while *ι* was spelled as <I> or <E>, suggesting that British Latin kept the two sounds apart as well.[41] I shall write the reflex of -*ī* as -*i*.

These sound changes affected the Classical Latin nominal paradigms as follows:[42]

I. type *filius* 'son'

Classical Latin		Late Spoken British Latin	Spelling
nominative	*filius*		
accusative	*filium*		
dative	*filiō*	*filio*	<U, O>
ablative	*filiō*		
vocative	*filī*		
genitive	*filī*	*fili*	<I>

II. type *hortus* 'garden'

Classical Latin		Late Spoken British Latin	Spelling
nominative	*hortus*		
accusative	*hortum*		
dative	*hortō*	*horto*	<U, O>
ablative	*hortō*		
vocative	*horte*	*hortι*	<I, E>
genitive	*hortī*	*horti*	<I>

III. type *filia* 'daughter'

Classical Latin		Late Spoken British Latin	spelling
nominative	*filia*		
accusative	*filiam*		
ablative	*filiā*	*filia	<A>
vocative	*filia*		
genitive	*filiae*		
dative	*filiae*	*filiɪ	<AE, E, I>

IV. type *civis* 'citizen'

Classical Latin		Late Spoken British Latin	spelling
nominative	*civis*		
accusative	*civem*		
ablative	*cive*	*civɪ	<I, E>
vocative	*civis*		
genitive	*civis*		
dative	*civī*	*civi	<I>

V. type *homō* 'man'

Classical Latin		Late Spoken British Latin	spelling
nominative	*homō*		
vocative	*homō*	*omo	
accusative	*hominem*		
ablative	*homine*	**om(ɪ)nɪ*	<I, E>
genitive	*hominis*		
dative	*hominī*	**om(ɪ)ni*	<I>

The Late Spoken British Latin column in these paradigms immediately renders visible the devastating effects of sound change: while each Classical Latin paradigm had four to five different forms in order to distinguish six different grammatical cases, British Latin retained only two to three different forms to perform the same job. Moreover, each type had its own pattern of syncretism: nominative, accusative, and ablative were expressed by the same forms in types I, II, III, and IV, but in type V there was one form expressing nominative and vocative and two others that expressed the other cases. Genitive and vocative had merged in types I and IV, but the other types had combined the form of the genitive with one or more of the other cases according to patterns unique to each type. A final weakness is that types II, IV, and V distinguished cases by means of the phonetically minimal opposition between *-i* and *-ı*, an opposition that readily disappeared during the early medieval period in the closest cognates of British Latin on the Continent (i.e. French, Occitan, Spanish, and Portuguese). We possess too little information about British Latin to be able to trace the following steps in the gradual breakdown of the British Latin cases, but they must have involved both sound change and analogy. Given the weaknesses listed above, it would be a natural development if the pattern of type I was extended to type II (nom./acc./abl./dat. *horto* beside gen./voc. *horti*), and if the pattern of case syncretism in types I and II (one form expressing gen./voc.) was extended to type III (nom./acc./abl./dat. *filia* beside gen./voc. *filiı*). The language of the medieval British inscriptions may in fact reflect exactly this system.

This interpretation of the development of the British Latin case system is heavily predicated on the idea that changes in the sound system of British Latin strongly suggest that the language survived as a spoken language well into the early medieval period, as was argued above. That idea automatically entails that we are justified in explaining the confusion of Classical Latin cases in the inscriptions in terms of natural changes in a living language. The correctness of that approach lies in the fact that it is so easy to reconstruct a chain of natural changes that lead to case confusion, based on the little we know about Late Spoken British Latin.

5.2.3. Conclusion

The approach taken here departs markedly from the widespread idea that the medieval British Latin inscriptions were carved by people who had lost nearly all connections with their Roman past and made a bad job of imitating good Latin. Even as meticulous and careful a scholar as Kenneth Jackson could label the engravers as 'lazy or ignorant' (1953: 188). That assessment makes as much sense as stating that Jackson wrote Modern English because he was apparently too lazy or ignorant to write Old English.

The language of the British Latin inscriptions of the early medieval period has all the hallmarks of being the product of a British community of Latin speakers that had survived the troubles of the fifth and early sixth centuries. At the same time, we see these Latin speakers in the process of gradually merging with local western British communities of speakers of British Celtic (most names that are commemorated are Celtic, and many show British Celtic sound changes) as well as speakers of Irish (as attested by the corpus of bilingual Irish-Latin epitaphs). It is this Latin community that gradually switched languages and became speakers of British Celtic, thoroughly Latinizing the sound structure of that language in the process (II.5.1).

5.3. Lowland British Celtic

Sources for Lowland British Celtic are very scarce indeed. There is one Roman-age inscription, which can halfway be interpreted, and a number of place names.

5.3.1. The Bath 'Pendant'

The presence of Latin in the Lowland Zone by the end of the Roman period was itself the result of a language shift from British Celtic to Latin. Among the 120 or so inscriptions on pewter sheets that have been found in the sanctuary of Minerva in Aquae Sulis (Bath) are the only two Celtic inscriptions of Roman Britain. One of them has become known as the Bath pendant. It is a small, round piece of pewter with an ear, on which a crude inscription consisting of seven lines has been scratched. Because of the ear, the object may have served as a pendant, but it looks rather like the lid of a seal box or of a small perfume or oil flask.[43] The text reads:[44]

ADIXOUI / DEUINA / DEUEDA / ANDAGIN / UINDIORIX / CUA-MIIN / AI

Efforts to read this text as either garbled Latin or an early form of Celtic have had to rely on a large portion of free speculation, in the sense that assumptions are made which lack parallels elsewhere in the late Latin or early Celtic corpora of texts. The situation has improved somewhat since the recent discovery of two Gaulish inscriptions on the Continent, which provide the Bath pendant with a new and interesting linguistic context. One is an inscribed roof tile found in 1997 during excavations in Châteaubleau (near Provins, east of Paris, just north of the Seine), the other a text on a small rolled-up sheet of gold, which has come to light in Baudecet (Gembloux, near Namur, Belgium). Both are relatively late texts, dating from the later second to early third century AD; both come from northern Gaul, an area in which only very few Celtic inscriptions have been found; and they share a peculiar innovation in the vowel system, whereby long vowels turn into diphthongs:

(1) Long close[45] vowels become mid-to-close diphthongs, probably only in word-final position

$*\bar{\imath} > ei$ (Châteaubleau: $*n\bar{\imath} > nei$ 'not')

$*\bar{u} > ou$ (Châteaubleau: $*-\bar{u} > -ou$ 1st person singular of verbs: *gniíou* '(may) do', *cluíou* '(may) hear'; Baudecet: $*pann\bar{u} > panou$ 'metal sheet, pan', an *o*-stem dative singular)

Another possible example is Châteaubleau $*p\bar{a}p\bar{\imath}\ s(t)or\bar{\imath} > papi\ ssorei$ 'of every *ssoros*', an *o*-stem genitive singular of $*p\bar{a}pos$ 'every' and a noun *ssoros* of unknown meaning. If the rule is formulated correctly, one wonders why the word-final $*-\bar{\imath}$ of $*p\bar{a}p\bar{\imath}$ did not become *-ei*. Perhaps the proposed analysis is incorrect, or this is an instance of conservative orthography. Another case of non-diphthongization is *-umi* in Châteaubleau *iegumi* and *liiumi*, both first person singular presents originally ending in **-ū* to which another first person singular marker, **-mi*, was added, so that **-ū* was not word-final and hence not diphthongized.

    (2) Long mid vowels become close-to-mid diphthongs, apparently without restriction

        *ē > ie (Châteaubleau: **ēg-* > *ieg-* '?cry out, accuse' in first person singular present *iegumi*, *iegui*, second person plural subjunctive *iexsete*, and other forms of this frequent verb; contrast Old Irish *éigid* 'cry out' < **ēg-*)

        ?**ō > *uo > ua* (Châteaubleau: **moinā > *mōnā > muana* 'gifts', if that is what it means; contrast Old Irish *moín* 'gift')

If we assume that the Bath pendant shares these developments, two problematic forms and thereby the interpretation of the text as a whole suddenly fall into place.

    (a) *Adixoui* can be interpreted as a first person singular verb, *adix-ou*, with the first person singular ending *-ou* coming from earlier Celtic **-ū*. This ending was followed by a puzzling element *-i*. However, the combination is also attested on the Châteaubleau tile in the form *iegui*. This consists of the verbal stem *ieg-*, which probably means something like 'cry out', the first person singular ending *ū*, and the mysterious *i*. *Adixoui* differs from *iegui* in showing diphthongization of **ū > ou* in spite of the fact that **-ū* is not word-final, which could be accounted for in two ways. Either the sound law **ū > ou* had wider application in the language of the Bath pendant. Or the sound law and condition were the same, but an analogy caused the word-final first person singular ending *-ou* to be introduced into all first person singular forms, including those with a following particle, according to the motto 'one function, one form':

	1 singular		1 singular + particle
Châteaubleau	*(clui-)ou*	≠	*(ieg-)u-i*
Bath	**(adix-)ou*	=	*(adix-)ou-i*

The particle *-i* may well be the same as the first person singular particle *-mi* which we find in Châteaubleau and elsewhere (Gaulish *iegumi* beside *iegui*, Châteaubleau; *uediiumi* 'I pray', Chamalières; Middle Welsh *kenif* 'I sing' < **kan-ū-mi*): in Celtic, all consonants between vowels were subject to so-called lenition, which changed the *m* in **-ūmi* to [ṽ].[46] In the Latin-based orthography of these Gaulish inscriptions, <ui> and <umi> would be equally appropriate renderings of what phonetically was [uːṽi]; accordingly, Bath's <oui> represents [ouṽi].

While the interpretation of this form as a first person singular verb can be plausibly established, it is unclear what the verbal stem is and what it means. The stem *adix-* could be the Latin perfect stem *addīx-* of the verb *addīcere* 'to dedicate', in which case *adixoui* means 'I have dedicated',[47] or it could be a native Celtic subjunctive **ad-dig-s-* meaning perhaps something like 'let me fix, curse' (Mullen 2007: 39).

(b) The other word in the text from Bath that can be understood in the light of the Châteaubleau tile is *cuamiinai*. This has a mysterious sequence *cua* which hitherto defied explanation.[48] It can now be interpreted as /kua/ from earlier **kō* according to rule 2. Just as Châteaubleau's *muana* reflects earlier **mōnā < *moinā*, so *cuamiinai* may reflect **kōmiināi < *koimiināi*. That would make perfect sense as a dative singular of the Celtic diminutive noun **koimignā* 'dearest, honey', which could also be used as a personal name—assuming, that is, that in the language of Bath, as in surviving British Celtic, **-gn-* regularly became **-jn-*. The entire inscription could be translated tentatively as either a dedicatory text: 'I, Vindiorix, have dedicated, o divine Deveda, an *andagin* to Cuamiina'; or as a curse: 'Let me, Vindiorix, fix an *andagin* on (i.e. "let me curse") Cuamiina, o divine Deveda'.

It is always best to be suspicious of full translations of Roman-age Celtic inscriptions because they usually result from informed speculation and educated guesses. So it is in this case. Yet the point of the exercise is not to insist that the full translation is correct but to establish that reasonable sense can be made of the Bath pendant, provided, that is, we assume that its language had undergone the same diphthongizations affecting long vowels as the language of Châteaubleau and Baudecet. Crucially, these diphthongizations did not affect Highland British Celtic. So the surprising conclusion is that the language of the Bath pendant is less like the Highland Celtic dialects that were spoken a few miles up the road than like the Celtic dialects spoken hundreds of miles away across the Channel, in northern Gaul. This strongly suggests that Lowland British Celtic differed from Highland British Celtic.

One might object that the Bath pendant looks like northern Gaulish because it was written not by a Briton but by a northern Gaulish visitor to the shrine of Minerva in Bath. That is a possibility that cannot be dismissed. However, the Bath texts in general are written on cheap material and deal with petty affairs, which at least suggests local provenance.

In northern Gaul, the rise of the diphthongs *ei*, *ou*, *ie*, and *ua* in the Gaulish language goes hand in hand with the rise of the same diphthongs in the local dialects of Late Spoken Latin, as in the following examples:

Latin	Late Spoken Latin	Old French
pīlum 'hair'	> **pēlu > *peilu*	> *peil*
lŭpa 'she-wolf'	> **lōba > *louba*	> *louve*
bĕne 'well'	> **bēne >*biene*	> *bien*
hŏmō 'man'	> **ɔmo > *uomo*	> *uem*

This diphthongization is widespread in Late Spoken Latin (French, Provençal, North Italian, Rhaeto-Romance; the *uo* and *ie* diphthongs also occur in Spain and middle and southern Italy). It is strictly local in Celtic, occurring only in areas that were bilingual in Celtic and Latin (Lowland British Celtic, late northern Gaulish). Hence the proclivity towards developing the system of diphthongs in Celtic may well have arisen in bilingual Latin-Celtic communities, where speakers copied the diphthongal pronunciation from their Latin into their Celtic speech. In view of this hypothesis and the general observation that British Late Spoken Latin was very similar to the Late Spoken Latin of Gaul, it stands to reason that British Latin had also developed the diphthongal system, even though British Latin written sources give no indication that it had.

5.3.2. *More on Lowland British Celtic: Southeastern Place Names*

The purpose of this digression is not just to highlight the oldest British text in a native language but mainly to establish whether reconstructed Highland British Celtic is a good proxy for the lost Lowland British Celtic with which the Anglo-Saxon colonists would have come into contact in eastern Britain. The test we performed was to compare what can be known about Lowland British Celtic through the Bath pendant with reconstructed Highland British Celtic. The outcome is that Highland British Celtic is not a good proxy for Lowland British Celtic but that northern Gaulish is—were it not for the fact that we know next to nothing about northern Gaulish.

Another way in which we can gauge the degree to which Lowland British Celtic resembled Highland British Celtic is by studying sound changes that occurred in Celtic place names which survived in the Lowland Zone. As long as such place names were being used by speakers of Celtic, they would undergo sound changes that affected the local variety of Celtic. Such sound changes are the smoking gun that shows that Celtic was still being spoken locally when the sound changes occurred. If, say, the area switched to Latin sometime during the Roman period, local place names would enter the local Latin dialect and undergo Latin sound changes. Finally, as the area switched to (pre-) Old English, typically Old English sound changes would affect the local place names. For example, the Old English river name *Bregent*, the modern *Brent* in Middlesex, seems to show that its second -*e*-, which at an earlier stage was *-*a*-, had undergone so-called Highland British Celtic final *i*-affection; that is, the original Celtic name *Brigantī became *Brigentī in Celtic. Subsequently, the name was adopted in Anglo-Saxon and became Old English *Bregent*. So it would seem that this toponym, which is squarely in the southeastern part of the Lowland Zone, arose in a type of Celtic that, like Highland Celtic, underwent final *i*-affection (Jackson 1953: 602). This kind of evidence is tricky, however, for Old English underwent a very similar sound change, called *i*-umlaut, which would have had the same effect (Parsons 2011: 133). So *Bregent* provides no evidence for the kind of Celtic that was spoken in Middlesex.

More problematic is the series *Andover*, *Candover*, and *Micheldever* in Hampshire. These names reflect Old English -*defer*, which ultimately goes back to Celtic *-*dubrī*, meaning 'waters'. The usual assumption is that the first -*e*- in Old English -*defer* requires the operation of Highland Celtic final *i*-affection of the Welsh type: *duvrī > **dyvr(ī)* (with *y* pronounced as in French *tu* 'you') > **dɪvr(ī)* (with *ɪ* as in *hit*), which was then adopted into Anglo-Saxon as -*defer* (Jackson 1953: 602). This particular case would seem to be stronger than *Bregent* because Old English *i*-umlaut should not have produced -*defer* but rather -*dyfer* (Parsons 2011: 133). Unfortunately, the assumption that -*defer* unambiguously shows Highland British Celtic *i*-affection is built on quicksand: the geographically closest Highland Celtic dialects are those of Devon and Cornwall, which survive as Breton and Cornish, and these show that the vowel -*y*- in such words as *-*dyvr(ī)* was retained until the ninth or tenth century (Schrijver 2011b: 20). That means that if the Anglo-Saxons adopted the names from a type of Celtic that had undergone Highland British *i*-affection, it should have still been *-*dyvr* rather than *-*dɪvr*. This *-*dyvr* would turn up as Old English -*dyfer* rather than the attested -*defer*. So the idea that the Hampshire names in -*defer* show Highland Celtic *i*-affection is just as problematic as the idea that they show Old English *i*-umlaut. It seems, however, that the initial problem has been overrated: -*defer* is unstressed in Old English, and *y* regularly became *e* in unstressed position (e.g. Campbell 1977: 82–83). Hence *-*dyvr*, irrespective of whether it shows Celtic *i*-affection or English *i*-umlaut, became -*defer* quite regularly. Whatever the details, the evidence for the Highland Celtic nature of this name has evaporated.[49]

5.3.3. The Name of London: Evidence for Lowland British Celtic or Late Spoken Latin?

The number of pre-Anglo-Saxon place names in the southeast that survived the transition from Roman to Anglo-Saxon Britain is very small. The one with the highest profile is no doubt *London*. At the same time, both its etymology and its transmission are bedevilled with problems; these require an extensive discussion because London offers a valuable but hitherto unrecognized piece of information for the linguistic map of late Roman Britain.

In Roman sources, the name is attested as *Londinium* and, rarely in late Antique sources, *Lundinium*. In early medieval sources, Latin forms beginning with *London*- and *Lundon*- turn up. Old English has *Lunden*, and Middle Welsh *Llundein*.[50] The history of the name abounds with difficulties at almost every stage of its development.

First of all, the origin and etymology are obscure. Richard Coates has undertaken a brave attempt to reconstruct it as Celtic *Lowonidonjon, meaning something like 'place at Boat River' or 'overflowing river' (Coates and Breeze 2000: 27), which he traces back ultimately to an ancient European language that survives only in place names spread throughout Europe, so-called Old European. Whatever the merits of this reconstruction, it is clear that on the way from the reconstructed *Lowonid-* to the attested Latin *Lond-* neither the loss of the -*o*- in the second syllable nor that of the -*i*- in the third syllable are explicable on the basis of our vast knowledge of Highland British Celtic sound changes. I shall let the etymology rest for the moment and return to it at the end of this section.

For the moment, let us concentrate on the transmission of the name from one language to another, because this brings us closer to the pre-Anglo-Saxon linguistic map. A general problem is that the medieval Welsh and English forms are impossible to derive from Roman-age Latin *Londinium* = Celtic *Londinjon*, with -*i*- in the second syllable. The opinion of linguists has tended to favour an alternative form *Londonium* = *Londonjon*, which allegedly is capable of generating Welsh *Llundein* and Old English *Lunden*. But this is not the case.

The Welsh name *Llundein* is attested from the early ninth century onwards (*Lundein* occurs in Nennius' *Historia Brittonum*). The only sound whose history is not problematic is the Welsh voiceless *Ll-*, which developed regularly from an earlier single *l* at the beginning of the word. The first problem concerns the origin of the -*u*- in Welsh *Llundein*. Celtic scholars have observed that the change from Latin *Lond-* to Welsh *Llund-* can be explained only if the Roman-period form was *Lōnd-*, with a long *-ō-*: compare, for example, Latin *Rōmānus*, which became Welsh *Rhufawn*. However, reconstructing long *-ō-* is impossible for another reason: neither Latin nor Celtic nor Germanic tolerated long vowels before a consonant group consisting of a nasal and a plosive, such as -*nd-*. In such cases, an originally long vowel was regularly shortened.[51] So a form *Lōndinium* cannot have existed. That means that *Londinium* did not originally have a long *-ō-* and that the -*u*- of Middle Welsh *Llundein* cannot have resulted from regular, known rules of Welsh sound change. This does not really come as a shock because it has been known for a long time that if it had complied with regular sound change, Latin *Lond-* should have become Welsh *Llunn-* rather than *Llund-* (compare the regular treatment in words like *descendere* > Middle Welsh *diskynn* 'descend'). A third problem is that the sequence *-nj-* at the end of the second syllable should probably have regularly become *-nn-* in Welsh, and this would have happened so early that the *j* could not cause *i*-infection of the vowel of the preceding syllable (Schrijver 1995a: 324). That in turn means that the Welsh -*ei*- cannot possibly be connected with Roman-age forms, be they *Londinjon* or *Londonjon*.

The only reasonable explanation for the problems facing Middle Welsh *Llundein* is to assume that it escaped regular sound changes because it was borrowed so late that it could not possibly take part in those changes anymore. That means that the name must have been borrowed well after almost all of the hundreds of Latin loanwords in British Celtic, which came in until the end of the Romano-British period (around 400). This brings us to a date of borrowing after approximately AD 600, when sound changes such as (Latin) *ō* > (Welsh) *u*, *nj* > *nn*, and *nd* > *nn* had already stopped operating.[52] Since *Llundein* must therefore be a borrowing, and a late one at that, the question arises from which language it was borrowed: was it from Old English, from Lowland British Celtic, or from Late Spoken Latin?

A problem that has already been addressed on the basis of Welsh *Llundein* concerns the vowel (or rather vowels) in the second syllable of Roman-age *Londinjon*, *Londonijon*: neither explains Middle Welsh *Llundein*, as we saw earlier, and likewise neither explains Old English *Lunden-*: whether it be based on *Londinjon* or *Londonjon*, and whether we assume a British Celtic or Latin intermediary, it seems that the form that should have come out in Old English is *Lynd-* rather than *Lunden* because according to all scenarios the first syllable should have undergone Old English *i*-umlaut of *u to *y (cf. Parsons 2011: 133).

As so often, problems provide keys to a solution. The first key is that since Middle Welsh *Llundein* was borrowed after around AD 600, there must have been available to seventh-century speakers of Welsh a name for London that was pronounced such that it was borrowed as *Llundein*. The second key is that Old English *Lunden-* is based on a form that prevented *i*-umlaut of *u to *y from happening in the first syllable. Both keys open the door to a basic form of the name that must have approximated *Lundein-*: that form explains the Welsh borrowing immediately, and it accounts for the absence of *i*-umlaut of the first syllable in Old English (*ei does not cause *i*-umlaut). This is encouraging, but how is it possible to make linguistic sense of *Lundein-? As it happens, there are two possible scenarios, both of which make eminent sense.

(1) *Lundein-* is Lowland British Celtic.

This presupposes that the early Latin form *Londinium* is a spelling for *Londīnium*, with long -*ī*- in the second syllable. *Londīnium* is a Latinization of earlier Celtic *Londīnjon*. This became *Lundīnjon* by the regular British Celtic and Gaulish development of *o > *u before nasal + plosive (in this case, *ond > *und). In the mouths of speakers of Lowland British Celtic, -*ī*- subsequently became *ei* (see II.5.3.1), so the name came to be pronounced as *Lundeinjon*. After the loss of final syllables, what remained was *Lundein*, which is exactly what is needed to explain the Welsh form as well as the Old English form. If this account is correct, there are two important corollaries:

- Lowland British Celtic must have survived long enough to have donated its name for London
  o to the Anglo-Saxons, probably at an early date around 400, given the importance of the town
  o to seventh-century speakers of Highland British Celtic (Welsh)

That must mean that even in the highly Romanized southeast, Latin had not supplanted Celtic altogether by 400. It also means that the

Lowland British Celtic name persisted at least until the seventh century, when it was adopted into Highland British Celtic.

- The fact that *Londīnion* became *Lundein* places the development of *ī to *ei firmly in Britain. That implies that the diphthongization of long vowels that is attested on the Bath pendant and in two northern Gaulish inscriptions (II.5.3.1) is indeed native to Lowland British Celtic, a conclusion that could be doubted as long as the only British attestation was the eminently transportable Bath pendant.

(2) *Lundein* is Late Spoken British Latin.

In the discussion of the language of the Bath pendant (II.5.3.1), it was observed that British Latin probably evolved the same set of diphthongs (*ei, ou, ie, uo*) as the Late Spoken Latin of Gaul. This is relevant to the assessment of the history of *Lundein*. In the Latin of Gaul, a Classical Latin short stressed *ī* had become *ei if it was followed by a single consonant plus a vowel. The example shown in II.5.3.1 was Latin *pĭlum*, which developed into *peilu*, whence Old French *peil* and Modern French *poil* 'hair'. If we suppose that its -*i*- was short, this development may be applied to Latin *Londĭnium*: according to the rules of Classical Latin stress placement, -*ĭ*- was stressed, and it was followed by a single consonant plus a vowel (-*ni*-). So in British Latin *Londinium* became *Londeiniu. Subsequently, final -*iu* was lost, and the -*o*-, which was positioned before a nasal plus plosive (-*nd*-), regularly became closed -ʊ- (as happened in prehistoric French), leading to early medieval British Latin *Lundein. If this interpretation is correct, we have lost the evidence for the retention of Lowland British Celtic in the southeast and have traded this in for evidence for the retention of spoken British Latin of the French kind.

I see no way of resolving whether *Lundein* originated in Lowland British Celtic or in Late Spoken British Latin. The choice depends on the answer to the question whether the Roman-age Latin form was *Londīnium* or *Londĭnium*, which as far as I can see cannot be decided. That is unfortunate. But what we have been able to establish regardless are three plausible ideas.

- The name of London was transmitted to English and Welsh in oral rather than written form: only in this way can the transmission of pronounced but never written [ei] be understood
- The people who informed the Anglo-Saxons and the Highland Britons about the name of the Roman town on the Thames themselves spoke either Latin of the French type or Celtic of the Gaulish type
- Either way, on the evidence of London the local population of the southeast did not speak the Highland British Celtic we know so well from Welsh, Cornish, and Breton.

Although it is not relevant to the present theme—the linguistic map of pre-Anglo-Saxon Britain around AD 400—I cannot resist the temptation to close this discussion of the name *London* with a speculation about its ultimate origin. The formation of *Londinium*, with its second part *-inium*, is reminiscent of the Romano-Celtic names of Cirencester, *Corinium*, and, on the opposite side of the North Sea, of *Helinium*, the estuary of the river Maas in the southwest of the present-day Netherlands. While the etymology of *Corinium* is not clear, *Helinium* probably contains the Celtic word for 'estuary, swamp', **hel-* from earlier **sel-*, followed by the Celtic suffix **-injo-*, feminine **-injā*, which forms specific, singular nouns derived from general collective nouns (e.g. **lukotes* 'mice in general', **lukot-injā* 'a single, specific mouse' > Middle Welsh *llygot* 'mice', *llygodenn* 'a mouse').[53] The first part of the name, *lond-*, looks very much like the Proto-Indo-European verbal root **lendʰ-*, meaning 'to sink, to cause to sink' and, figuratively, 'to be subdued, to subdue'.[54] In the surviving Celtic languages, there are two nominal representatives of that root:

- **landā*, denoting 'low-lying, uncultivated land' (e.g. Middle Welsh *llann*, Old Irish *land*, which are related to the corresponding Germanic term in English *land* and German *Land*); this preserves the literal meaning
- **londos* 'subduing', whence 'fierce', continues the figurative meaning (Old Irish *lond*).

It seems conceivable that *lond-* in *Londinium* is the same item as **londos* but preserves the literal rather than the figurative meaning: 'going under', whence 'submerging, flooding'. So *Londinium* would reflect an earlier Celtic **Londinjon*, meaning 'place that floods (periodically, tidally)'. That would be an apt descriptive name: before the embankments of the Thames were created, much of London was at the mercy of its tidal regime.[55]

This brings us back to the main question that we tried to answer before we became distracted by the name of London: does the place name evidence of the Lowland Zone provide information about the type of British Celtic that was spoken there? The answer, after the discussion of London, is that the Celtic dialect of the southeast was either British Latin or Lowland British Celtic rather than Highland British Celtic.

Matters may have been different in a strip of land just east of the Highland Zone, where Highland British Celtic developments seem to turn up. We will have occasion to turn to that issue in the following section.

5.4. What Eastern Britons Spoke around 400

After this lengthy survey of the thorny evidence for the pre-Anglo-Saxon linguistic map of the Lowland Zone, it is time to summarize the conclusions. When Anglo-Saxon settlers first engaged with native Britons in eastern Britain, those Britons spoke either Late British Latin or Lowland British Celtic or both. Since those languages disappeared without leaving substantial traces in the written record, we know next to nothing about them. It is possible to reconstruct a few details of sound changes and developments of the case system of British Latin, but that is all. Of Lowland British Celtic we know only that it underwent a number of diphthongizations of long vowels. Yet what little we know suggests that both languages show strong connections across the Channel, with the Latin and Celtic of northern Gaul. Reconstructed Highland British Celtic, of which much more is known because it underlies the surviving British Celtic languages Welsh, Cornish, and Breton, has turned out to be an imperfect proxy for lost Lowland British Celtic.

The traditional claim that the Old English language was not influenced by the language of the pre-Anglo-Saxon inhabitants of Britain is based on a confrontation of Old English and Highland British Celtic, which has turned out to be irrelevant. We have been searching for a language contact situation that never existed, based on incorrect premises. The correct way of posing the question is to ask whether Old English was influenced by Lowland British Celtic and/or by Late Spoken British Latin. Since we know next to nothing about either language, the question seems impossible to answer. We may be pleased with the amount of acuteness and discernment that was invested in reaching this conclusion, but that hardly makes up for the inability to make further headway. But before that conclusion can be embraced, we may try to approach the issue from a different perspective: is there anything in the Old English language itself that betrays that it may have been in contact with another language?

6. OLD ENGLISH AS EVIDENCE FOR A SUBSTRATUM IN OLD ENGLISH

If a population originally speaking another language had switched to Old English, the sound system of that language—whether it was some form of Celtic, Latin, or something else—may have managed to shine through in the Old English sound system, like the original writing on a palimpsest. It may be worthwhile to concentrate completely on Old English itself and to investigate whether it shows the features of a palimpsest: is it possible to discern two different layers in Old English, one reflecting the speech of the first Germanic colonists who came from the Continent, and the other reflecting the speech of British natives who switched to Germanic? Theoretically, this approach has the advantage that it does not presuppose any knowledge about the speech of the British natives. It is an exercise in finding a substratum language just by observing its traces in the language that engulfed it.

The linguist's task of distinguishing two layers in the sound system of a language differs in one important respect from the task facing a palaeographer who deciphers a palimpsest. A palimpsest contains two (or more) texts written over one another. Each text is a unit by itself: overwriting does not result in a meaningful merger of the texts. The two layers of a sound system, however, form one single, functional system of hybrid origin in the same way that a child's DNA is a single, functional system that results from a merger of both of its parents' DNA.

There is no straightforward way in which a sound system of such hybrid origin can be reconstituted into the parent sound systems of which it is composed—unless, that is, the substratum language has been identified and consequently the linguist knows which substratum features to look for. In the case of Old English, such knowledge has turned out to be too vague to be usable, so we need to devise a search method that enables us to identify the presence or absence of a substratum without it. As a rule of thumb, a sound system betrays the presence of a substratum (i.e. a language shift event) if one or more of the following criteria are met:

(1) The sound system changes in a way that cannot be explained plausibly on the basis of general structural principles, such as economy, simplicity, and symmetry (hence the dice are loaded in favour of an explanation on the basis of that other great cause of change, language contact).

(2) The initial state of the sound system does not pre-programme the language to undergo those changes (hence the impetus probably did not come from the language itself but from a contact language).

(3) The changes are linked, that is, form a coherent system in themselves (so that in combination with (1) and (2) the idea is strengthened that a foreign sound system is steering the changes).

(4) The changes do not spread gradually from a centre to the periphery of the area in which the language is spoken (gradual spread of changes is explained by people speaking to one another across a dialect continuum, not by a common substratum; if there is no gradual spread but the changes are 'suddenly' there, that is an argument in favour of a substratum).

The more criteria are met, the more plausible is the idea that a substratum (i.e. a language shift event) triggered the changes involved. Since it makes high demands, the application of this search method probably drastically underestimates the total amount of language shift events in the history of languages. Changes that are known to have been caused by a substratum would easily escape detection by the proposed method: they can be open to an alternative explanation according to (1) or (2); they can be relatively isolated rather than linked serially, thus defying (3); and a feature can emerge as a substratum feature in one dialect before spreading across a dialect continuum in wave-like fashion, so that its substratal origin goes unnoticed by (4).

Take the example of the replacement of the English sounds /θ/ and /ð/[56] by /t/ and /d/, respectively, in most varieties of Anglo-Irish (*think* and *father* are pronounced as *tink* and *fader*). The explanation for this change is language contact: native speakers of Modern Irish (Gaelic) would have found it difficult to pronounce English /θ/ and /ð/ because those sounds do not exist in Modern Irish. Therefore, they replaced them with the phonetically closest equivalents that do exist in Modern Irish, /t/ and /d/. Had the Irish background of the sound change been unknown, linguists would have tried to make sense of it in different ways, and they would have been reasonably successful. Dental slit fricatives, as /θ/ and /ð/ are known to phoneticians, are much rarer sounds than the plosives /t/ and /d/ and the grooved fricatives /s/ and /z/ in the languages of the world, so getting rid of them would make English more 'normal'. Indeed, this normalization may well have been pre-programmed in the Germanic ancestor of English because all modern Germanic languages have replaced the slit fricatives with /t/ or /d/, except the particularly conservative Icelandic and Faeroese languages and, notably, English itself. In English the old /ð/ was turned into /d/, but /θ/ was preserved and subsequently a new /ð/ was created. It seems that the pre-programming of the loss of /θ/ and /ð/ did not make much of an impact on English, so it probably did not have any impact at all on Irish when it came into contact with English. One might think that turning /θ/ into /t/ would create a large number of homonyms, e.g. *thick* and *tick*, *third* and *turd*, and would therefore be avoided. This did not happen because in fact Anglo-Irish /t/ and /θ/ do not merge: as old /θ/ became /t/, old /t/ moved slightly out of the way and became an approximant (i.e. the front part of the tongue only approaches but does not come into contact with the front part of the palate). Only the untrained ear confuses the Anglo-Irish pronunciations of *third* and *turd*.

So the Anglo-Irish change fails criteria (1) and (2). It fails criterion (3) because it does not form part of a conspicuously large set of sound changes (other fricatives, such as /f/, /v/, and /s/, are left intact). There is no information about the way in which the change spread throughout Anglo-Irish, so criterion (4) is useless. All in all, therefore, the Anglo-Irish change /θ/, /ð/ > /t/, /d/ would go unnoticed as the substratum feature that it is.

But the aim of the search method is not to estimate the number of language shift events that have happened in the past. What is required here is a method by which we can convince ourselves that, in the absence of evidence about a language contact situation, language shift offers a better (and not just an alternative) explanation of observed linguistic changes than all other explanations that could be suggested. Let us now turn to Old English in order to observe how the method works in practice.

6.1. Developments of the Old English Vowel System

The Old English system of consonants changed very little between c. 450 and 700, so evidence in favour of (or against) language shift cannot be distilled from it. By contrast, the situation of the vowel system is very different. The initial state is the vowel system of c. 450, which the Anglo-Saxon settlers brought with them to Britain from their homelands in northern Germany and Denmark. This vowel system is accessible to linguistic investigation only by reconstruction. The procedure is the same as I have outlined for the reconstruction of Highland British Celtic on the basis of Welsh, Cornish, and Breton (II.4.2):

- Draw up all prehistoric (i.e. pre-seventh-century) sound laws of English and of its closest cognates: Frisian, Coastal Dutch (ancient dialects of Dutch along the North Sea coast) and northwestern Saxon, which together with English are called North Sea Germanic.
- Put the sound laws in a relative chronology, one for each language.
- All sound laws that the North Sea Germanic languages have in common are posited to have taken place when those languages still formed a unity, so they are shared innovations.
- Deviate from this procedure only if there is an explicit reason to do so; for example, differences in the conditioning of the sound laws can mean that they are separate sound laws; seemingly identical sound laws occupying different positions in the relative chronologies of the different languages are probably different sound laws (sound laws which are just similar rather than identical are interesting in themselves and require careful consideration, but they are put aside for present purposes).

The result is the following reconstruction of the vowel system of pre-settlement North Sea Germanic:[57]

Pre-settlement North Sea Germanic (c. 400)[58]

	long vowels			short vowels		
	front	central	back	front	central	back
close	$\bar{\imath}$		$\bar{u}$	i		u
mid	$\bar{e}$		$\bar{o}$	e		[o]
open	$(\bar{æ})$		$\bar{\jmath}$		a	

diphthongs: *ai, au, iu, eu*

The long vowel *æ* existed only in the predecessor of the West Saxon and Kentish dialects of Old English, not in that of Anglian.

In the course of the seventh century, the Old English dialects begin to appear as written languages. By this time, a number of different dialects have formed: Northumbrian in the northeast (north of the river Humber, as the name says) and Mercian, between the Humber and the Thames, are together named Anglian. South of the Thames is West Saxon. The dialect of Kent is for obvious reasons designated as Kentish. At this time all dialects, whatever their differences in other segments of grammar, share the same vowel system, with one small exception: the diphthongs *īe, ie* exist only in West Saxon.

The Old English vowel system (c. 700)

	long vowels and diphthongs					short vowels and diphthongs				
	front	front + back	front round	central	back round	front	front + back	front round	central	back round
close	*ī*	*īo*	*ȳ*		*ū*	*i*	*io*	*y*		*u*
mid	*ē*	*ēo*	*ō*		*ō*	*e*	*eo*	*ø*		*o*
open	*ǣ*	*ēa*		*ā*		*æ*	*ea*		*a*	

West Saxon has additional *īe, ie*

As can be observed at a glance, the vowel system has changed dramatically in the course of a little more than two centuries. There is a new series of front-to-back diphthongs (*io, īo*, etc.), and the rounded front vowels *y* and *ø* have made an appearance.[59] So has the long vowel *ā*, which arose out of earlier **ai*. The sound laws that affected the vowel system between c. 450 and c. 700 are varied and complex, but most of them express relatively simple general tendencies, which can be represented as follows:

- *Backing in back contexts*: the long and short front vowels **i, *e, *æ* became opening front-to-back long and short diphthongs *io, eo, ea* before consonants and vowels that are back (developments include so-called breaking in front of certain consonants and consonant groups, and *a/u*-umlaut, which occurred if the following syllable contained *a, o*, or *u*). Examples:

  *melkanan > meolcan 'to milk'; **kældaz > ceald* 'cold' (breaking before *ld, lk*)

  *eburaz > eofor 'boar'; **hæbukaz > heafuc* 'hawk' (Anglian; *a/u*-umlaut)

- *Opening of diphthongs*: the inherited diphthongs **iu, *eu, *æu* underwent opening of the second element to become *īo, ēo* (part of Northumbrian *ēa*), and *ēa*, respectively. These merged with the long diphthongs that arose as a result of breaking (see first bullet). The development of **ai* to *ā*, which created a new long vowel phoneme, may be described in terms of opening of the second element as well: **ai > *aæ > aa = ā*. Examples:

  *ainaz > ān 'one'; **æugān > ēage* 'eye'; **deupaz > dēop* 'deep';

  *liudi- > līode, lēode 'people'; results coincide with the results of breaking in e.g. **nǣhwaz > nēah* 'near'; **līhtaz > līoht, lēoht* 'light'

- *Fronting in front contexts*: long and short back vowels (**u, *o, *a*) and diphthongs (**io, *eo, *ea*) became front vowels before **i* and **j* in the following syllable (*i*-umlaut), from which resulted the rounded front vowels *y* and *ø* (long or short; /ø/ is conventionally spelled <œ>). Examples:

  *bankiz > benc 'bench'

  *kuningaz > cyning 'king'

  *dōmijanan > dǣman (later *dēman*) 'to judge, deem'

The processes of *a/u*-umlaut (backing) and *i*-umlaut (fronting) share a common characteristic: the vowel that was present in the second syllable in the Proto-Germanic forms was anticipated in the first syllable (this is in fact what the term 'umlaut' means). More precisely, it is the feature axis 'front-back' that copies itself from the second into the first syllable. For instance, if the first syllable contained the rounded, close, *back* vowel **u* and the second syllable contained the unrounded, close, *front* vowel **i*, as in **kuningaz* 'king', the feature *front* of the second syllable was drawn into the first, where it replaced the feature *back* of the **u*. The result is a rounded, close, *front* vowel, i.e. /y/ in *cyning* (as in French *pur*, German *Brücke*). Similarly, if the first syllable contained the unrounded, mid, *front* vowel **e* and the second syllable contained the rounded, close, *back* vowel **u*, as in **eburaz* 'boar', the feature *back* of the second syllable was drawn into the first, where it followed (rather than replaced) the feature *front* of the **e*. The result is a mid, front-to-back diphthong, i.e. /eo/ in *eofor* (/o/ is the back counterpart of /e/ and happens to be also rounded; in English as in most European languages, close and mid back vowels are automatically rounded).[60]

So the grand scheme behind the radical changes in the vowel system between c. 450 and c. 700 is that back vowels in the first syllable are fronted before front **i*, **j* in the second syllable (*i*-umlaut), and front vowels in the first syllable are backed before back **o*, **u*, **a* in the second syllable (*a/u*-umlaut) as well as before certain back consonants or consonant groups (breaking).[61] The result of fronting in front contexts includes the rise of the new phonemes /y/ and /ø/. The result of backing in back contexts, however, consists of front-to-back diphthongs, which are combinations of vowels that already existed as single vowel phonemes. In this respect, the results of fronting and backing are asymmetrical: fronting *could* have turned /o/ into a back-to-front diphthong such as */oe/ rather than into the rounded front vowel /ø/, but it did not; similarly, backing *could* have turned /e/ into a simple back vowel such as /o/ rather than into a front-to-back diphthong /eo/, but again it did not. In this respect, the exact results of fronting and backing are unpredictable and specific to Old English.

6.2. Explaining the Developments of the Old English Vowel System: Language Shift or Not?

Let us now investigate whether the changes in the Old English vowel system betray the presence of a substratum, i.e. of a population shifting to Old English and steering its developments, by setting off Old English developments against the criteria that were suggested earlier.

(1) The sound system changes in a way that cannot be explained plausibly on the basis of general structural principles, such as economy, simplicity, and symmetry (hence the dice are loaded in favour of an explanation on the basis of that other great cause of change, language contact).

It seems safe to say that the linguist's toolbox of general structural principles, however sophisticated, does not contain the gear necessary to turn the vowel system of pre-settlement North Sea Germanic into that of Old English. In fact, the initial state is a rather trivial and common type of vowel system, which betrays no inherent structural inclination to develop into the far from trivial Old English system, with its rounded front vowels and highly uncommon long diphthongs opposed to short ones. But if the development of the vowel system is not amenable to an explanation based on general principles of linguistic change, perhaps the individual changes that affected the vowel system are. The general principle behind those changes is, after all, fairly simple: first-syllable front vowels acquire the feature back from a back vowel in the second syllable, and first-syllable back vowels acquire the feature front from a front vowel in the second syllable; in other words, the second, unstressed syllable is anticipated in the first, stressed syllable. Eventually, unstressed syllables even reduce or lose the relevant features. Perhaps this anticipation is quite a natural thing for a language to do? It has indeed been claimed that languages in which the stressed syllable is marked by greater intensity rather than higher or lower tone, such as is the case in English, naturally have less intensity in the following, unstressed syllables, which predisposes them towards reduction and towards bleeding of their features into the first syllable: umlaut. As it turns out, however, the combination of unstressed vowel reduction and umlaut is just typical of some western European languages, whether they be Romance (e.g. French), Celtic, or Germanic, and it peaks in Germanic languages. It is not a general property of languages with intensity stress at all. Since most linguists speak a western European language, the familiar soon feels as if it is the norm, which in this case it is not. Finnish has had word-initial intensity stress for thousands of years yet shows neither unstressed vowel reduction nor umlaut (what it does have is its reverse, vowel harmony: features of the first, stressed syllable spill over into unstressed syllables). Saami is a close cognate of Finnish and shares its word-initial intensity stress as well as the absence of unstressed vowel reduction, but it does have extensive umlaut. Russian has intensity stress and unstressed vowel reduction but no umlaut. So languages with intensity stress may show umlaut or unstressed vowel reduction, or even both, or they may show neither. The absence of a compelling link between intensity stress, on the one hand, and unstressed vowel reduction and umlaut, on the other, means that we need to look elsewhere for an explanation of the Old English vowel changes. Hence criterion (1) in favour of language shift is met.

(2) The initial state of the sound system does not pre-programme the language to undergo those changes (hence the impetus probably did not come from the language itself but from a contact language).

In a general sense, fronting in front contexts (*i*-umlaut) and backing in back contexts (*a/u*-umlaut and breaking) are attested in Old English and all its closest relatives within the Germanic language family: the histories of Frisian, Dutch, German, and Norse are littered with phenomena that fall under this heading. So perhaps umlaut phenomena date back to the Proto-Germanic period, around the beginning of our era, when Germanic had not yet diversified into its various daughter branches?

As we saw in section II.6.1, sound laws can be ascribed to a common ancestor if they occur in identical form in identical chronological sequence in the daughter languages. By this token, umlaut fails to make it as a Proto-Germanic development: the sound laws are different in each language, and there are wide chronological differences (Old English had full-fledged *i*-umlaut when first attested around 700, while Old High German had to wait until around 1100 to reach that stage). The closest match, as always, is between Old English and Old Frisian: the rules for *i*-umlaut are the same, and they occur earlier than in any other Germanic languages (sixth to early seventh century at the latest). The difference is that *i*-umlaut operates on a vowel system that has already become slightly different in Old Frisian than in Old English. The rules for breaking and *a/u*-umlaut, however, are very different and much more restricted in Old Frisian. At a slightly further remove is Old Norse, which shows extensive *i*-umlaut but according to partially different sound laws, which operate centuries later than in Old English; Old Norse has a restricted *a/u*-umlaut which affects only original short **e*. At the furthest remove from Old English in terms of umlaut are two languages: Gothic shows no umlaut whatsoever, but that may have to do with its eccentric position: it is a language that split off from the bulk of Germanic at a particularly early date before it was written down in fourth-century sources. The other language is after Frisian the next closest cognate of English, however: western Dutch shows *i*-umlaut of only short **a* and, perhaps, **u*, and no *a/u*-umlaut whatsoever (see chapter IV). So while umlaut is a particularly frequent phenomenon in Germanic, it is not omnipresent, and it is not strictly speaking a phenomenon of Proto-Germanic.

Yet the mere fact that umlaut is so frequent in Germanic *although* it is not a Proto-Germanic phenomenon only adds to the puzzle: what made umlaut so popular among speakers of early medieval Germanic? A conceivable scenario is that umlaut arose at some point in the Germanic-speaking world after the break-up of Proto-Germanic and subsequently spread to the other languages. But how did it spread? Intensive contact among speakers of Germanic across a large area would certainly have been favourable for umlaut to spread like a rolling wave, and it would leave enough leeway for local differences to develop, but it is hard to see how umlaut could become so virulent as to spread across an area that stretched all the way from Britain (English) and Scandinavia (Norse) to northern Italy (High German). A linguistic change that spreads across areas by contact does so because speakers who do not have the change want to identify with speakers who do for some social, economic, or political reason: we want to speak like the people on whom we model our better selves. Hence the spreading of a linguistic feature presupposes a similar social, economic, or political setting across the area, and this is patently lacking in the case of the early medieval Germanic languages.

Alternatively, it is possible that umlaut was present in Proto-Germanic, not as a set of fully fledged sound laws, but as a predisposition that had just started to emerge as the parent language gradually broke up. If so, Old English umlaut is explainable as the unfolding of an innate tendency whose roots lie on the Continent before the migration period. According to this scenario, other Germanic languages inherited the same innate tendency, which then expressed itself differently in different areas and languages. It is necessary to explain what veiled terms like 'predisposition' and 'innate tendency' might mean in the real world, and that involves the notion of phonemicization.

Some sound laws start as gradual processes.[62] Take *i*-umlaut of **a* in Old English. The eventual sound law is **a > e* if the following syllable contains **i* or **j* (**i*, **j* may themselves be lost or changed subsequently). An example is Proto-Germanic **antiz >* Old English *ent* 'giant' (where indeed the *i* that caused the umlaut was subsequently lost as a result of another sound law). The initial stage of this *i*-umlaut was nowhere near as drastic as changing *a* into *e* but consisted of a slight fronting and closing of [a] (with a sound as in *high* [haɪ]) in the direction of [æ] (as in *hat* [hæt]). This change would not normally have been perceptible to speakers of early Germanic at the time: only someone with a very sharp ear or a trained phonetician might have noticed it. That is because the difference between [a] and [æ] was not functional in Germanic at the time (as it is not in English nowadays). A test of the functionality of the difference between [a] and [æ] in the language is to find two words with different meanings such that the only sound difference between them consists of the fact that the one contains [a] where the other contains [æ]. If you succeed, you have found a so-called minimal pair (i.e. a pair of words that differ from one another only in the feature that is investigated), and you have established that [a] and [æ] are functionally different: they are elevated from the status of phones (sounds) to the state of so-called phonemes. Phones are written in phonetic transcription, in square brackets, as [a], [æ]. Phonemes are written in phonemic (also called phonological) transcription, as /a/ and /æ/. The implication is that /a/ and /æ/ are different psychological entities for speakers of the language, of whose difference they are now conscious. If you fail to find a minimal pair for [a] and [æ], the difference between [a] and [æ] is not phonemic (= subphonemic). In most modern European languages, including English, German, and French, the difference between [a] and [æ] is non-phonemic, and therefore speakers of these languages cannot normally hear the difference even though a trained ear can. An example of a phonemic difference in Modern English is that between [æ] and [ɛ]. While the difference is phonetically just as subtle as that between [a] and [æ], there are in this case minimal pairs which promote the phonetic (sound) difference to a functional, phonemic (mental) difference, distinguishing between *bat* [bæt] and *bet* [bɛt], *can* [kæn] and *ken* [kɛn]. As a result, we have established the phonemes /æ/ and /ɛ/ for English. Native speakers of English are aware of the sound difference between the two. By the same procedure, phonetically obvious sound differences can be stamped as phonemic, such as that between English /l/ and /p/ on the basis of minimal pairs such as *lot* [lɔt] and *pot* [pʰɔt], *pope* [pʰoʊp] and *pole* [pʰoʊl].

Hence, initially, the effect of *i*-umlaut in words such as */antiz/ > *[æntiz] was so subtle (to an early Germanic ear, that is) as to be subphonemic. Native speakers would be unaware that a change had occurred at all. A trained ear would notice it and would at the same time be able to establish that it is governed by a strict rule: /a/ automatically changes to [æ] if there is an *i* (or *j) in the following syllable, not only in the word */antiz/, but in all words with /a/ in the first syllable and *i* or *j in the second syllable, such as */mari/ 'sea, lake', */satjan/ 'to set', and */gastiz/ 'guest', which were pronounced as *[mæri], *[sætjan], and *[gæstiz]. So [æ] was a conditioned variant (conditioned, that is, by the presence of *i*, *j in the following syllable) of the phoneme /a/. The conditioned variant was predictable on the basis of its environment. As long as this predictability lasted, [æ] was bound to remain subphonemic, hence subconscious. This situation implies that [æ] would have been unstable: speakers could replace [æ] with the original [a] with impunity, because doing so would not lead to problems of comprehension. There are various ways in which phonemicization of [æ] to /æ/ would put an end to the instability of [æ]:

(a) *Phonetic distance*: if [æ] continued to move in the directions 'front' and 'close', it would come so close to pronunciations of the phoneme /e/ as to become disassociated with /a/ by sheer phonetic distance; it could merge with the existing phoneme /e/, or it could develop into a new, independent, *e*-like phoneme. Either way, from that point onwards the effect of *i*-umlaut on /a/ would be phonemicized and perceptible to speakers. Importantly for linguists who deal with old, written sources, perceptibility means that the phoneme would now be able to enter to the written record.

(b) *Loss of condition*: if the sounds that originally conditioned *i*-umlaut changed, [æ] would no longer be a predictable variant of /a/, and this would have the same phonemicizing effect as (a). Thus, */antiz/ > *[æntiz] at a certain point lost its final syllable, which contained the *i* that caused the umlaut, resulting in *[ænt]; the effect is immediate phonemicization of the variant in the first syllable, whence the Old English form, written <ent>, phonemically /ent/.

(c) *Interference in a bilingual setting*: if early Germanic, at a stage at which it had */antiz/ > *[æntiz], would attract new speakers whose first language contained a quite different vowel system, including, say, a phoneme /æ/, or a different distribution of [a] and [æ] across phonemes, [æ] could become a phoneme /æ/ in their variant of Germanic.

This process leads to phonemicization without the changes described in (a) and (b): suddenly */antiz/, pronounced *[æntiz], would jump to a new phonological state */æntiz/.

When historical linguists formulate sound laws, they almost invariably (and without saying so explicitly) formulate phonemic rather than phonetic sound laws. They do not bother with the initial stages of sound changes but focus on the finished product. This book is no exception. There are good reasons for doing so. Firstly, phonemicized sound laws have crossed an essential threshold in the sense that their outcome has become psychologically real and recognizable by native speakers. Secondly, historical linguists usually deal with written sources that document past stages of a language. In as far as they are devised by native speakers, writing systems generally encode the conscious, phonemic level rather than the unconscious, subphonemic (phonetic) level of a language. Hence it is generally the phonemic level of a language that is accessible to study by historical linguists. This understandable preoccupation of linguists with phonemic, finished sound laws rather than their subphonemic, unfinished precursors does not diminish the fact that both levels are equally real.

All this is relevant to understanding what is meant by the idea that Proto-Germanic may have had an 'innate tendency' or 'predisposition' towards *i*-umlaut. It means that on the subphonemic level, vowels may have already begun to be slightly raised and fronted if the following syllable contained *i*, *j*. From this starting point, the Germanic daughter languages in the course of time developed their different forms of phonemicized *i*-umlaut, which are encoded as different sound laws in the historical grammars of the Germanic languages. A similar case could be made for *a/u*-umlaut, although it is a lot weaker because *a/u*-umlaut is a much rarer phenomenon in Germanic languages. The whole idea that umlaut was subphonemically present in Proto-Germanic, it must be remembered, is based on the need to explain the particular virulence of *i*-umlaut in medieval Germanic languages. If the idea is correct, the seeds of the extensive umlaut phenomena of Old English were indeed sown on the Continent, and explaining umlaut on the basis of a substratum in Britain becomes unnecessary. So the second criterion for assuming a substratum in Old English then fails to be met. There are two reasons not to be altogether satisfied with this approach, however.

Firstly, even if a predisposition towards umlaut was already present in the speech of the Anglo-Saxon colonists of the fifth century, we would like to be able to explain why this relatively fluid predisposition was ultimately phonemicized in the particularly striking and far-reaching umlaut sound laws of Old English, which differ so much from those in other Germanic languages.

Secondly, *i*-umlaut is not limited to Germanic but is also characteristic of its Celtic neighbour, Highland British Celtic, e.g. *donjos* 'man, person' > *dynjos* > Old British /dyn/ (spelled in Old Breton as <don>, pronounced approximately as French *dune*) > Breton *den*, Welsh *dyn*. When final syllables were regularly lost around AD 500, *i*-umlaut was phonemicized (in other words, the stage /dyn/ had been reached by c. AD 500). As we will see in section II.8, a very similar development was characteristic of Irish, too, but was phonemicized differently. So explaining the apparent polygenesis of umlaut in Germanic by turning umlaut into a phonetic tendency of the Proto-Germanic ancestor reintroduces monogenesis and consequently simplifies the explanation of Germanic umlaut, but it does not get rid of polygenesis of *i*-umlaut in the wider areal context of northwestern Europe. Monogenesis could be restored by assuming, arbitrarily, that Celtic took over the phonetic tendency towards umlaut from Germanic by contact, that Germanic took it over from Celtic, or that both took it over from an unknown third party. But that means that we either settle for polygenesis of umlaut, which undermines the compellingness of the idea of monogenesis in Germanic, or that language contact is required to save monogenesis, which undermines the compellingness of the idea that Old English umlaut is not due to language contact.

Given those difficulties, the best approach is to be both strict and practical: the presence of umlaut in Old English does not require the presence of a British substratum, even though perhaps the details of its unfolding do. If for other reasons than criterion (2) a substratum is required and happens to explain the striking details of the unfolding of umlaut in Old English, that would clearly support the idea that there was a substratum.

Let us turn to the next criterion in favour of substratum influence.

(3) The changes are linked, that is, form a coherent system in themselves (so that in combination with (1) and (2) the idea is strengthened that a foreign sound system is steering the changes).

This criterion in favour of a substratum in Old English is fulfilled: a host of Old English sound laws conspire for the vowel of the first syllable to anticipate phonetic features that are located later in the word, which gives rise to the impression that a particular sound system is engineering the changes.

(4) The changes do not spread gradually from a centre to the periphery of the area in which the language is spoken (gradual spread of changes is explained by people speaking to one another across a dialect continuum, not by a common substratum; if there is no gradual spread but the changes are 'suddenly' there, that is an argument in favour of a substratum).

Since the sound changes involved are prehistoric sound changes, the way in which they have spread cannot be tracked down in our written sources of the seventh and later centuries, by which time the sound changes were ancient history. Yet there are indirect indications that the Old English sound changes between c. 450 and 700 did not behave as a gradual spread from a centre to its periphery. As is well known in Old English studies, the almost identical vowel systems of the Old English dialects arose by similar processes but with many differences in the details of applying those processes. The differences concern not only the application of *i*- and *a/u*-umlaut but also breaking, the influence exerted by word-initial *c*- and *g*-, the so-called Anglian smoothing (which turned diphthongs into long vowels), and the so-called second fronting characteristic of one particular Mercian dialect. Processes of change that look similar if described in general terms (such as umlaut, breaking, diphthongization, and monophthongization) upon closer observation break up into rather different sound laws. The result is that cognate words, which had one and the same form in ancestral North Sea Germanic, could turn out quite differently in the various Old English dialects. Compare the following examples:

North Sea Germanic	Anglian	West Saxon	meaning
*hauhaz	hǣh > hēh	hēah	'high'
*skǣpaz	scēp	scēap	'sheep'
*hauzjan	hēran	hīeran	'to hear'
*seukaz	sēc	sēoc	'sick'
*eduraz	eodor	edor	'enclosure'
*niman	nioman	niman	'to take'
*herdijaz	hiorde	hierde	'shepherd'
*fallan	fallan	feallan	'to fall'
*fatō	featu (fatu)	fatu	'vats'

Hence we observe that on a macroscopic level the Old English dialects all underwent highly similar and distinctive changes leading up to an almost identical vowel system in all dialects. But we also observe, on a microscopic level, that these changes take the form of slightly different sound laws in the various dialects. Those slightly different sound laws led to a potentially confusing array of differences between the dialects on the level of individual words. The inevitable consequence of these observations is that the similarity of the vowel systems and of the processes leading up to them cannot be explained just on the basis of contact between the speakers of the Old English dialects, because speaker contact should have led to easy mutual comprehension.[63] Instead, the processes produced such different results that they impaired rather than improved mutual comprehension. It is as if the dialects adopted the same phonemic and phonetic system *without* contact with one another. That, I submit, is one of the best possible indicators of a common substratum, more explicitly, of a language shift by a non-Anglo-Saxon population to Old English in the period between c. 450 and 700.

Criteria 1, 3, and 4 in favour of language shift steering change are applicable to the developments of the Old English vowel system, with criterion 2 remaining inconclusive. On balance, it is therefore likely that a substratum language was involved in the formation of Old English. One of the features of that substratum language is that it shows a particular system of long and short diphthongs as well as extensive anticipation of second syllables in the first syllable (umlaut), which involves the rise of diphthongs and rounded front vowels in the first syllable. That is a very specific profile to work with for someone on the hunt for possible candidates.

7. TRACKING DOWN THE SUBSTRATUM LANGUAGE UNDER OLD ENGLISH

In section II.5, Late Spoken British Latin and Lowland British Celtic were established as obvious candidates for having been the languages of the British natives who shifted to speaking Old English. Since detailed enough information on British Spoken Latin is unavailable, northwestern Gallo-Romance serves as a proxy; it is the geographically closest Latin dialect, from which Picardian French developed. A reconstruction of its vowel system around the middle of the first millennium looks as follows:

Northwestern (Picardian) pre-Old French[64]

long vowels and diphthongs			short vowels and diphthongs		
ī	ȳ		i	y	
ē		ō	e		o
ǣ > ie		uo > ye	æ		ɔ
ā > ǣ				a	

Obviously, this system is not suspiciously like the Old English system as cited earlier:

The Old English vowel system (c. 700)

	long vowels and diphthongs					short vowels and diphthongs				
	front	front + back	front round	central	back round	front	front + back	front round	central	back round
close	ī	īo	ȳ		ū	i	io	y		u
mid	ē	ēo	ō		ō	e	eo	ø		o
open	ǣ	ēa		ā		æ	ea		a	

(additional īe, ie in West Saxon)

Nor does the Old English system resemble the Highland British Celtic vowel system around AD 500:

Highland British Celtic (ca. 500)[65]

long vowels			short vowels			
ī	*ȳ*	*ū*	*i*	*y*		*u*
ē			*e*	[ø]		
ǣ		*ɔ̄*	*æ*			*o*
					a	

That is not entirely unexpected, as it has already been established that Highland British Celtic is probably not a good proxy of the Lowland British Celtic with which the first Anglo-Saxons would have come into contact. Therefore, we can be pretty sure that neither Gallo-Romance nor Highland British Celtic fits the brief of the substratum language hiding in Old English. What is significant in a different context is the obvious similarity between the Gallo-Romance and the Highland British Celtic vowel systems, but this is irrelevant for present purposes.

An idea that cannot be discarded is that Lowland British Celtic had a vowel system similar to Old English and that it is the substratum we are looking for. But neither can that idea be supported, it seems, due to the absence of information. By a stroke of good fortune, however, there may well be an indirect way of accessing the sound system of Lowland British Celtic. This brings us on an unexpected excursion to Ireland.

8. THE ORIGIN OF IRISH

The oldest known native language of Ireland is called Irish (or Gaelic). Irish is also spoken in the Highlands of western Scotland, where it is called Scots Gaelic. Irish is a Celtic language, and Celtic languages belong to the Indo-European language family. Nobody has ever seriously argued that the Celtic or Indo-European language families originated in Ireland, and there is general consensus that Irish—or rather its ancestor language—must at a certain point in time have been imported into Ireland. How and when this happened is a big question, one people have been arguing about for well over a century. Only the most basic issue is undisputed: since languages live within the heads of speakers, they can travel only when their speakers do. So the question when and how Irish arrived in Ireland translates to the question: when did speakers of Irish (or its ancestor) first reach Ireland? Apart from this trivial point, everything else about the coming of Irish is hotly disputed. While some have argued for a date around the beginning of the Neolithic, shortly after 4000 BC (e.g. Renfrew 1987) and others have put forward arguments for a Bronze Age date (Koch 1991, 1994 argues for the twelfth century BC), those who have expressed opinions on the matter have mostly favoured an arrival date sometime during the Iron Age between c. 500 and 100 BC,[66] when Celtic languages spread across large areas of middle and southern Europe, presumably from a homeland north of the Alps. The modus operandi of the first immigrant speakers of ancestral Irish could have been anything from a military invasion and a colonization movement to the opening of trading posts along the Atlantic seaboard. The immigrants may have been so numerous that they linguistically swamped whoever lived in Ireland before them, or they may have come in small numbers and then been very successful in culturally assimilating the aboriginals. In short, we can imagine almost anything and know almost nothing.

Much of the difficulty arises from the fact that the disciplines that are brought to bear on the question, historical linguistics and archaeology, are ill equipped to answer it. Historical linguists are very adept at reconstructing the Celtic languages and at describing how the Proto-Indo-European mother tongue changed to become Proto-Celtic, and how the Proto-Celtic language step by step broke up into its various daughter languages, one of which is British Celtic and another Irish. While over the last two centuries progress in uncovering the history of Celtic speech has been spectacular, it has turned out to be almost impossible to get a handle on the history of Celtic speakers. Hence most linguists steer clear of tackling the issue altogether. Archaeologists, on the other hand, are well equipped to deal with the prehistory of speakers (i.e. people) but only in the limited sense that they can reconstruct culture on the basis of material remains that have been preserved well enough to be excavated thousands of years after their deposition. That provision means that they cannot usefully deal with language: prehistoric peoples were illiterate and did not leave inscriptions. Archaeologists use the name Celtic, if they do not avoid it altogether, as a term for a particular configuration of materials and ideas from Iron Age Europe. Historical linguists define Celtic as a particular subgroup of the Indo-European linguistic family. Based on such different definitions, discussions about Celtic are bound to end in utter confusion.

Hence, while historical linguistics and archaeology are both successful in reconstructing prehistoric culture, their reconstructions cover such different fields of culture that as a rule they do not meet. An archaeologist's Celt is quite a different kind of bird from a linguist's Celt. The consequences are easy to imagine. Archaeologists and linguists are able to draw highly informative maps showing the distribution of their respective prehistoric Celts, but there is no more reason why those maps should match up than a map showing the density distribution of owners of German cars in Europe should match up with a map showing the density distribution of speakers of the German language. Language and other aspects of culture very often do not travel together. A map of the extent of the Western Roman Empire shows a resemblance, even though it is only a very rough one, to a map showing the distribution of medieval and modern Romance languages, which descend from Latin. We happen to know that both maps are historically linked and that in this case language and history marched together. But a map plotting the gradual conversion of late Antique and medieval peoples to Christianity simply has no linguistic counterpart. The spread of Christianity is culturally one of the most incisive developments in Europe of the first millennium, but it had hardly any effect on the linguistic map. Archaeologists and linguists, it seems, are predisposed not to get along.

Over the last decades, this uneasy marriage has been joined by a third party, from the fast-developing field of human evolutionary genetics.[67] By using mainly modern DNA, and especially mitochondrial and Y-chromosome DNA in order to trace female and male lineages, respectively, geneticists are capable of contributing their share to the reconstruction of European history over the last 10,000 years by concentrating on relatively small and fast-developing regions of the genome and by exploiting the notion that mutations in those regions accumulate at a regular rate. In this way they are capable of distinguishing ancient from more modern genetic variants, drawing family trees of those variants, and approximately dating the various branching points on family trees. Since both genes and languages travel within people, it would seem to be an easy thing to align gene family trees with language family trees and accordingly solve puzzles like the date of the coming of the Irish language to Ireland by applying the following procedure:

- Identify a genetic variant that is significantly more frequent in present-day Ireland than elsewhere and label this an Irish variant.
- Plot its position on the family tree of all variants of that particular stretch of genome.
- Identify where on the map of Europe other variants of that stretch of genome are nowadays most frequent.
- Assume that a genetic variant is nowadays most frequent where it first originated.
- Date all variants.
- Draw arrows on the map that connect areas of high incidence of an innovative variant to areas of high incidence of its ancestral variant, in accordance with the genetic family tree; the ancestral variant is the point of origin of the arrow.
- If the arrow pointing at the Irish gene originates in, say, the present-day Basque Country, assume that the gene came to Ireland from the Basque Country as a result of a population movement and that the population movement occurred at some point in time between the date of origin of the Basque variant and the date of origin of the Irish variant.
- Conclude that the movement that has been identified in this way offers a possible conduit for the Irish language to have moved into Ireland.

Geneticists are aware of numerous practical and theoretical problems that may disturb this relatively simple procedure. A well-known practical problem is the problem of sampling: how many people's genes do we need to investigate in order to claim a variant as an 'Irish variant'? One million, one hundred, two? Computational limitations usually mean that samples are at the lower end of the scale. A theoretical problem is the assumption that an area with a high incidence of a genetic variant today is the area of origin of that variant and of all variants descended from it. This is a very crude assumption—as geneticists acknowledge. The problem is that high incidence today does not mean high incidence in the past, and high density of a feature at a particular spot on the map does not mean that the feature originated there. A linguistic parallel may help to clarify the point. Suppose we wish to identify the place of origin of the Celtic languages as the area which nowadays shows the greatest density of speakers of a Celtic language. That area is without a doubt North Wales. We may subsequently draw a map that shows the past expansion of Celtic on which all arrows ultimately depart from North Wales. This would be a completely incorrect map, first of all because the modern linguistic map is an incorrect point of departure: a twentieth-century linguistic map has Celtic languages in Ireland, Scotland, Man, Wales, and Brittany as well as some patches in the Americas. A linguistic map from a period that is much closer to the date at which Celtic started to spread, say, a map of the first century AD, shows Celtic languages being spoken across vast areas of central and southern Europe, from Spain to Turkey and from Poland to the British Isles. It is impossible to estimate speaker density at such a remote period, but if the incidence of Celtic personal names in Roman-age Latin inscriptions is anything to go by, the greatest density of Celtic speakers was in the province of Noricum, in present-day Austria (Raybould and Sims-Williams 2007: 22–25). That is much closer to our best present guess at where the Celtic homeland may have been, somewhere between eastern France and the Czech Republic, north of the Alps.

So geneticists' maps with arrows that indicate prehistoric population movements need to be taken with a grain of salt. But even if we allow for the rapid progress in the field and conceive of future perfect genetic maps showing reliable dates and arrows, we will still be nowhere near solving the issue of when and how languages spread. That is because languages and genes often do not spread in tandem. While genes, which are transmitted from parents to children, are part of our unalterable nature, the particular language or languages we speak are part of our culture: they can be acquired for any reason in the course of our lives as the opportunity arises. It is true that gene transmission and language transmission are similar in one respect: infants are immediately exposed to the language of their parents, which they pick up and then learn to use perfectly. But dissimilarities predominate: consider what has been happening to the Breton language during the twentieth century, within a few generations. Put simply, a first generation speaks Breton as its first language, and to a greater or lesser degree French as a second language. Their children, the second generation, grow up in communities and visit schools in which the active use of Breton outside the home is strongly discouraged, even penalized. That generation grows up bilingually but is convinced that speaking Breton is a sign of backwardness and a hindrance to a socially and economically successful life. Since they wish the best possible future for their own children, they expose the third generation to Breton as little as possible and to French as much as possible. Typical third-generation speakers will have no active command of Breton but are able to understand it because they picked some up in the homes of their grandparents. Fourth-generation speakers have not been exposed to Breton in this way and grow up as monolingual speakers of French. They are as Breton, in the linguistic sense, as most readers of this book, and the whole process of language loss has been accomplished within a few generations over less than a century. Since this scenario has been extremely common in rural Brittany, the Breton language is in very serious decline. Yet the exchange of Breton for French in four generations is not accompanied by a comparable genetic watershed: a monolingual French speaker is an ordinary great-grandchild of a monolingual Breton speaker.

Language shifts of this kind occur all over the world and have probably been common since linguistic diversity first arose tens of thousands of years ago. They are the most important means by which languages spread. Shifts play havoc with the desire to align language family trees with genetic trees. Nowadays, native speakers of English grow up in communities as genetically diverse as North American Inuit and Hopi, Australian Dyirbal, South African Zulu and Xhosa, and English Scousers. It is quite plausible, if we return to Ireland, that the Irish language originally spread across Ireland as a result of language shift. Irish must have been brought to Ireland by a group of speakers, who by necessity brought along their genes, but there is no saying how big that group of primaeval Irish speakers was, nor by what means they managed to cause their language to spread, nor whether their genes were as successful in spreading themselves around.

If, then, the results of genetics, archaeology, and historical linguistics do not align, how is it possible for those disciplines to conduct a meaningful conversation about human history? First of all, they need to acknowledge their differences and avoid metaphors borrowed from one another. Celtic is a well-defined linguistic term, and its application to archaeological cultures and to genes is a metaphor that is bound to cause confusion and misunderstandings. A second means of meaningful exchange is to concentrate on windows of opportunity: if, say, a fairly uniform archaeological culture is seen to spread across a wide area, this is a window of opportunity for a language to have spread along with the culture (but by no means a necessity). If this happens to coincide with independently recovered data from historical linguistics, we may surmise that language and culture in this particular case spread in tandem. A third precondition to cross-disciplinary co-operation is that we abstain from propping up a weak linguistic argument with archaeological or genetic data and vice versa. An argument from linguistics should be able to stand on its own two feet and be viable by itself.

I shall attempt to stick to those rules of conduct by producing a strictly linguistic argument for dating the coming of Irish to Ireland. When the argument is complete, we may search for a suitable window of opportunity in the archaeological record. There are a number of linguistic items that can be used to fix an approximate date for the coming of Irish to Ireland.

8.1. The Name of Ireland

The oldest linguistic piece of information we have relating to Ireland is its name, which has been variously assumed to be of Celtic or non-Celtic origin. The earliest name form is used by the Greek historian Strabo (first century BC), who calls Ireland *Iernē*. A very similar form is used by the Latin author Avienus, who wrote as late as the fourth century AD but seems never to have used sources later than the fourth century BC. He mentions the *insula Hiernorum* 'the island of the *Hiernī*'. Both *Iernē* and the tribal name *Hiernī* probably go back to a form *Hiwern-*, which was borrowed from an unknown source into the Ionic dialect of Greek, probably at some point between the sixth and fourth century BC. Ionic Greek was originally spoken in what is now western Turkey, which is so far from Ireland that one wonders why the Ionic form of the name became so popular. Ionic sailors were experienced traders who founded a number of colonies in the Mediterranean basin. Most famous among those colonies is Marseille, which was founded around 600 BC by merchants from the Ionic town of Phocaea. For centuries, Marseille was one of the most important Greek gateways to the western Mediterranean and Atlantic trading routes, and its citizens sailed as far north as the British Isles and Scandinavia, where they may have picked up the name for Ireland.

The reconstruction *Hiwern-* fits in well with the names *Iuverna*, *Iverna* attested by Latin authors of the first and second century AD and by the geographer Ptolemy, who wrote in Greek and used the names *Iouernías nēsos* 'the island of Ivernia' and *Iouérnioi* 'the tribe of the Ivernii'. But beside this well-supported *(h)iwern-* there is also Latin *Hibernia*, which Caesar used (first century BC), as did many authors after him. It is conceivable that this form with -b- is based on a Greek spelling IBEPN-, pronounced [hivern]-, in which case it is just another spelling for the name we have already met.

This name for Ireland in Classical Greek and Latin sources is similar but by no means identical to its name in the Celtic languages themselves, Irish and Welsh. The Old Irish name for Ireland is *Ériu* (Modern Irish *Éire*), which goes back to Proto-Celtic *ēwerjon-*. This is also the form that underlies Middle Welsh *Ywerddon*.[68] This form differs from the Classical forms in its initial vowel (*ē-* instead of *i-*) and in the form of the suffix (*-jon-* instead of *-no-*, *-nā-*, *-niā-*). A cross between this Celtic name for Ireland and the Classical name, *in Hiverione* 'in Ireland', is already attested in the

'Maritime Itinerary', a Latin text of the third or fourth century AD that lists place names along sea routes. Medieval Latin texts from Ireland show a similar cross: *Ebernia*, *Evernis*, and *Hebernensium*, instead of showing *(H)i-*, contain the *ē-* of Irish *ēwerjon-.*[69]

The Classical form *Hiwer-n-* is closer to the Celtic *Ēwer-no-* that underlies the Middle Irish name for an ancient tribe of southern Ireland, the Erainn: nominative plural *Érainn*, accusative *Érnu*; this has *ē-* rather than *i-*, exactly like the Celtic name for Ireland.[70] According to Irish tradition, a mythical ancestor figure of the *Érainn* is called *Iär*, which goes back to an older form *Ēweros.*[71]

Taking stock of the relevant material, we have seen forms with or without initial *h-*, with first-syllable *i* (long or short is unclear) or *ē*, and with a variety of consonants and vowels in the final syllables. This variety towards the end of the word can be accounted for in terms of word formation, meaning that there is a basic stem *ēwer-* (or *(h)iwer-*) to which different suffixes can be added, which turn the basic stem into an actual word with a particular function (e.g. abstract noun, material adjective, etc.). From these basic words new words can be derived, as in English the noun *friend* forms the basis of the adjectival derivation *friendly*, from which in turn the abstract noun *friendliness* is derived. The pattern of derivation of the stem *ēwer-* probably started from the basic noun *ēweros*:

Ēwer-o-s (name of a tribal ancestor figure: Irish *Iär*)
→ *Ēwer-no-s* 'person belonging to the tribe of *Ēweros* (Irish *Érainn*)'
  → *Ēwer-n-ā* or *Ēwer-n-iā-* 'land belonging to that tribe' (Classical names of Ireland)
  → *Ēwer-ion-* (probably modelled after the native Celtic word *īwer-ion-* 'land': Irish *íriu*, Welsh *Iwerddon*) (Latin *Iverione*, Irish *Ériu*, Welsh *Ywerddon* 'Ireland')

While there is nothing intrinsically un-Celtic about the suffixes and the derivational patterns of the words involved, things are rather different with respect to the stem *ēwer-*: the interchange of *i-* (perhaps long *ī-*) in the Classical sources with *ē-* in Celtic sources is impossible to explain if the word is native Celtic.[72] This difficulty mars any attempt to squeeze a Celtic or Indo-European etymology out of *ēwer-* and rather suggests that the name has been borrowed into Celtic as well as into Greek and Latin from an unknown language.[73]

Hence, the name of Ireland cannot provide evidence for a Celtic presence in Ireland when the name first entered Greek sometime between the sixth and the fourth century BC. There are two reasons for that conclusion: it is highly questionable that the name of Ireland is etymologically Celtic at all, and even if it were, there is no way of knowing whether the name was used by the inhabitants of Ireland themselves (in which case it shows that Celtic was spoken in Ireland) or rather by their Celtic-speaking neighbours elsewhere in western Europe (in which case it is irrelevant to the issue).

8.2. Ireland in Claudius Ptolemaeus' *Geographia*

Claudius Ptolemaeus was a productive scientist who lived in Alexandria (Egypt) during the second century AD and wrote in Greek. Among his many works, the *Geographias Hephegesis* (in short, Ptolemy's *Geographia*) ranks foremost. It is a geographical description including maps of the entire known world, and it was composed around the middle of the second century. Ptolemy's main source was a geography of Marinus of Tyre, who worked earlier in that same century and may himself have used a first-century AD source. Ptolemy's map of Ireland is our first known source dealing with the island. It mentions names of tribes, towns, rivers, and other geographical features. Some of those names are clearly Celtic: examples are the tribal names *Brigantes* ('Nobles'), *Ouenniknioi* ('Family Descendants'), and probably also *Rhobogdioi* ('Very Poor'?) and the river names *Bououinda* ('White Cow') and *Ouidoua* ('Widow' or 'Wooded').[74] The tribal name *Manapioi* and the town *Manapia* may be compared to the name *Menapii*, which in Roman sources is applied to a Belgic tribe inhabiting southern coastal areas of the Low Countries. This name can be reconstructed as Celtic $*Menak^{w}io$-, but it does not have a plausible Celtic etymology. Its importance lies in the fact that the Irish forms show the typically Celtic sound change of $*eRa$ to aRa (where R is a cover symbol for a resonant l, r, or n). It is one of the very few Irish names in Ptolemy's work that survived into the medieval period, surfacing as the Middle Irish tribal name *Manaig* (or *Monaig*, under the influence of the word *monach*, *manach* 'monk') and in the name of the modern county *Fermanagh*.

Ptolemy is our first cornerstone: around the middle of the second century AD (when the *Geography* was composed) and possibly by the late first to early second century AD (the date of his main sources), peoples and places in Ireland bore Celtic names, which presupposes that the first speakers of Celtic must have entered Ireland before that time. How much earlier is impossible to say on the basis of the place name evidence alone: Celtic may have been present for thousands of years, or it may have arrived only in the course of the first century AD.

This wide window of opportunity is perhaps disappointing, but it is also sobering: while Ireland may have been Celtic-speaking since time immemorial, there is nothing to stop us from believing that it was by far the last piece of land in Europe that Celtic had conquered. Fortunately, there is more evidence, which is capable of narrowing down the time frame.

8.3. Irish and British Celtic

The closest cognate of Irish is British Celtic, or rather Highland British Celtic, the ancestor of Welsh, Cornish, and Breton that was spoken in the west and north of Britain. Although on the face of it the Old Irish of the seventh century and Old Welsh and Breton of the eighth century look very different from one another, almost all of the differences between them had arisen in a relatively short period between the fifth and seventh centuries

AD, when masses of sound changes affected both languages. In fact, during the Roman period Irish and British Celtic must have been so similar that Celtic speakers on either side of the Irish Sea had little difficulty in understanding one another's language.

The earliest datable linguistic development that was not shared between Irish and British is the development of the Proto-Celtic diphthong *ai to *$\bar{\bar{e}}$ (as in English *bed* but long), which affected British Celtic but not Irish, probably at some point during the later first century AD at the earliest.[75] Before this happened, Irish and British Celtic were not just mutually comprehensible dialects; they were indistinguishable from one another.

The only possible exception is the development of Proto-Celtic *k^w (pronounced as *qu* in *queen*) into British Celtic *p*, while Irish retained *k^w until at least the fifth century AD and then turned it into *k*, spelled *c* (as in Proto-Celtic *k^writus* 'form' > Middle Welsh *pryd*, Old Irish *cruth*). It is indeed generally assumed that British Celtic developed along with Gaulish when it turned *k^w into *p*. This idea has been translated into a labelling of Irish as Q-Celtic (Q stands for the sound *k^w*) and of British and Gaulish as P-Celtic, as if these were two different dialects of Celtic. But since British and Irish were identical in all other respects, the labels P- and Q-Celtic are diagnostic of that single feature alone, which renders them virtually useless. Moreover, the issue of *k^w > p* is itself beset with problems. Gaulish is predominantly P-Celtic, but there are Gaulish words that indicate that Q-Celtic dialects existed as well (e.g. *eqos* 'horse' on the Coligny Calendar and the river name *Sequana* 'Seine'). Surviving British Celtic, that is, Highland British Celtic, is solidly P-Celtic, but we do not have enough information about Lowland British Celtic to state that it was uniformly P-Celtic rather than mixed, like Gaulish. Another complication is that while Irish is uniformly Q-Celtic, Ptolemy's map of Ireland contains the P-Celtic names *Manapioi* and *Manapia* (see II.8.2). There are three different ways in which this can be understood:

1. Two different Celtic waves swept into Ireland, an earlier P-Celtic wave, as witnessed by Ptolemy, and a later Q-Celtic wave, which became Irish. The latter translated the tribal name *Manap-* from its P-Celtic form into Q-Celtic *$Manak^w$-*. Given the limited usefulness of the *p/k^w* development as set out earlier, it is far too weak to support anything as ambitious as two Celticization waves.

2. Ptolemy or his sources may have got the names *Manapioi* and *Manapia* from British or Gaulish spokespersons rather than from the Irish themselves. Since at the time P-Celtic British and Gaulish used the sound *p* (e.g. *$pempe$* 'five') whenever Q-Celtic Irish used *k^w* (*$k^w enk^w e$* 'five'), and vice versa, *Manap-* would be no more than a British or Gaulish pronunciation of Irish *$Manak^w$-*.

3. If we turn the *p/k^w* issue on its head, the earliest Celtic of Ireland was indeed P-Celtic, as Ptolemy's names indicate, but then shifted to being Q-Celtic by a sound law *p > *k^w*, possibly as a result of

the assimilation to Irish of a large number of non-Celtic speakers who in their native language (whatever that may have been) lacked a phoneme /p/. This is, after all, what Irish itself did when in the fifth century it was confronted by Latin loanwords with a *p* in them: Latin *Pāscha* 'Easter', for instance, was borrowed in Irish as *$k^w\bar{a}sk\bar{a}$, which became Old Irish *Cásc*.

However this may be, the *p*/k^w difference is too problematic, too isolated, and too trivial to single-handedly carry the burden of representing an important early split between Irish and British Celtic.

So, to all intents and purposes, in the first century AD Irish and British Celtic were one single undifferentiated language. This is highly relevant to us if we wish to determine when Irish first arrived in Ireland. If Irish had been geographically isolated from British Celtic for any length of time before the first century AD, one would expect to find at least some early differences between them, although it is impossible to say how many: language does not change at a particular rate comparable to a molecular clock, and periods of little change follow short bursts of rapid change. It seems safe to say, however, that any scenario that has Irish arriving in Ireland before, say, 1000 BC, is impossible for linguistic reasons: more than a thousand years of relative isolation seeing no linguistic change whatsoever simply strains our credulity. Beyond that, dating becomes more difficult, but it seems safe to say that an Irish arrival in Ireland close to or in the first century AD is much easier to unite with the linguistic evidence than an arrival around, say, 500 or 1000 BC.

8.4. Rapid Change in Irish

After the Irish names in Ptolemy, the next and fortunately much larger corpus of Irish language material is the inscriptions written in the curious Ogam alphabet.[76] They are short funerary texts containing little more than the name of the deceased and his or her affiliation, but this spareness hides a wealth of linguistic information about the state and development of the Irish language between approximately 400 and the inception of Old Irish literature in Latin script in the seventh century. What they show is that Irish underwent radical phonological developments that changed the entire fabric of the language. A name that in 400 was *Lugudixs*, genitive *Lugudikas*, had by the seventh century become Old Irish *Lugaid* /lluɣəð/, genitive *Luigdech* /lluɣ́ðəx/. The nominative *wiras*, genitive *wirī* 'man' had become *fer* /fer/, *fir* /fif/. The result of all those changes was a complete overhaul of the sound system and an extreme rise in the complexity of the morphological structure of the language: each Old Irish verb, for instance, had about 160 different forms, many of which contained a complication or two. The intensive changes that affected Irish between AD 400 and 600 turned a moderately complex language of the Latin type into one of the morphologically most complex languages in the world. It is not clear why so many changes occurred in such a short period of time, nor what triggered this avalanche. At around the same time, British Celtic turned into Old Welsh, Cornish, and Breton by an equally spectacular set of phonological changes, which took British Celtic in an entirely different direction from Irish and mercifully did not lead to languages as complicated as Old Irish. It is much clearer what went on in this case. Almost all changes that affected British Celtic have counterparts in contemporary Late Spoken Latin, and it is probable that those changes entered British Celtic from Latin. The explanation for this remarkable Latinization of British Celtic after the collapse of Roman Britain is probably that large numbers of speakers of British Latin switched to become speakers of British Celtic but in doing so imported a strong Latin accent into British Celtic (see II.5.1, with references).

So intensive change in British Celtic between 400 and 700 was caused by a language shift, which we are fortunate enough to be able to trace because we happen to know so much about Late Spoken Latin, from which people shifted to British Celtic. In Ireland between 400 and 600 something very similar occurred, which strongly suggests a similar explanation: language shift. But in this case we know nothing about the language from which people shifted to Irish.

If indeed there was a massive language shift in Ireland from an unknown language to Irish between 400 and 600, the spread of the Irish language across Ireland apparently took place at approximately that period in time. This is much easier to combine with a late first-century AD arrival of the first speakers of Irish in Ireland (II.8.2 and II.8.3) than with any other scenario that has Irish arriving earlier.

8.5. Survival of a Pre-Irish Language in Ireland: The *Partán* Argument

If the expansion of Irish in Ireland occurred as late as between the second and sixth centuries AD, we would expect to find at least traces of a different, pre-Irish language surviving in the medieval period. The medieval Irish sources are remarkably silent about language, which conveys the impression that everybody spoke Irish (and, in clerical circles, Latin). Yet there is indirect evidence that a pre-Celtic language was spoken in Ireland at least until the sixth century AD. The argument centres around a number of Irish words that lack a Celtic or Indo-European etymology and are therefore likely to have been borrowed into Irish from a non-Celtic language that was spoken in Ireland before Irish replaced it. It is usually impossible to date when such words entered Irish, so they offer no help in answering the question of when Irish first arrived in Ireland. There is one category of words, however, which does provide datable evidence: those that contain the phoneme /p/, such as Middle Irish *petta* 'pet', *pait* 'bottle made from skin', and *partán* 'crab'.

One of the earliest sound changes that differentiated the Celtic language family from its closest Indo-European cognates, the Italic languages, is the loss of Indo-European *p, which via *φ (an f produced by releasing compressed air between the two lips rather than between lower lip and upper incisors) usually became *h before it was lost altogether. Late Indo-European *$pat\bar{e}r$ 'father', for instance, accordingly developed into Celtic *$at\bar{\iota}r$, which ultimately became Old Irish *athair*. So the ancestor language of Celtic did not have a phoneme /p/. While most dialects of Gaulish and British Celtic remedied the situation by creating a new /p/ from Proto-Celtic *k^w, Irish for a very long time remained p-less (see II.8.3). This situation persisted into the fifth century. When the Briton Patricius came to convert the Irish, they found it impossible to pronounce the first letter of his name and substituted it by its closest counterpart in Irish, *k^w: *$K^w atrikias$ developed into the oldest Irish name for the saint, *Cothraige*.[77] So it went with all Latin loanwords that entered Irish in the fifth and early sixth centuries: Latin *purpur* 'purple' became Old Irish *corcor*, and *Pāscha* 'Easter' yielded Old Irish *Cásc*. Only after in the course of the sixth century a development called syncope had given rise to a new native phoneme /p/ did Irish adopt Latin loanwords with retained p, such as Old Irish *peccad* 'sin' from Latin *peccātum*.

What this means is that words such as *partán*, *petta*, and *pait* cannot have been borrowed into Irish before the sixth century. This implies that during the sixth century the pre-Irish language of Ireland must have been in good enough shape to donate words into Irish. So there is evidence that a pre-Irish, probably non-Indo-European language survived in Ireland into the early medieval period.[78]

8.6. Old Irish Is Proto-Irish

The Old Irish literary language, which is attested from the seventh century AD onwards, is famously monolithic: initially, it showed no dialectal variation. This is odd for an early medieval literary language: as soon as Welsh, English, Dutch, German, and Norse appear in the written record, they show a variety of dialects. Yet in as far as a literary language is a conscious creation by a small cultural elite, it is quite conceivable that the early Irish literati operated differently from their counterparts elsewhere in western Europe and picked just one Irish dialect as the basis of the Old Irish literary language. In that case the Old Irish written language was monolithic, whereas the Old Irish spoken language, of which we have no direct knowledge, may have distinguished various dialects which never surface in our records.

That is most unlikely to have been the case, however. Modern Irish, Manx, and Scots Gaelic distinguish many different dialects, but in all cases the differences between them do not go back very deep in time. Occasional slips in Old Irish texts show that the first dialectal differences start to appear only in the course of the Old Irish period. One instance is a difference in expressing the Irish equivalent of so-called prepositional relatives. While standard Old Irish and the later northern dialects express 'the house in which I live' as 'the house *in which* I live', with a preposition followed by the relative pronoun, southern Irish uses 'the house *that* I live *in it*'. Modern Irish follows the southern pattern. It seems, however, that this difference did not exist before the eighth century and that Old Irish originally used the construction 'the house *that* I lived', so without explicit expression of *in* (McCone 2006: 33–34). Another early difference concerns the word for 'house', which in modern Scots Gaelic and northern Irish is *taigh*, while the central and southern Irish form is *teach*. Both forms originate by a split of one and the same paradigm, which still existed in the eighth century when the Würzburg glosses were written, which show nominative-accusative singular *tech* 'house' (the basis of the southern form *teach*), dative singular *taig* (the basis of the northern form *taigh*: Würzburg glosses 9b23, 23b9 (2x), 33a6), and genitive singular *tige* (southern again: Würzburg glosses 7c9).

All evidence points to the fact that Old Irish is not monolithic just because it is a literary standard language but because the Irish language of around AD 700 was in fact monolithic. Old Irish is Proto-Irish. This is really unusual and almost impossible to explain if Irish had been spoken in Ireland for a long period before our earliest texts of the seventh century: Ireland is not so small that if Irish had been present there for, say, a thousand years no dialectal differences would have arisen. By contrast, the monolithic nature of Old Irish is easier to explain if its expansion was of very recent date, as was suggested in II.8.4.

There is a way in which this conclusion can be avoided: it is conceivable that Irish was once widespread across Ireland, then almost died out, and then expanded again in the form of Old Irish as we know it. The dying phase needs to have been relatively drastic: the number of speakers must have been decimated to such a degree that almost all dialectal varieties perished and the remaining differences then disappeared when the surviving speakers got together and started speaking to one another, a process that usually leads to avoidance of differences that endanger mutual comprehension, which disappear as a result. In other words, if the language passed through a bottleneck before it expanded again, its monolithic nature hides former diversity. This is what must have happened to British Celtic: Welsh, Cornish, and Breton can be reconstructed as a monolithic sixth-century AD dialect, which hides the fact that British Celtic had been widespread across all of Britain for probably a millennium or more. The ancestor of Welsh, Cornish, and Breton reflects the tiny portion of British Celtic that survived the Roman and early Anglo-Saxon periods (this is the bottleneck), and the assimilation of large numbers of speakers of Latin led to simplification, Latinization, and unification, which pushed out the remaining differences. If this is what happened in Britain, it could have happened in Ireland, too, without us knowing it. Mercifully, we can exclude this possibility because of the argument presented in II.8.3: Irish

must have arrived in Ireland recently because Irish and British Celtic are
so closely related to one another that they were one and the same language
until the first century AD.

8.7. Conclusion

In order to tackle the question of when Irish first arrived in Ireland, five
independent lines of linguistic argumentation were presented:

(1) The first linguistic evidence for the presence of Celtic in Ireland dates
from as late as the second century AD (Ptolemy's map of Ireland):
while Irish may have arrived much earlier, there is no reason to
believe that it actually did.
(2) British Celtic and Irish are so closely related to one another that their
common ancestor must have been spoken as recently as the first century AD; this cannot be squared with a much earlier arrival of Irish
in Ireland.
(3) Similar developments in British Celtic suggest that the rapid and deep
sound changes that affected Irish between approximately 400 and
600 can be explained by a language switch to Celtic by an originally
non-Irish population; this recent switch suggests that the spread of
Irish in Ireland is a recent event.
(4) The evidence that a pre-Irish, possibly non-Indo-European language
survived in Ireland until at least the sixth century AD but subsequently disappeared from the radar during the Old and Middle Irish
periods (600–1200) suggests that the language was in the course of
disappearing by the early medieval period; this implies a contemporary switch of its speakers to Irish, which in turn suggests that the
spread of Irish in Ireland is a recent event.
(5) The absence of any dialectal differences in Irish that predate the Old
Irish period shows that Old Irish is Proto-Irish; this strongly suggests
that Old Irish resulted from a recent spread.

These considerations conspire towards a surprisingly coherent conclusion:
the ancestor of Irish arrived in Ireland shortly before Ptolemy's time (around
AD 150), i.e. probably during the first century AD. Given its close relationship with British Celtic, Irish came to Ireland from Britain. Once in Ireland,
it met with a pre-Celtic language, whose speakers gradually switched to Irish
between approximately 300 and the early medieval period and by doing so
caused the deep changes that affected Irish during that period. The fact that
medieval Irish continues the type of Irish spoken by those new speakers indicates that they probably heavily outnumbered the immigrants who imported
Celtic from Britain. That the immigrants were nevertheless very successful
in making the natives adopt Irish suggests that they must have been role
models, but we do not know in which respect.

Since these conclusions are based on five independent considerations, they are robust. Since they are entirely founded in linguistic argumentation, they can be falsified only by linguistic arguments, which makes the conclusions even more robust. In other words, no amount of rummaging around in the archaeologists' or geneticists' toolboxes can provide us with an instrument that is capable of shaking the conclusion that Ireland became Irish as late as approximately the first century AD. The other side of that coin is that archaeology and genetics are called upon to put flesh and bone to the linguistic scenario, which gives rise to many questions that linguistics cannot answer: who were the people who imported Irish into Ireland? Why did they leave Britain in or around the first century AD, and where exactly did they come from? If they were few, what proportion of Ireland's population at the time were they? How did they manage to make the natives adopt Irish so successfully?

This is where speculation begins, however well informed. If during the first century British immigrants imported Irish into Ireland, it is quite possible that this movement was connected with the Roman conquest of Britain, which started in AD 43 and intermittently lasted well into the 80s of the first century. The gradual and invariably brutal destruction of British independence may well have persuaded people to seek refuge and new fortunes to the west. In one particular case, archaeological evidence indicates that such a movement had indeed taken place: on Lambay Island, in the Irish Sea near Dublin, a number of inhumation burials have been found which were accompanied by objects that evidently stem from the late first-century kingdom of Brigantia, north of the Humber.[79] Brigantia had been a nominally independent Roman vassal state under Queen Cartimandua until in 74 Roman legions, facing an uprising that had lasted several years, crushed its independence. It may well be that on this occasion Brigantian exiles moved to Lambay Island as well as further afield onto the Irish mainland: Ptolemy records a tribe *Brigantes* in County Wexford.[80]

There is little continuity between Ptolemy's map of the second century and the early medieval constellation of Irish tribes, which suggests political instability and change in the intervening period.[81] The period from 200 BC to the beginning of the third century AD is known as the 'Irish Dark Ages', when a cooler, wetter climate and a strong decline of agriculture combined with reforestation suggest that population numbers dropped significantly.[82] From the third century onwards, improved climatic conditions were accompanied by a strong growth of agriculture. Economic prosperity led to increasing demands for manual labour. One way of meeting those demands was slave raiding in Roman Britain, which among many others brought the young St Patrick to Ireland. Increased contacts with Roman Britain also resulted in the establishment of Irish settlements in Roman Wales, the invention of the Ogam alphabet on the model of Latin, and, ultimately, the introduction of Christianity. It is tempting to connect the spread of Irish with this period of economic and social upheaval. It is particularly the area of 'Greater Leinster', along the east coast, that may be implicated. This was a new socio-economic configuration, which cut across the traditional Iron Age divide between the La Tène north and the south. Numerous finds of Roman imports and its involvement in the establishment of the Irish colonies in Wales show that this Greater Leinster was oriented towards Britain.[83]

Since enough information about the coming of Irish to Ireland has been gathered, we are in a favourable position to return to the main argument of this chapter: the origin of English.

9. THE CELTIC INFLUENCE ON OLD ENGLISH

Irish probably came to Ireland from Britain and as late as the first century AD. Those who brought the language to Ireland may well have been exiles who fled their native lands in the wake of the fierce fighting and extensive destruction which resulted from the Roman conquest of Britain.

Consequently, the Celtic language that those immigrants introduced into Ireland was spoken by a population that had always lived outside of the Roman Empire. It escaped the type of Latin influence that turned Highland British Celtic into a phonologically Latinized variety of Celtic during the fifth and sixth centuries (see II.5.1). Therefore, Old Irish may well give a better insight into the sound structure of British Celtic before the Roman conquest than Highland British Celtic does. Let us assume, for the sake of the argument, that that is correct. Let us further assume that Celtic speakers who stayed behind in Roman Britain continued to speak Celtic with this 'Irish' sound structure for some centuries. In the course of time, many of those British Celtic speakers would switch to Latin and would tend to speak Latin with an 'Irish' accent. In the same way, it is reasonable to suspect that when British natives (both speakers of Celtic and speakers of Latin with an 'Irish' Celtic accent) switched to Old English during the early medieval period, they may have introduced an 'Irish' accent into English. All of this falls under the heading of reasonable assumptions: an 'Irish' accent may have slipped into Old English in this way, but so far we have seen no reason whatsoever to think that this is what actually happened.

It turns out, however, that this suspicion is confirmed by linguistic data. It so happens that the sound system of Old Irish is strikingly similar to the Old English sound system. The similarities are obscured if we compare the phonological systems, but on a phonetic level they are immediately apparent.

9.1 Old English *i*-umlaut and Old Irish Palatalization

As was explained in section II.6.1, Old English underwent *i*-umlaut. This a *fronting in front contexts*: long and short back vowels ($*u$, $*o$, $*a$) and diphthongs ($*io$, $*eo$, $*ea$) became front vowels before the front sounds $*i$ and $*j$

in the following syllable, as in *bankiz* > *benc* 'bench' , *kuningaz* > *cyning* 'king', and *dōmijanan* > *dǣman* (later *dēman*) 'to judge, deem'.

The Irish counterpart of Old English *i*-umlaut is called palatalization. This a complex process—indeed, one of the banes of every student of the history of Irish—according to which consonants become palatalized by a following front vowel.[84] Simplifying somewhat, the rules for palatalization state that consonants between front vowels (long or short *e* and *i*) and consonants before (long or short) *i* become palatalized; additionally, any *i* or *e* that is being lost at the end or in the middle of a word by the processes called apocope and syncope causes palatalization of the preceding consonant. As a result of palatalization, Celtic *kannīnā* 'leek' became *kańńīnā*, where palatalized *ńń* denotes something like the middle *n* in English *onion* or *minion*. Its palatalization was caused by the following long *ī*. The form *kańńīnā* underwent various other changes before it turned out as Old Irish *cainnenn* /kańńənn/.

Old English *i*-umlaut and Irish palatalization are similar in the sense that the front vowel *i* is drawn from a non-initial syllable towards the preceding syllable, with the effect of making that syllable more like *i*. The difference is that English *i*-umlaut affects a preceding vowel, while Irish palatalization affects a preceding consonant. But if we take a closer look at what happens, that difference turns out to be a phonological (psychological) rather than a phonetic difference: in English, original *kuningaz* became phonetic [kyńingaz], with fronting of both *u* > *y* and *n* > *ń* as a result of the following *i*. And in Irish, *kannīnā* became phonetic [kæńńīnā], with fronting of both consonant and vowel. The difference between English and Irish arose by the process of phonemicization: psychologically, speakers of English assigned the fronting effect in [kyńingaz] only to [y], while the fronting of [ń] was considered to be an automatic consequence of standing after the front vowel [y]. In other words, *i*-umlaut was phonemicized on the vowel /y/ rather than on the consonant [ń], and this stabilized the fronting on /y/ but not on [ń], where it could subsequently be easily lost again: *kuningaz* > Old English /kyning/, spelled *cyning*. In Irish, the converse happened: the fronting effect in [kæńńīnā] was psychologically allotted to the /ńń/ but not to [æ], where fronting was considered, subconsciously, to be an automatic consequence for any /a/ standing in front of /ńń/. So [kæńńīnā] was ultimately phonemicized as Old Irish /kańńənn/, spelled *cainnenn*. This difference in the phonemicization of fronting between Old English and Old Irish occurred in the early medieval period. Before phonemicization, the phonetic effects of English *i*-umlaut and Irish palatalization would have been identical.

In Old Irish, the effects of palatalization phonetically trickled through from a consonant into a preceding vowel. Here are some examples, in which approximate phonetic representations accompany the Old Irish (OIr.) phonological forms. They show that a phonemic central or back vowel becomes a phonetic front vowel before a palatalized consonant.[85]

*gabitih > OIr. *gaibid*	/gaˈvəð/	[gæˈvɪð]	'takes'
*kaneti > OIr. *canaid*	/kanəð/	[kanɪð]	'sings'
*tolā > OIr. *tol*	/tol/	[tol]	'will'
*tolen > OIr. *toil*	/tolʲ/	[tolʲ]	'will' (accusative)
*mori > OIr. *muir*	/murʲ/	[myrʲ]	'sea'
*ūros > OIr. *úr*	/ūr/	[uːr]	'fresh'
*ūrī > OIr. *úir*	/ūrʲ/	[uːʲrʲ]	'fresh' (genitive)
*māros > OIr. *már*	/mār/	[mɑːr]	'big'
*mārī > OIr. *máir*	/mārʲ/	[mɑːᵆrʲ]	'big' (genitive masculine)

9.2 Old English Breaking/*a*-umlaut and Old Irish Velarization

As a result of Old English *a*-umlaut, *u*-umlaut, and breaking, the long and short front vowels **i*, **e*, and **æ* became the opening front-to-back long and short diphthongs *io*, *eo*, and *ea* (see II.6.1). Breaking and *a/u*-umlaut can be called *backing in back contexts*: they have in common that front vowels develop a back element (e.g. front *e* becoming front-to-back *eo*) and that their triggers are following back sounds (back vowels *a*, *o*, *u* or back consonant groups such as *lk*). Examples include **melkanan* > m*eo*lcan 'to milk', **kældaz* > c*ea*ld 'cold' (breaking before *ld*, *lk*) and **beranan* > beoran 'to carry' (Anglian; *a*-umlaut).

Old Irish has two counterparts. One is velarization: any consonant that is not palatalized (because the consonant or consonant group resisted palatalization by **i* or because it was followed by the back vowels **a* or **o*) is velarized, which means that the soft palate at the back of the mouth is brought into near contact with the back of the tongue whilst the consonant is pronounced (try pronouncing *d* simultaneously with *w*, then remove lip rounding, and the result is a velarized *d*, phonetically [dˠ]). Such velarized consonants affect a preceding front vowel by turning it into a front-to-back diphthong, as in Old Irish *benn*, which is phonemically /benʲnˠ/ and phonetically approximately [beənˠnˠ]. The cause and effect are very similar to those of English *a*-umlaut and breaking, and the difference, once again, is one of phonemicization: in English the front-to-back diphthong is phonemicized, while in Irish it is the velarized consonant. A few Old Irish examples follow, with Modern Irish (MoIr.) equivalents.

*līnon > OIr. *lín*	/lʲīn/	[lʲiːˑnˠ] 'number' (MoIr. *líon*)
*kanton > OIr. *cét*	/kʲēd/	[kʲeːˑdˠ] 'hundred' (MoIr. *céad*)
*kʷennon > OIr. *cenn*	/kʲenn/	[kʲeənˠnˠ] 'head' (MoIr. *ceann*)

In the case of one reconstructed vowel, *ē (< Proto-Celtic *ei), the development to a front-to-back diphthong before a velarized consonant transcended the phonetic level and was phonemicized, however.

*slēbos > OIr. *sliab*	/śĺiav/	[śĺiavˠ]	'mountain' (MoIr. *sliabh*)
*slēbesā > OIr. *sléibe*	/śĺēv́e/	[śĺeːj́v́e]	'mountains'

The Old Irish counterpart of Old English *u*-umlaut is so-called *u*-infection, which produced front-to-back-rounded diphthongs if the following syllable contained a *u. In such cases, the front-to-back diphthong was phonemicized in some instances but not in others:[86]

*kinuts > OIr. *cin*	/ḱin/	[ḱiunˠ]	'crime' (MoIr. *cion*)
*wirū > OIr. *fiur*	/f́iur/	[f́iurˠ]	'man' (dative singular)
*karuts > OIr. *caur*	/kaur/	[kˠaurˠ]	'warrior'

So, on a phonetic level, Old Irish has consistently pulled features of a second-syllable vowel into the first syllable: second-syllable *i caused palatalization, *a and o caused velarization, and *u caused rounding of a first-syllable vowel. This is very similar to the effects of *i*-umlaut, *a*-umlaut, and *u*-umlaut in Old English. Where Old Irish and Old English differ is on the phonemic level: with the exception of *u*-infection and the diphthong *ia*, Old Irish phonemicizes only consonantal features (palatalized and non-palatalized consonants), whereas Old English phonemicizes vowel features (rounded front vowels and front-to-back long and short diphthongs).

Within this general pattern of correspondence between Old Irish and Old English, there is an even more specific correspondence. In Old English, vowel + *u + *i in subsequent syllables became vowel + *i + *i, and the vowel underwent *i*-umlaut. This is so-called double umlaut.[87] Its prehistoric Irish counterpart is that vowel + *u + *i became vowel + *i + *i, and if the *i in the second syllable was lost by syncope, it palatalized the preceding consonant.[88] Examples:

Old English *lat-umista- > *latimista- > *lætemest* 'last'
Old Irish *Lugudikos > *Luγiδex > *Luigdech* /luγ′δ́ˊəx/ [lyγ′δ́ˊəx], genitive singular of the personal name *Luguid*

Other, less specific features that the prehistory of Old English and Old Irish have in common are the following:

- placement of stress on the word-initial syllable
- loss or shortening of final unstressed syllables (apocope)

- loss of unstressed syllables in the middle of the word (syncope)
- a much richer vowel system in stressed than in unstressed syllables
- the presence of the voiceless fricatives *χ, *θ, and *f (as in Scots Gaelic *loch*, English *think* and *few*, respectively; they were inherited from Proto-Germanic in Old English; they reflect lenited *k, *t, *sp/*sw, respectively, in Old Irish).

In conclusion, prehistoric Old Irish and prehistoric Old English, although separated by thousands of years of language evolution along separate branches of the Indo-European family tree, appear to share a common phonetic basis. The correspondences in the vowel system in particular are non-trivial and highly specific, and they strongly indicate a causal link. It is at this point that all the threads that have been woven in this chapter come together to form a coherent story: the Old Irish sound system offers access to the sound system of Lowland British Celtic as it was before the Roman occupation. It is this sound system that, 400 years later, influenced the language of the Anglo-Saxon colonists, as a native British population shifted to speaking their language.

10. SYNTHESIS

Four independent strands of argumentation constitute the building blocks of the linguistic history of early Anglo-Saxon England:

(1) In as far as Anglo-Saxon colonists met with Celtic speech in eastern Britain, it was Lowland British Celtic, whose sound system differed from that of Highland British Celtic (Welsh, Cornish, Breton) whilst agreeing with the Celtic spoken in northern Gaul (the inscriptions of Châteaubleau and Baudecet). Consequently, the question whether Celtic influenced the Old English sound system cannot be answered on the basis of the Highland British Celtic sound system. Crucial support for this idea comes from a study of the language of the Bath pendant and the history of the name of London.

(2) A study of the developments of the Old English sound system between c. 450 and 700 reveals that it probably underwent influence from contact with another language in Britain. Since this influence is found in all Old English dialects, the contact language must have been spoken in a vast area between southeastern Scotland and the Isle of Wight. Obvious candidates are Lowland British Celtic and Late Spoken British Latin.

(3) The Irish language is a recent offshoot of British Celtic, probably as recent as the first century AD and in that case possibly identifiable with the language of immigrants from the Brigantian area in northern England. This idea explains why Old Irish happens to show a phonetic

basis that is strikingly similar to the Old English phonetic basis both in general outline (second-syllable features are anticipated in the first syllable) and in specifics (development of rounded front vowels and front-to-back diphthongs under comparable circumstances; 'double umlaut' involving original *u): Old Irish phonetics reflect Lowland British Celtic phonetics, which were introduced into Old English by a native British population's language shift to Old English.

(4) In contrast to the phonetic Celticism of Old English, the syntactic Celticisms of Middle English arose in the southwest and the north of England, where as a result of Anglo-Saxon conquests after c. 600 a native British population adopted Old English speech with interference from Celtic. This Celticized variety of Old English surfaced in the written record only after the Old English period as a result of the backward socio-political and economic position of its speakers at the time.

The Old English sound system betrays the otherwise invisible assimilation of a British Celtic population to the language and culture of the Anglo-Saxon colonists. The degree to which linguistic features of the British population who shifted to the Germanic language of the colonists were taken over in the speech of the colonists themselves reflects a social compromise whose background is no longer accessible. Why it was that only features of the British sound system—and none of its syntactic features—managed to become generally accepted in Old English can only be guessed at. Perhaps the nascent tendency of North Sea Germanic to anticipate second-syllable features in the first syllable made Anglo-Saxon receptive to the British natives' vowel anticipation, which was comparable in nature but much more pervasive in its execution. Apart from this, it seems safe to say that the compromise between Anglo-Saxons and assimilated British Celts left little room for linguistic initiatives by the latter. This indicates a broader pattern in Anglo-Saxon attitudes towards the first native British with whom they came into contact: if British natives were prepared to be completely assimilated, linguistically and in a more general sense culturally, they were accepted into Anglo-Saxon society. That fits in with the general idea of a clean cultural break between sub-Roman Britain and Anglo-Saxon England.

A similar background may account for the success of the only other Celtic feature of Old English: the double paradigm of the present tense of 'to be', one having a general meaning and based on the stem *es-, and the other meaning 'is normally, usually' and based on the stem *bi-. Accordingly, the West Saxon dialect of Old English has *eom* 'I am' beside *bīo* 'I am wont to be, am usually'. This system is present in Highland British Celtic and in Irish (cf. Middle Welsh *wyf* beside *byðaf*, and Old Irish *am* beside *biuu*), so it can be reconstructed back to Proto-British. One might therefore argue that Old English borrowed it from Lowland British Celtic, as in the case of the vowel system. But things are more complicated because the double system of 'to be' can be reconstructed for all West Germanic languages: English, Saxon, Dutch, and High German. This correspondence between Celtic and West Germanic to the exclusion of all other Indo-European languages is so specific that one must have borrowed from the other. Stefan Schumacher argued convincingly that Germanic borrowed the distinction from Celtic on the Continent and used native Germanic verbs to express it, which etymologically, since Celtic and Germanic are related Indo-European languages, happened to be the same verbs that Celtic employed.[89] But Old English stands out from among the other West Germanic languages in that it has preserved the distinction, while the rest of West Germanic contains only its debris. It seems likely that the twofold paradigm of 'to be' was given a new lease of life in Old English when contacts with Celtic were resumed in Britain.

The story of the twofold paradigm of 'to be' in Old English picks up a strand that was left lying at the end of section II.3.3, when we were discussing the origin of Celticisms that surfaced in English no earlier than the late Middle Ages. Some of those Celticisms, such as the auxiliary 'do' and the progressive, make an appearance not only in English but also in German and Dutch. The story of 'to be' suggests that such phenomena may indeed go back to a contact zone on the Continent, where Celtic and West Germanic met at some time during the first centuries AD. This is the first and earliest contact event in the histories of Celtic and Germanic.

The British natives of the southeast who were assimilated to Anglo-Saxon society spoke Celtic or Latin with a heavy Celtic accent when the first Anglo-Saxons arrived, for it was a Celtic sound system that influenced Old English. Interestingly, the British natives who fled west into the Highland Zone and were assimilated into Highland British Celtic society spoke relatively standard Late Spoken Latin rather than Celtic (see II.5.1). It stands to reason that the degree of a person's Romanization corresponded to his socio-economic status under the Empire. The correlation between a person's language and his decision to stay put or to move west is surely significant and requires an explanation. Apparently, those who managed to throw in their lot with the Anglo-Saxons belonged to the Romano-British lower classes, who still spoke Celtic or heavily Celticized Latin by the end of the Roman period. Many of them may have been agricultural labourers, who would have constituted a welcome work force for the early Anglo-Saxons. The successful linguistic assimilation of the British Celts and their inevitable intermarriage with the Anglo-Saxon colonists probably welded a society in which the Romano-British origins of part of the population were soon forgotten. It was a society in which a man with the British Celtic name *Cerdic* could become the founder of the Anglo-Saxon dynasty of Wessex.[90] Romano-British city folk and landed gentry, however, who stood a good chance of being speakers of standard Late Spoken Latin, did not possess any of the qualifications that would have been valued by the new powers. They may have been offered no alternative but to leave the occupied areas and move west, where they led an ignoble life before being assimilated to their Highland Celtic environment.

III. The Origin of High German

1. INTRODUCTION

For many centuries, the Rhine and the Danube formed the northern boundary of the Roman Empire, separating it from what in the Roman imagination were the wild lands of *Germania* to the east and north. There an infinite variety of barbarians roamed, who constantly needed to be kept at bay. Along those rivers a long chain of military structures was built for both defensive and offensive purposes, which was called the *limes*. Rather than forming an impenetrable wall, the *limes* developed into a zone of intensive traffic and contact, which attracted large quantities of people and capital as well as the relentless scrutiny of those in power. At times when Rome prospered, friendly relationships were struck up with peoples beyond the *limes*, while commercial activities were intense on either side. Barbarian fortune seekers offered their services, which were usually of a military nature. When the Empire's fortunes waned, roving bands of warriors would grasp the opportunity to cross the frontier looking for easy plunder and an opportunity to strike a deal with one claimant or another to the imperial purple. In other cases, whole populations crossed into the Empire in the hope of securing a livelihood within the Roman state. As a consequence, the peoples who lived just outside the *limes* were not only strongly influenced by their powerful neighbour but also periodically churned by population movements.

Gradually, the dynamics of those areas intensified to such a degree that the patchwork of local tribes with which the Romans were confronted during the early centuries of the Roman Empire evolved into a landscape of large and changing confederations, whose identity and coherence cannot be explained without recourse to the fact that they flanked the Empire. This is the period of the so-called Germanic Migrations. Most of those tribal constellations carry Germanic names, and so do the people who formed their elites, but that is not to say that they were necessarily linguistically or ethnically homogeneous. Over the last decades, researchers have come to the conclusion that the confederations were ethnically complex and changed over time. The long periods over which names such as Suebi, Burgundones, Franci, and Langobardi were used suggest an ethnic stability over time among those who carried those names that is not borne out by the data.[1]

A case in point is the Suebi, which first turns up as the name of people who lived between Rhine and Main around the middle of the first century BC. They formed part of the powerful groups of migrants who had crossed the Rhine into Gaul and formed one of the catalysts of Caesar's conquest of Gaul. Their leader's name, *Ariovistus*, although not unambiguously clear, suggests a Germanic or Celtic provenance. Etymologists have frequently tried their hand at the name *Suēbī*, too.[2] The closest and hitherto unrecognized match, it seems, is with an Indo-European verbal stem **(k)sweib^h-* that means 'move in a curving path, roam':[3] 'nomads' would be an appropriate designation for Ariovistus' roving war bands. If this is correct, the name is linguistically Celtic, for the development of **ei* to *ē* is typically Celtic (the verb survives in Welsh *chwyfu* 'stir, move', among others) and certainly not Germanic because in Germanic **ei* became *ī* (as in the cognate Old Norse verb *svífa* 'to rove, ramble'). A probable scenario that explains the Celtic name is that the Gaulish natives of the first century BC, who spoke Celtic, used their Celtic word for 'roamers, nomads' to designate Ariovistus' immigrant bands. Subsequently, the name *Suēbī* stuck to them and was used by Romans in later centuries to designate various constellations of presumably mainly Germanic-speaking peoples. It seems quite unlikely that the *Suēbī* of the first century BC were ethnically identical with the *Suēbī* or *Suēvī* who in AD 406 joined the Vandals and Alans on a massive expedition deep into the Roman southwest, or with the inhabitants of the Suebian kingdom which those migrants subsequently founded in northwestern Spain.[4] Nor can the early *Suēbī* be identified ethnically with the inhabitants of the area in southern Germany that is nowadays called *Schwaben*, even though it is clearly the same name (the development of *ē* to *ā* in this form of the name is typical of early medieval Germanic on the continent). What joins all these instances of the name *Suēbī* is geographical origin and a Roman view of history rather than native ethnicity.[5]

The Langobardians are first attested as inhabitants of northern Germany east of the Lower Elbe by the geographer Strabo, who died in AD 22. In the second century they disappear from history, only to turn up again as the name of the inhabitants of Bohemia and Lower Austria by 500. A large confederation headed by the Langobardians migrated into Italy in 568, where their language is preserved in isolated words in Latin law texts. Although the linguistic and ethnic integrity of the Langobardians across six centuries has been claimed (most notably by Vennemann 2008), a different analysis of the material suggests a story of repeated episodes of ethnic churning and a formative period of the Langobardian language on Italian soil. We will have more to say about the Langobardian language in section III.5.

From the later second century onwards, such tribal constellations developed into significant powerhouses that were capable of posing a serious threat to the integrity of the Roman Empire. In the second half of the second century, the *Marcomanni*—literally meaning 'Horse-Men' in Germanic – entered a long period of warfare with Rome. Around the middle of the third century, at a time of great political instability, Germanic units broke into the Empire across a wide front. The *limes* never really recovered. Along the Lower Rhine, from the North Sea coast to beyond Nijmegen, the line of Roman fortresses was never rebuilt. It is here for the first time that we hear of the Germanic constellation called *Franci* or *Francones*, the Franks. Much of what is now southwestern Germany saw the rise of the *Alamanni* ('All-People'), a name that seems to have denoted much the same as *Suebi*. In southeastern Germany and Lower Austria, complex processes of assimilation gave rise to a population called the *Baiuwari*, the Bavarians. In spite of several attempts, Rome was incapable of regaining control over the area. The names of the Franks, Alamannians, and Bavarians stay with us during the many power struggles over the next centuries of the Empire's life and well into the medieval period. They have a special significance for linguists, too, for Franconian and Alamannian are labels that play an important role in the history of the rise of three modern languages of the area: French, German, and Dutch. It is this history that is the subject of the present and following chapters.

2. GERMAN AND DUTCH

Although the modern standard languages Dutch and German are rather different from one another in many aspects of the sound system, grammar, and lexicon, they represent chunks of one and the same linguistic continuum that stretches from the North Sea in the northwest to the Polish frontier in the east and northern Italy in the south, including much of the area of the Netherlands, northern Belgium, Germany, Austria, Luxembourg, and the northern half of Switzerland. The Dutch-speaking area includes the Netherlands, Flanders, and historically also the area around Dunkerque in northwestern France.

Additionally, there are German-speaking enclaves in many other European countries, which are remnants of an earlier much larger extension of German in eastern Europe and eastern France (Alsace and Lorraine). The later medieval and early modern period saw the linguistic spread of German into mainly Slavic-speaking territory in eastern Europe. This movement continues an earlier medieval movement of German-speaking settlers into Slavic territory (now German and Austrian soil), which started by the ninth century after a concerted military campaign by Charlemagne had destroyed what remained of the Avar Khanate (AD 796). In fact, much of present-day Germany east of the rivers Elbe, Saale, and Naab (so almost all of the former German Democratic Republic and northeastern Bavaria) as well as the Austrian provinces of Styria and Carinthia were largely Slavic-speaking before this German expansion began. Since German settlers generally moved from west to east, taking their speech with them, many important dialect boundaries in Germany run from west to east, too.

In a long process that began in late Antiquity, Germanic has been steadily encroaching on areas of Romance (Late Latin) speech as well. This includes the German-speaking areas west of the Rhine, where Germanic and Latin must have been well represented during the Roman period, as well as Germany south of the Danube and large parts of Switzerland and Austria. The Dutch-Flemish area south of the Lower Rhine formed part of the Roman Empire for centuries, so that we might expect a significant former presence of Latin speakers in that area, too, but since it passed out of direct Roman control by the middle of the third century it is unclear whether Latin survived here as a spoken language into the medieval period.

In the course of the early medieval period Dutch and German surface from an area where previously contact with Latin (in the west and south) and Slavic (in the east) must have been substantial. The influence of Latin has a special significance, for it is on the geographical interface of the Roman world and Germania that the early medieval Dutch and German centres of economic and political power arose. They are associated with the expansion of the power of the Franks. Let us keep these historical facts in mind when we delve into the linguistic histories of Dutch and German, which initially take us far away from Latin and the early Middle Ages.

3. THE HIGH GERMAN CONSONANT SHIFT

The so-called High German consonant shift (henceforth HGCS) is the signature sound change of German. It is also one of the most heavily commented sound changes in the history of linguistics. The HGCS is a sound change, or rather a complex of sound changes, the intensity of which increases the further south we move: Dutch and Flemish as well as the adjacent area of northern Germany stretching all the way to the linguistic boundary with Polish were hardly affected by the HGCS at all. This is the Dutch–Low German area, and the absence of the HGCS is one of the main reasons why traditionally a speaker of the Groningen dialect in the north of the Netherlands was able to converse effortlessly with a speaker of a dialect spoken east of Berlin. By contrast, the southernmost German dialects of Switzerland and of Austrian and Italian Tyrol have been affected by the HGCS to the full extent of its capabilities. In between the extremes is a wide band of dialects that were affected by the HGCS to varying degrees, with its intensity increasing from north to south. The modern German standard language is based on those intermediary dialects. It is seductive to compare this state of affairs to an earthquake that had its most devastating effects in its epicentre in the southernmost German dialects and gradually petered out the further north it travelled.

The sounds that are affected by the HGCS are the Proto-Germanic voiceless plosives $*p$, $*t$, $*k$. Usually, it is not only the sounds themselves but also the sounds that surround them in a word that determine whether and how sounds are affected by a sound change. So it is with the HGCS. In order to capture all relevant intricacies, the behaviour of **p*, **t*, and **k* in six different phonetic contexts needs to be studied:[6]

(1)	/#_	i.e. at the beginning of the word
(2)	/V_V	i.e. between vowels
(3)	/V_#	i.e. between a vowel and the end of the word
(4)	/VL_	i.e. after a vowel followed by a liquid (*r* or *l*)
(5)	/VN_	i.e. after a vowel followed by a nasal (*n* or *m*)
(6)	geminate	i.e. double **pp*, **tt*, **kk*

Example words illustrate the behaviour of **p*, **t*, and **k* in each of these six contexts in the various dialects. The first diagram represents the initial state, before the HGCS occurred. This is the stage that Dutch and German had reached by approximately AD 400.

	/#_	/V_V	/V_#	/VL_	/VN_	geminate
*t	**tehun*	**lātan*	**θat*	**bolt-*	**planta*	**katta*
	'ten'	'to let'	'that'	'bolt'	'plant'	'cat'
*p	**panna*	**kaupōn*	**ūp*	**helpan*	**damp*	**appl*
	'pan'	'to buy'	'up'	'to help'	'vapour'	'apple'
*k	**kald*	**makōn*	**ik*	**merkōn*	**drinkan*	**akkr*
	'cold'	'to make'	'I'	'to mark'	'to drink'	'crop field'

In those cases where the English translation preserves the same Old Germanic word, it can be observed that in English **t*, **p*, **k* are retained without change. The only exception is English *I*, which has lost its final **k* via a stage [tʃ] (Old English still has *ic* 'I'). The words **kaupōn*, **damp*, and **akkr* survive with a different meaning in English *cheap*, *damp*, and *acre*.

Dutch and Low German are like English in that they generally preserve **p*, **t*, **k* unaltered because they are not affected by the HGCS. The example words in the following diagram are the modern Dutch equivalents of the Germanic words in the previous diagram:

Proto-Germanic	/#_	/V_V	/V_#	/VL_	/VN_	geminate
*t	*tien*	*laten*	*dat*	*bout*	*plant*	*kat*
*p	*pan*	*kopen*	*op*	*helpen*	*damp*	*appel*
*k	*koud*	*maken*	*ik*	*merken*	*drinken*	*akker*

By contrast, a fully developed HGCS can be observed in the southernmost dialects of German: all instances of *p, *t, *k are affected, but the way in which they are affected depends on the phonetic context. Typical reflexes of the example words in those dialects are as follows (only the relevant sounds are adapted; other dialectal features characteristic of southernmost German, of which there are many, are ignored in order not to confuse the reader):[7]

Type I: full-flung shift

Proto-Germanic	/#_	/V_V	/V_#	/VL_	/VN_	geminate
*t	/ts/ehn	la/ss/en	da/s/	bol/ts/en	pflan/ts/e	ka/ts/e
*p	/pf/anne	kau/ff/en	au/f/	hel/f/en	dam/pf/	a/pf/el
*k	/kx/alt	ma/xx/en	i/x/	mer/(k)x/en	trin/kx/en	a/kx/er

Boldface indicates words affected by the HGCS, so we can see that all words were affected in type I dialects. The basic rules that underlie type I dialects are relatively simple:

Stage (a): the voiceless plosives *t, *p, *k first became voiceless affricates *ts, *pf, *kx in all contexts.

Stage (b): in some contexts, these affricates shift further towards the voiceless fricatives *s(s), *f(f), *x(x). The latter shift occurs without exception in the case of single *t, *p, *k after vowels (V) and erratically after liquids (L = r, l) and nasals (N = n, m).

There are modern dialects that underwent stage (a) but not stage (b) in the southernmost German-speaking part of Switzerland (Goblirsch 2005: 185) as well as much further north, at some localities in the Rhineland (Goblirsch 2005: 192–193). There is one medieval source that represents the same state of affairs, the so-called *Pariser Gespräche*. This is a German-French phrase book which may well contain a long-lost Old German dialect that was spoken somewhere in northern France (Gusmani 1996).

Moving north of the area where type I dialects occur, we enter a wide band consisting of most of southern Germany and the northern and eastern parts of Austria. The HGCS system that is attested here comes closest to the modern High German standard language. This is type II:

Type II: almost full-flung shift

Proto-Germanic	/#_	/V_V	/V_#	/VL_	/VN_	geminate
*t	/ts/ehn	la/ss/en	da/s/	bol/ts/en	pflan/ts/e	ka/ts/e
*p	/pf/anne	kau/ff/en	au/f/	hel/f~pf/en	dam/pf/	a/pf/el
*k	/kh/alt	ma/xx/en	i/x/	mer/x~k/en	trin/k/en	a/kk/er

Again, forms that show the HGCS are printed in boldface. The example *helpfen ~ helfen* represents the fact that after a liquid (*r, l*) the HGCS did not progress beyond stage (a) in some words and in some dialects of type II. The main difference between type I and type II, however, resides in the treatment of Proto-Germanic **k*: in type II dialects, there is no trace of the affricate stage (a), *kx*. After a vowel, we find the fricative stage (b) (*maxxen, ix*), while in other phonetic contexts there appears to have been no HGCS of **k* at all. Strikingly, the example *merken ~ merxen* seems to show a hesitation between a form with no HGCS at all (*merken*) and a form that has reached stage (b) (*merxen*), but the intermediate stage (a) form, **merkxen*, is absent. How can this complicated state of affairs be understood?

The simplest scenario that accounts for the difference between type I and type II dialects takes its cue from a difference in pronunciation between /x/ in type I and /x/ in type II. In type I, /x/ is generally articulated further back in the mouth, as a uvular [χ], and with intense friction, much like the Liverpool English fricative in [kχ]*old* 'cold', *loo*[(k)χ] 'look!' and the *ch* in Scots *loch*. In type II dialects, however, /x/ is pronounced more to the front, as a velar [x], with relatively less intense friction, much like in standard German ma[x]en 'make'. Bearing this in mind, let us propose a scenario according to which originally type II dialects behaved exactly like type I dialects and had a full-flung shift of **k* to **kx* (stage (a)) in all positions in the word:

(a) **kxalt*	**makxen*	**ikx*	**merkxen*	**trinkxen*	**akkxer*

Subsequently, **kx* became **x(x)* in the same positions it did in type I dialects:

(b) **kxalt*	**maxxen*	**ix(x)*	**merkxen ~ *merxen*	**trinkxen*	**akkxer*

Next comes a crucial development which interfered with the HGCS in type II dialects: since the friction of velar (rather than uvular) *x* was slight in these dialects, **kx* became aspirated **kh* (as in standard English [kh]*old* 'cold'): *h* is similar to *x* but has no friction.

(c) **khalt*	**maxxen*	**ix(x)*	**merkhen*	**trinkhen*	**akkher*

Finally, the aspiration in **kh* shared the general fate of its counterpart in **ph* and **th* in type II dialects as well as further north: it was preserved word-initially but lost in all other contexts.

(d) **khalt*	**maxxen*	**ix(x)*	**merken*	**trinken*	**akker*

The attractive feature of this scenario is its parsimony. Stages (a) and (b) are the two stages of the HGCS already required by type I dialects; (d) is a development that is required anyway to account for the loss of aspiration of all voiceless aspirated plosives in type II and more northern dialects. So the only real 'cost' of the explanation is stage (c), which, though new and typical of type II, ties in with the general phonetic properties of the sound *x* in type II dialects. In short, it seems that the HGCS in type II dialects behaves almost exactly as in type I dialects, the only difference being a peculiar treatment of the sound **x* in **kx*.

In central and eastern Germany, type II hits an area that corresponds roughly to the southern half of the former German Democratic Republic, where Slavic was prominent in the early medieval period and German can be considered a colonial language. Here, typical characteristics are the development of word-initial type II *pf-* to *f-* (*pfanne > fanne*) and the absence of shift in *pp* (*appel*, not *apfel*), which corresponds to type III, discussed below. North of this area lies the boundary with Low German, where the HGCS did not take place at all.

Things become significantly different as soon as we move from type II to the northwest, towards the medieval heartland of Franconian power. First of all, there is the area that roughly corresponds to present-day Hessen and Rhineland-Palatinate which includes the important medieval towns of Worms, Mainz, and Frankfurt. Geography is dominated by the Middle Rhine, the Nahe, and the lowermost Main. To linguists, the local dialects are known as Rhine Franconian. They show the following type of HGCS:

Type III: Rhine Franconian

Proto-Germanic	/#_	/V_V	/V_#	/VL_	/VN_	geminate
*t	/ts/ehn	la/ss/en	da/s/	bol/ts/en	pflan/ts/e	ka/ts/e
*p	/ph/anne	kau/ff/en	au/f/	hel/f~pf/en	dam/p~pf/	a/pp/el
*k	/kh/alt	ma/xx/en	i/x/	mer/k/en	trin/k/en	a/kk/er

It is useful to discuss this type in conjunction with its northern neighbours, types IV and V. Leaving Rhine Franconian and moving towards the northwest, we enter an area in which the HGCS reaches its greatest complexity. This is the so-called Rhenish Fan (German: *Rheinischer Fächer*), a triangle that encloses the Rhine between Düsseldorf and Koblenz as well as its western and eastern tributaries, the Lahn, Moselle, Ahr, Sieg, and Erft. It encompasses the central western part of Germany, the southeast of the Netherlands, eastern Belgium, Luxembourg, and French Lorraine (Lothringen) along the Moselle. Because of its importance to an understanding of the origins and causes of the HGCS, the Rhenish Fan merits close scrutiny. Despite its relatively small size, the area is split up into many dialects. This fragmentation has been favoured by the natural landscape: the many rivers attracted habitation and functioned as axes of contact, while the hilly ranges of the Taunus, Hunsrück, Eiffel, Westerwald, and Schiefergebirge, which separated the river valleys, were traditionally rural and sparsely populated and formed barriers to exchange, as is evident from the fact that they serve as dialect boundaries. The towns of Trier and Cologne have been dominant centres since the Roman period.

The southernmost zone of the Rhenish Fan is called Moselle Franconian, with its ancient urban centre of Trier. It has the following variant of the HGCS:

Type IV: Moselle Franconian

Proto-Germanic	/#_	/V_V	/V_#	/VL_	/VN_	geminate
*t	/ts/ehn	la/ss/en	da/t/	bol/ts/en	plan/ts/e	ka/ts/e
*p	/ph/anne	kau/ff/en	u/f/ ~ o/p/	hel/f/en	dam/p/	a/pp/el
*k	/kh/alt	ma/xx/en	i/x/	mer/k/en	trin/k/en	a/kk/er

North of Moselle Franconian is the Ripuarian (or Ribuarian) zone, whose urban centre is Cologne. This has a very similar version of the HGCS:

Type V: Ripuarian

Proto-Germanic	/#_	/V_V	/V_#	/VL_	/VN_	geminate
*t	/ts/ehn	la/ss/en	da/t/	bol/ts/en	plan/ts/e	ka/ts/e
*p	/p/anne	kau/ff/en	o/p/	hel/p/en	dam/p/	a/pp/el
*k	/k/alt	ma/xx/en	i/x/	mer/k/en	drin/k/en	a/kk/er

Types III, IV, and V share a complex form of the HGCS. Its characteristics are as follows:

- Proto-Germanic *t is affected in all positions of the word, except word-finally. The most important examples of that exception are *dat* 'that', *et* 'it', *dit* 'this', *allet* 'everything', *wat* 'what', and *bit* 'until, to', all of which have shifted word-final -s in type I and II dialects.[8] Rhine Franconian (type III) nowadays has -s in these forms, but medieval sources suggest that -t was originally common here (Schützeichel 1956).
- Proto-Germanic *p is universally affected only between vowels. After liquids (*r*, *l*), modern dialects show that type III and type IV have shifted *p, while type V has not (the line separating them is the so-called *dorf/dorp* isogloss, referring to the pronunciation of the model word for 'village', which corresponds to the English place name elements *thorp* and *throp*). In the medieval period, however, the line separating

shift in the south from non-shift in the north lay much further to the south and included at least part of type III dialects (Schützeichel 1956). There is only one word that gives information about the fate of originally word-final *p, and that is Proto-Germanic *ūp 'up, on'. The line that separates unshifted northern *up, op* from shifted southern *uf, auf* nowadays cuts across zone IV, but in this case, too, there is medieval evidence to suggest that the boundary between the two originally lay further south (Schützeichel 1956: 116ff., 1960: 113–114).

- Proto-Germanic *k is affected by the HGCS if it stood between vowels or at the (medieval) end of the word. In all other positions, *k remains unaffected. Medieval sources confirm the antiquity of this situation.

Unshifted word-initial *p- and *k- are aspirated (i.e. pronounced as *ph-, kh-*) in types III and IV, which agrees with type II. They are unaspirated in type V, which agrees with northern dialects and with Dutch. In this sense, as in many others, the dialects of the Rhenish Fan are intermediate between High German in the south and Low German and Dutch in the north.

What is striking about the HGCS in types III (in the medieval period), IV, and V is something that does not follow at all from the intermediate nature of these dialects: the asymmetry of the behaviour of *t, *p, and *k:

- *t is affected in all positions within the word except word-finally.
- *p is affected only between vowels; medieval evidence shows that the shift after liquids and at the end of the word in types III and IV is a secondary development which moved in from type II dialects because type II dialects determined the shape of the high-status standard language.
- *k is affected between vowels (like *t and *p) as well as word-finally (unlike *t and *p)

In order not to lose track of what is essential amidst the confusing richness of the data, the following diagram summarizes the state of the HGCS in zones III–V as it can be reconstructed for the medieval period. This type will be called Rhineland Franconian:

Type III–V in the medieval period: Rhineland Franconian

Proto-Germanic	/#_	/V_V	/V_#	/VL_	/VN_	geminate
*t	/ts/ehn	la/ss/en	da/t/	bol/ts/en	plan/ts/e	ka/ts/e
*p	/p(h)/anne	kau/ff/en	o/p/	hel/p/en	dam/p/	a/pp/el
*k	/k(h)/alt	ma/xx/en	i/x/	mer/k/en	drin/k/en	a/kk/er

Before we can attempt an explanation for the asymmetry with which the HGCS operated in Rhineland Franconian, two other types remain to be discussed.

Type VI is exemplified by the famous dialect of Wermelskirchen (Hasenclever 1905), which has attracted much attention in recent years.[9] Wermelskirchen lies just north of the northernmost boundary of the area in which the HGCS operated, the so-called Benrather Line. Yet Wermelskirchen does undergo a very special brand of the HGCS: it limits the operation of the shift to the position between vowels, and that only if the first vowel was short during the early medieval period and not *a. Accordingly, examples of shift are ɛsən 'eat' < *etan; ɔfən 'open' < *opan; kɔxən 'cook' < *kokan, a loanword from Latin *coquere*. The shift is absent after long vowels in e.g. lɔtən 'let' < *lātan; rīpən 'ripen' < *rīp-; brūkən 'need' < *brūkan. It is also absent after old short *a, as in mākən 'make' < *mak-. The Wermelskirchen dialect agrees with the more southern Rhenish Fan dialects by preserving word-final *t and *p and shifting *k, as in iç /ix/ 'I' < *ik.

Type VI: Wermelskirchen

Proto-Germanic	/#_	/*V_V	/*V:_V /*a_V	/V_#	/VL_	/VN_	geminate
*t	/t/ehn	e/ss/en	la/t/en	da/t/	bol/t/en	plan/t/e	ka/tt/e
*p	/p/anne	o/ff/en	kau/p/en	o/p/	hel/p/en	dam/p/	a/pp/el
*k	/k/alt	ko/xx/en	ma/k/en	i/x/	mer/k/en	drin/k/en	a/kk/er

Finally, the northernmost portion of the Rhenish Fan, which stretches into the southeastern part of the Netherlands and into northeastern Belgium, has a system in which the HGCS is limited to *k in word-final position:

Type VII: northenmost Rhenish Fan

Proto-Germanic	/#_	/V_V	/V_#	/VL_	/VN_	geminate
*t	/t/ehn	la/t/en	da/t/	bol/t/en	plan/t/e	ka/t/e
*p	/p/anne	kau/p/en	o/p/	hel/p/en	dam/p/	a/pp/el
*k	/k/alt	ma/k/en	i/x/	mer/k/en	drin/k/en	a/kk/er

Examples of the shift of word-final *k are *ich* 'I' < *ik; *mich* 'me' < *mik; *sich* '(one)self' < *sik; *och* 'also' < *auk; adjectives and adverbs ending in -*lich* '-ly' < *-līk.

4. MAKING SENSE OF THE HGCS

Amongst the features that characterize the HGCS, the one that cries out most for an explanation is the asymmetrical treatment of *p, *t, and *k in the dialects of the Rhenish Fan. On the theory that the HGCS started out as a type I dialect, showing full-flung shift that affected **p*, **t*, and **k* in all relevant positions in the word, the Rhenish Fan is a product of petering out: at the limits of the area affected by the HGCS, its effects gradually become less and less, like the sun's radiation towards the outer reaches of the solar system, until they die down completely beyond the icy Plutonian realms, where Dutch and Low German are spoken. The imagery is misleading in so far as there is nothing wave-like about the HGCS, however. It is not the case that as we move from south to north in the German-speaking area, shifted /ts/ gradually becomes more and more like unshifted /t/ across a continuum. The HGCS rather behaves in a particle-like, binary fashion: given a number of phonetic positions in the word, in each position old **t* either becomes /ts/ or remains /t/. And if it becomes /ts/, it either moves on to /ss/ or remains /ts/. There are no intermediaries. Given this modification, the idea that the HGCS gradually peters out means that it affects fewer and fewer positions in the word as we move north. The implication of the petering-out scenario is that the way in which the HGCS peters out is essentially arbitrary, as long as the number of affected contexts decreases the further north we move. In other words, the fact that in type VII dialects only word-final **-k* is affected (and not, say, word-final **-p* or **-t-* between vowels) should be due to chance. That turns out not to be the case, however, which is where the problems for the petering-out theory begin.

4.1. The Uerdingen Line

As we have seen earlier, the northernmost portion of the Rhenish Fan limits the operation of the HGCS to word-final **-k*, which turns into *-x*. This is type VII. To the north and west of type VII, there is no HGCS at all. The line that separates type VII dialects (*ich* 'I') from dialects that lack the HGCS altogether (*ik* 'I') is known to dialectologists as the Uerdingen Line. On its westward stretch, this line cuts across Dutch northern Limburg before curving down through Belgian Limburg until it hits the linguistic boundary with French between Tienen and Leuven.

What is striking about the Uerdingen Line is that at the approximate point on the map where it stops at the linguistic boundary with French, an important dialectal boundary within French takes over, viz. the so-called *bec/bètch* line. This separates Walloon and Lorraine French in the east from Picardian French in the west. It is as if the Uerdingen Line does not bother about the language boundary and runs on deeply into French-speaking territory. As the Uerdingen Line deals with the treatment of word-final **k* in Germanic, so the *bec/bètch* line concerns the treatment of Old French word-final **k*: while western French dialects retain this, eastern dialects such as Walloon turn it into the affricate [tʃ], spelled <tch> (as in English *catch*). Examples beside the model word, Late Latin **bekku* 'beak, mouth', which becomes Picardian *bec* and Walloon *bètch*, are Late Latin **sakku* 'bag', which becomes *sac*, *satch/sètch*, and Late Latin **sikku* 'dry' (masculine), which yields *sec, sètch*.[10]

It is hard to believe that the Germanic and French lines are holding hands purely by accident. This impression is strengthened by the fact that in both languages the development of $*k$ (to x in Germanic and $tʃ$ in French) is linked to palatalization: in southeastern Dutch and eastern Flemish dialects that preserve word-final $-k$, it is usually pronounced as [kʲ]. That is a noticeable feature of many French dialects that preserve word-final $-k$, too, in words such as *sac*, *banque*, and *cinq*, which have word-final [kʲ]. It is true that Dutch and German x, a (palato-)velar fricative, is phonetically not identical to French $tʃ$, but that difference may easily be the result of later developments. Some varieties of Limburg Dutch and many varieties of Rhineland German have turned palatovelar x into $ʃ$, using *iʃ* instead of *ix* for the pronoun 'I'. As a result, they are therefore phonetically very close to Walloon. Step by step, the development probably went as follows:

[-k	>	-$kʲ$	>	-$kᶜ$	>	(German and Dutch) -$xʲ$ (> x, $ʃ$)]
					>	(Walloon) -$tʃ$]

As there can be little doubt that the French and the Dutch and German developments are ultimately one and the same, language contact must have played a role. This idea is reinforced by the non-trivial nature of the change: there is no intrinsic phonetic reason why word-final $-k$ should undergo palatalization. It is not clear, however, which process lies at the bottom of this uniformity. Roughly, six possible interpretations might be entertained:

- It is possible that Dutch and German started the development and influenced the neighbouring French dialects. That implies a degree of bilingualism, which is quite plausible in this linguistic border region, and an incentive for speakers of Walloon to 'speak like a German', which would arise if speakers of German had relatively high social, political, or economic prestige.
- Alternatively, the process started in Romance (French), and speakers of neighbouring Germanic dialects took it over. In that case, speakers of Dutch and German must have felt pressure to 'speak like a Roman (Frenchman)'.
- A third possibility is that the Walloon area shifted from Germanic to French and retained the peculiar pronunciation of word-final $-k$ as a Germanic accent; this again implies social pressure in favour of the speakers of French.
- Conversely, the population of the Rhenish Fan shifted from Romance (of the Old French type) to Germanic and retained the peculiar pronunciation of word-final $-k$ as a Romance accent; this would imply social pressure in favour of the speakers of Germanic.
- The population of an unknown language, which had a particularly palatalized pronunciation of word-final $-k$, shifted towards French

(Walloon) in the west and towards Dutch and German in the east and north but retained their pronunciation of -*k*, thus introducing it into French, Dutch, and German. Given its geographical position, one might consider a variety of Celtic a likely candidate.

- Given enough time for the social prestige of French, Dutch, and German to change, a combination of two or more of these scenarios may have occurred in sequence.

In order to narrow things down, it is useful to consider the date of the developments and their geographical extension.

The earliest instance of *-*k* > -*x* in type VII dialects appears to date from the 1400s.[11] As to French, there is no evidence for -*k* > -*tʃ* in Old French texts from the Walloon area. That does not mean, however, that the developments must have occurred as late as the late medieval or early modern period. The first attestation of a development in written sources only indicates a *terminus ante quem*: the development must have occurred earlier than the date of the first written attestation, but unless other arguments intervene it is impossible to say how much earlier it had arisen in the spoken language. Written language usually adapts itself to supra-regional norms, which tend to exclude regionalisms like the ones we are discussing. Moreover, as long as the development had not reached beyond the stage [kᶜ], it is unlikely that a scribe would have felt the urge to spell this in any other way than with traditional <c> or <k>, and even if he had, there was no unambiguous symbol available in the alphabet to spell [kᶜ] differently than non-palatalized [k]. So the chronological data are of little avail.

Geographical extension is somewhat more helpful. The development of -*k* to -*tʃ* in French is not just limited to Walloon but also occurs in Lorraine and Burgundian French, in other words, stretches down south in a broad band into eastern central France.

The extension of -*k* to -*x* in Dutch and German at first sight appears to encompass an even vaster area because it occurs in all dialects that are affected by the HGCS, whether it be those of the Rhenish Fan or those of northern Italy. But that probably is a misinterpretation. For we have now established that two different sound changes are involved: one is the palatalization of word-final -*k*, which leads to -*x*, and the other is the HGCS. The fact that both have the effect of turning *k into *x* should not lead us to conflate the rules that are responsible for the effect (if it helps: one can get sick as a result of a stomach infection or because of consuming too much alcohol, but that does not mean that catching a bug is the same as a night of heavy boozing).

There is another good reason for excluding the palatalization of final -*k* from the HGCS: it eliminates half of the disturbing asymmetry that characterizes the HGCS in the Rhenish Fan and in the type III dialect to the south of it. What we found earlier is that in those dialects -*p* and -*t* were not affected by the HGCS in word-final position while -*k* was. Or, to put it more exactly: word-final position *disfavoured* the operation of the HGCS on *t* and *p*, whereas it *favoured* its operation on *k*. The puzzle is solved if we ascribe the development of -*k* into -*x* to a palatalization rule rather than the operation of the HGCS. Symmetry is restored: word-final plosives are not affected by the HGCS in the Rhenish Fan and type III dialects, and there are no exceptions.

The consequence of all this is that we can be relatively sure that the palatalization rule applying to word-final -*k* affected the entire Rhenish Fan and its southern type III neighbour (because in this area the HGCS did not affect word-final consonants, yet -*k* became -*x*). Outside of that small area, in the vast terrain covered by type I and II dialects, word-final -*t* and -*p* were affected by the HGCS, so it seems probable that -*k* was, too. In other words, in type I and II dialects the development of word-final -*k* to -*x* is more plausibly ascribed to the HGCS than to the palatalization rule.

How is this helpful in weighing the probability of each of the six contact scenarios that were suggested earlier? Well, it is surely important to establish that on the Germanic side the palatalization rule -*k* > -*x* is characteristic only of the type III–VII dialects along the Middle Rhine, Moselle, and Meuse. In the late Roman period, this was a densely populated area with important towns along major traffic axes, where Latin must have been strongly represented: after 275 Trier became the imperial residence, which it remained until around 400, and it is known that Latin survived along the Moselle well into the medieval period. The Germanic-speaking population of the area may well have adopted palatalization of final -*k* from those high-prestige Romans (scenario 2). Later on, when power devolved to Germanic speakers, the Late Latin-speaking population would have been encouraged to speak Germanic, and palatalized final -*k* survived as a Latin accent in their form of Germanic (scenario 4). Both scenarios may have occurred in sequence (scenario 6). What they have in common is that they presuppose a degree of population continuity between late Antiquity and the present day along the Middle Rhine, Moselle, and Meuse, because only in this way can we explain how a linguistic feature that arose among the Latin-speaking population of late Antique or early medieval times survived the shift to the German and Dutch dialects of today.

By contrast, scenarios (1) and (3) are a lot less likely to be on the mark. It is difficult to see why the vast French-speaking area between Liège and Dijon would feel inclined to want to 'speak like a German', and specifically using the German from the small Rhenish Fan area (scenario 1). Scenario (3) fares little better: although in late Antiquity and the early medieval period the Walloon area, Lorraine, and Burgundy must have harboured a percentage of Germanic speakers, who subsequently shifted to speaking Latin (which became French), those Germanic speakers are unlikely to have all come from the Rhenish Fan (Burgundy, for instance, took its name from the Burgundians, who presumably came from what is now eastern Germany or Poland and spoke an East Germanic dialect).

The conclusion is that palatalization of word-final -*k* is more likely to be a Latin (French) feature in Dutch and German than a Germanic feature in French. The conclusion that the development of word-final -*k* to -*x* in type III–VII dialects is the result of language contact with Latin (French) and has nothing to do with the HGCS brings us halfway to finding an explanation of the curiously asymmetrical impact of the HGCS in the Rhenish Fan. Type VII dialects now turn out not to have been affected by the HGCS at all. We will leave type VI, the Wermelskirchen type, aside for a moment and return to types V, IV, and III. The HGCS system in those dialects was reconstructed as follows:

Type III–V in the medieval period: Rhineland Franconian

Proto-Germanic	/#_	/V_V	/V_#	/VL_	/VN_	geminate
*t	/ts/ehn	la/ss/en	da/t/	bol/ts/en	plan/ts/e	ka/ts/e
*p	/p(h)/anne	kau/ff/en	o/p/	hel/p/en	dam/p/	a/pp/el
*k	/k(h)/alt	ma/xx/en	i/x/	mer/k/en	drin/k/en	a/kk/er

If we adapt the diagram to the conclusions of the present section by subtracting the development of word-final -*k* to -*x*, it comes out as follows:

Type III–IV in the medieval period without -k > -x: Rhineland Franconian

Proto-Germanic	/#_	/V_V	/V_#	/VL_	/VN_	geminate
*t	/ts/ehn	la/ss/en	da/t/	bol/ts/en	plan/ts/e	ka/ts/e
*p	/p(h)/anne	kau/ff/en	o/p/	hel/p/en	dam/p/	a/pp/el
*k	/k(h)/alt	ma/xx/en	i/k/	mer/k/en	drin/k/en	a/kk/er

It can be observed that the asymmetry is now limited to the different treatment of *t* on the one hand and *p* and *k* on the other: while *t* is affected in all phonetic contexts, *p* and *k* are affected only in the position between vowels. It is to this asymmetry that we can turn next.

4.2. The HGCS, Aspiration, and Late Latin Affricates

The sounds on which the HGCS operated were the Proto-Germanic voiceless plosives *p*, *t*, and *k*. In modern Germanic languages, such as most varieties of English, northern German, Scandinavian, and northeastern Dutch, these are aspirated; i.e. they are pronounced as [pʰ, tʰ, kʰ]. We have already seen that most German dialects have aspirated pronunciations in contexts where these sounds were not affected by the HGCS. In general, aspiration is most noticeable and best preserved in Germanic languages in word-initial position. In word-internal or word-final position, aspiration was only rarely preserved. Western Moselle German dialects (type IV) preserve aspiration in almost all positions within the word, except perhaps word-finally and following *s* and *x*; they share this property with the archaic Norse dialects of northern and eastern Iceland (Goblirsch 2005: 127, 190). By contrast, Germanic dialects that lack aspiration are bound to have lost it: in the case of Finland Swedish, this loss was caused by contact with Finnish. In most varieties of Dutch, loss of aspiration may be attributed to contact with Romance, as we shall see in chapter IV. In English, word-initial *p*, *t*, *k* show aspiration, but where they stand after a vowel (as in *water*, *cat*), aspiration *after p, t, k* is replaced by glottal constriction *before* them (at least in many English dialects in England; the effect is that of combining a glottal stop, as in Cockney [wɑʔɐ] 'water', with the *p*, *t*, or *k*; these are preglottalized plosives). That feature is also famously characteristic of the West Jutish dialects of Danish. In Icelandic and Faeroese, aspiration *precedes p, t, k*, as in *bak* 'back' [b̥ɑʰk], whence the term *pre-aspiration*. All these special features could be regarded as different outcomes of the retraction of post-aspiration: [pʰ, tʰ, kʰ] > [ʰp, ʰt, ʰk] (pre-aspiration) or [ʔp, ʔt, ʔk] (pre-glottalization).

While Germanic voiceless plosives were originally probably aspirated, Latin and Romance voiceless plosives were, and still are, unaspirated. This difference potentially caused problems of perception when Germanic and Romance came into contact. There is a body of early medieval names that suggests that Romance speakers in France did not identify the Germanic aspirated [tʰ] with Latin unaspirated [t] but rather with the Late Latin affricate [tsʲ]. The common Germanic personal name element **Gauta-* appears in early medieval Latin sources with spellings that suggest a pronunciation **Gautsʲ-*: examples comprise *Gaucio-bertus*, *Gautio-bertus*, *Gauts-uini*, *Gauts-elinus*, *Gauts-elmus*, *Gauts-aldus*, and *Gauts-inius*. Similarly, the Germanic name **Buttō* underlies spellings such as *Bucc-elenus*, *Buccio-valdus*, and *Butio-valdus*.[12] The interpretation of these names is ambiguous, however. The orthography may be an attempt to capture the aspiration of the Germanic voiceless plosive [tʰ], which was foreign to Romance, by a native Romance sound that came closest, viz. the affricate [tsʲ], spelled <c, cc, ti, ci, cti>. Or it may be an attempt to render a Germanic **t* that had already become **ts* by the HGCS by means of its closest counterpart in Romance.

The association of aspiration with affrication may seem surprising, but it popped up time and again even within Germanic itself. Danish and northeastern dialects of Dutch show aspiration of word-initial *p-* and *k-* but affrication of *t-* to *ts-* (which is not recognized in standard orthography). In northeastern Dutch, *ts* instead of *t* occurs in other contexts, too, such as between vowels; after *n*, *r*, *l*; and at the end of the word (as in *taart* [tsɑrts] 'cake, tart'). The Bavarian salutation *pfiat* 'bye bye' contains the labial affricate [pf]. It goes back to an earlier aspirated *phiat* and ultimately to the formula (*Gott*) *behüte* (*dich*) 'may God protect you'. Given this close relationship between aspirated plosive and affricate, it would not be surprising if speakers of early Romance did indeed perceive their native affricates as the closest possible counterparts to the Germanic aspirated plosives which they heard all around them.

It is this possibility that will be pursued further in the form of an experiment. Let us suppose that the form of Germanic with which Late Latin speakers in Gaul and along the Rhine came into contact indeed had aspirated [p^h, t^h, k^h]. Late Latin lacked voiceless aspirated plosives of this kind. Hence speakers of Late Latin who wanted or needed to learn Germanic would be confronted with the well-defined problem of how to render them. Let us suppose that they substituted them with Late Latin voiceless affricates because within the Late Latin sound system the affricates approximated the Germanic aspirated plosives most closely.

In order to assess the effects of this substitution, we need to determine first of all which voiceless affricates existed in Late Latin between approximately 400 and 700. This is the period in which Latin was gradually breaking up into the various Romance languages, all of which developed slightly different sets of affricates. For present purposes developments in German's closest Romance neighbour, northern Gallo-Romance (i.e. the earliest stages of French), are most relevant. During the period in question, Gallo-Romance started with three and ended with two voiceless affricates. Those affricates have the following Classical Latin sources:[13]

- Classical Latin *c* = /k/ > */ts^j/ before the vowels *e* and *i*, as in *centum* '100' > */ts^{j}entu/; this */ts^j/ occurred only word-initially and word-internally after a consonant; after a vowel a voiced affricate resulted; in ninth-century Old French, the affricate had become /ts/, spelled <c>: *cent*
- Classical Latin *t* + *i* or *e* + vowel > */tj/ + vowel; here */tj/ became /ts^j/, as in *spatium* 'space' > */espats^{j}u/; in ninth-century Old French, the affricate had become /ts/, spelled <c>: *espace*
- Classical Latin *c* = /k/ + *i* or *e* + vowel > */kj/ + vowel; this developed into two different affricates, depending on its position in the word:
  - after consonant, */kj/ > */ts^j/, as in *lancea* 'lance' > */lants^{j}a/; in ninth-century Old French, the affricate had become /ts/, spelled <c>: *lance*
  - after vowel, */kj/ > */kx^j/, as in *faciem* 'face' > */fakx^{j}e/; at some point in time between the fifth and ninth century, this had merged with /ts^j/: Old French *face*
- Classical Latin *p* + *i* or *e* + vowel > */pj/ + vowel; this developed into */pf^j/ > */pʃ/, as in *sapiat* 'may taste, know' > */sapf^{j}at/; by the ninth century, it had become Old French /tʃ/, spelled <ch>, as in *sache* 'may know'[14]

Those are the sources from which early Gallo-Romance had acquired three different voiceless affricates: */ts^j/, */kx^j/, */pf^j/. It so happened that these affricates had significantly different distributional patterns. While /ts^j/ could appear in all positions in the word except at the end, /kxʲ/ and /pfʲ/ occurred only between vowels:

Gallo-Romance	/#_	/V_V	/V_#	/VL_	/VN_	geminate
*tsʲ	yes	yes	no	yes	yes	yes
*pfʲ	no	yes	no	no	no	no
*kxʲ	no	yes	no	no	no	no

The striking fact is that if we compare the positional constraints on the occurrence of affricates in Gallo-Romance with the constraints on the occurrence of the HGCS in type III–V dialects of German, called Rhineland Franconian, we observe a perfect match:

Proto-Germanic	/#_	/V_V	/V_#	/VL_	/VN_	geminate
*t	/ts/ehn	la/ss/en	da/t/	bol/ts/en	plan/ts/e	ka/ts/e
*p	/p(h)/anne	kau/ff/en	o/p/	hel/p/en	dam/p/	a/pp/el
*k	/k(h)/alt	ma/xx/en	i/k/	mer/k/en	drin/k/en	a/kk/er

Rhineland Franconian applies the HGCS only in those positions in the word in which voiceless affricates occurred in Gallo-Romance. In view of its precision and non-trivial nature, the match can hardly be accidental.

We started this section with an experiment: suppose speakers of Gallo-Romance substituted Germanic /pʰ, tʰ, kʰ/ by Gallo-Romance affricates, and study the effect that would have on how they spoke Germanic. The perfect match between the positions where Gallo-Romance affricates occurred and those in which the Rhenish Fan applied the HGCS legitimizes the experiment, which can now be translated into a probable scenario: the HGCS in Rhineland Franconian is the result of speakers of Gallo-Romance learning Germanic and replacing Germanic aspirated voiceless plosives with voiceless affricates but only in the phonetic positions in which these affricates occurred in Gallo-Romance.

This scenario has the great virtue that it not only describes but also explains the Rhineland system of the HGCS. It also explains why Germanic *single* /pʰ, tʰ, kʰ/ between vowels became *double* /ff, ss, xx/: the Gallo-Romance affricates after vowels were long because they developed from groups of consonants (*pj, *tj, *kj).

It also explains the most striking feature of the Wermelskirchen variety of the HGCS (type VI), which, the reader may recall, limited the operation of the shift to single /pʰ, tʰ, kʰ/ but only if they stood after an originally short vowel:

Proto-Germanic	/#_	/*V_V	/*V:_V /*a_V	/V_#	/VL_	/VN_	geminate
*t	/t/ehn	e/ss/en	la/t/en	da/t/	bol/t/en	plan/t/e	ka/tt/e
*p	/p/anne	o/ff/en	kau/p/en	o/p/	hel/p/en	dam/p/	a/pp/el
*k	/k/alt	ko/xx/en	ma/k/en	i/x/	mer/k/en	drin/k/en	a/kk/er

According to specifically Gallo-Romance rules, the affricates were long consonants, and as a consequence the preceding vowels were automatically short. By this token, the Wermelskirchen variety goes back to a system in which Gallo-Romance rules of pronunciation were assiduously applied to Germanic. There is therefore every reason to agree with authors who have claimed that Wermelskirchen represents the fossilized first stage of the application of the HGCS.[15] An aspect that still requires an explanation is why the Wermelskirchen dialect replaced the expected *ts* with *t* in word-initial position, after liquids, after nasals, and in geminates. It is probably relevant to know that Wermelskirchen lies just outside the area in which the HGCS took hold and that it is surrounded by dialects that were unaffected by it. Those dialects lacked the affricate /ts/, but they did have /ss, ff, xx/, evidently from other sources than the HGCS. It stands to reason that Wermelskirchen adapted its sound system to those neighbouring dialects by replacing its 'foreign' /ts/ with 'native' /t/.

That it should be the Rhineland, or more precisely the strip of land between the Rhine and the Meuse, which saw speakers of Romance not only shift to Germanic but also ultimately cause their particular variety of Germanic to prevail over that of the Germanic immigrants is not unexpected: the area was a densely settled administrative and military centre in the later Roman period.

5. SOCIOLINGUISTICS IN THE RHINELAND, AND LANGOBARDIAN AND ROMANCE IN NORTHERN ITALY

The way in which the HGCS conducted itself in the Rhineland is the result of intensive contact between Latin and Germanic, more specifically of bilingualism and of Late Latin speakers' ultimate shift to Germanic. In general, the effects of language contact on language change are determined by specific social circumstances at a particular time and a particular place. In the case of the Rhineland, several ingredients come together to mix the cocktail that resulted in Rhineland Franconian (types III–V): it is located at the ancient frontier of the Roman Empire and harboured a dense Latin-speaking population; it was an important power centre of the Western Roman Empire; speakers of Germanic moved in and took over permanent control; they were sufficiently tolerant of the way in which former Latin speakers pronounced

Germanic with a Latin accent for that variety to not only survive but also spread at the expense of their own variety; and, finally, the Rhineland became an early medieval powerhouse of strong Franconian dynasties, who expanded their power well beyond its boundaries. If any of those ingredients had been different, Rhineland Franconian might never have arisen. If, for instance, the area between the Rhine and the Meuse had been largely depopulated in late Antiquity as a result of frequent military activities, there would not have been a Latin-speaking population to be exposed to Germanic. If the Germanic speakers had not been tolerant of Germanic with a strong Latin accent, which enabled the local Roman population to rise socially in spite of their 'funny accent', the Rhenish Fan type of HGCS would have been nipped in the bud. And if this Latinate form of Germanic had not been propelled by the powerful Franks but had remained a marginal dialect of German, it is questionable whether it would have survived to the present day.

It would be interesting to know whether what happened to Germanic in the Rhineland was so tied up with specific socio-political events in the Rhineland that it could not have occurred elsewhere. This brings us to the Langobardians and the fate of their variety of Germanic in northern Italy.

The Langobardians enter the full light of history around AD 500.[16] They lived in Bohemia, in the present-day Czech Republic, as well as in adjacent areas of Lower Austria and western Hungary, where they had occupied an area previously abandoned by the Rugii. Under the long and prosperous reign of king Wacho, they consolidated their power by forging alliances with neighbouring polities and by crafty diplomatic arrangements with the great adversaries of the time, the Ostrogoths and the East Romans of Byzantium. Wacho's successor Audoin pursued a more expansionistic policy, which brought him into frequent, though ultimately restrained, conflict with his eastern neighbours, the Gepids. Audoin's son Alboin succeeded his father in 560. He set out to destroy the Gepid ruling dynasty, presumably in order to gain control of the powerful Gepid warrior aristocracy. The final act of this episode was played out in a battle of 567, in which the Gepids suffered a devastating defeat. Alboin is reputed to have slain the Gepid king himself.

These developments should be seen in the light of greater changes in the region. Byzantium had hitherto pursued a policy of containment and peaceful diplomatic relations with its barbarian neighbours along the Danube. After the death of the Emperor Justinian in 565, tactics became based on military strength rather than diplomacy. At about the same time, the formidable Avar people from Central Asia had arrived on the steppes near the Black Sea and started expanding their power towards the west, having an eye on the territory of the Gepids, which was handed to them in 567 in consequence of a treaty between the Avars and the Langobardians. Although the Langobardians had emerged from the battle of 567 as victors and although their relations with the Avars seem to have been friendly, they gave up their territory in what was the last of the Great Migrations: in 568, Alboin collected a vast army consisting of a confederation of Langobardians, Gepids,

Suebi, Bulgars, Sarmatians, Saxons, and Roman provincials from the provinces of Pannonia and Noricum and set off to Italy. Why he did so has been a mystery for a long time. Walter Pohl explains the migration as an entirely voluntary and well-planned act, which Alboin and his followers undertook in order to come into the prize possession of the heartland of the old Roman Empire. Alboin thereby stepped into the shoes of many barbarian leaders before him, of the Ostrogoths, Visigoths, Burgundians, Suebi, Alans, and Vandals, who all sought to live in the Empire and exploit its resources.[17]

Weakened by a century of war and pestilence, most Italian towns opened their gates to the immigrants, and resistance was in general weak to non-existent. The area that came under Langobardian rule comprised northern Italy, Tuscany, and the southern Italian regions around Spoleto and Benevento. Over the next centuries, the immigrants gradually merged with the local population.

Linguistically, the Langobardian forces comprised many speakers of Germanic. The name means 'Men of Long Beards' in Germanic (although ironically the Langobardian origin myth connected that feature to women who tied their long hair around their faces in such a way that it seemed they were wearing beards). In 643, the Italian Langobardians produced a law code in Latin which contains a wealth of Germanic words. This is the so-called *Edictum Rothari* (Edict of Rotharius), which was promulgated by the Langobardian king Rotharius. Among the immigrants there must have been speakers of other languages as well, as the indications about Sarmatians, Bulgars, and Roman provincials would seem to show. Their languages are lost to us.

The Langobardian migration is one of the few migrations that are completely borne out by the archaeological record: Langobardian graves almost disappear in their northern homeland and suddenly start appearing all over Italy in the second half of the sixth century. The epicentre of Langobardian grave finds is Italy north of the Po. That is where we may presume Langobardian settlement was densest.

It so happens that the Germanic words in the Edict of Rotharius have undergone a form of the HGCS. In as far as can be made out from the spelling of those words, the pattern of distribution of the HGCS in Langobardian is strongly reminiscent of the HGCS in the Rhenish Fan:[18]

The Langobardian HGCS

Proto-Germanic	/#_	/V_(V)	/VL_ /VN_	geminate
*t	/ts/	/ss/	/ts/	/(t)ts/
*þ	/p/	/ff/	/p(f)/?	/pp/
*k	/k/ or /(k)x/	/x/?	/k/ or /(k)x/	/kk/ or /(k)x/

The status of the shift of *k is unknown for orthographical reasons: in words such as *march* 'frontier area' and *champhio* 'champion', written <ch>

may represent an affricate *kx*, a fricative *x*, or simply an aspirated k^h. A similar problem affects the interpretation of written <ph> in *champhio*: this may have been *f*, *pf*, or plain aspirated p^h. The unambiguous shift of *k* after a vowel is found only in relatively late attestations, the oldest of which is the personal name *Herih* in a cartulary of 845 (this contains -*rih* from earlier -*rīk* 'king').

Since the asymmetry of the HGCS system in Langobardian strongly resembles that of the Rhenish Fan, it invites the same type of explanation of its origin. Since the Edict of Rotharius dates from 643 and its earliest preserved manuscript, the *Codex Sangallensis*, from approximately 675, the language represented in it reflects a form of Germanic spoken in northern Italy at least four to five generations after the migration. So it is quite possible that the Germanic of the Edict of Rotharius had been influenced by the Latin of northern Italy. If this influence expressed itself in the same way as in the Rhineland, Latin speakers would have replaced Germanic aspirated p^h, t^h, k^h, which to them would have been foreign sounds, with Late Latin affricates. In order to establish whether this was indeed what happened, we need to observe whether there is a match between the positions in which the HGCS occurred in Langobardian and the positions in which affricates occurred in the Latin of northern Italy. It turns out that there is. Based on a reconstruction of the northern Italian dialects it is possible to posit the existence of the following set of affricates for the local variety of Latin in the early medieval period:[19]

Latin of northern Italy	/#_	/V_V	/VL_/VN_	geminate
t-type	*ts/*$tʃ$[20]	*ts	*ts	*$(t)ts$
p-type	–	*pf^j (> *$tʃ$)	–	–
k-type	–	*kx^j(> *ts)	–	–

The Latin origins of these affricates are closely comparable to those of their French counterparts: *k in front of *e, *i; and *pj, *tj, *kj. Given the close match between the HGCS in Langobardian and the occurrence of affricates in the Latin of northern Italy, it is reasonable to assume that the situation here was the same as in the Rhineland: speakers of Latin acquired Germanic and substituted Germanic aspirated plosives by Latin voiceless affricates but only in those positions in the word in which they occurred in Late Latin. It is this type of Germanic that is reflected in the Edict of Rotharius.

While Germanic in the Rhineland continued to flourish, Langobardian ultimately died out,[21] probably in the later medieval period: although the Langobardians had come in great numbers (how great is unclear) and continued to play an important political role for centuries, once in Italy they were gradually submerged in a sea of Latin speakers.

What is significant is that language contact between Germanic and Late Latin yielded identical results in the Rhineland and in northern Italy: Langobardian and Rhineland Franconian had a well-nigh identical version of the HGCS. That can be explained only if the conditions of contact were almost identical. In the case of northern Italy, historical and archaeological evidence suggests that numerous Germanic-speaking immigrants—rather than just a warrior elite—moved in with a plan to stay and gained control of a dense sub-Roman population. Although the historical and archaeological evidence for such a scenario unfolding in the Rhineland is less clear cut, linguistics now suggests that the situation there must have been very similar.

Another feature that jumps out is that the way in which Rhineland Franconian and Langobardian changed was determined by the local contact situation rather than by the migrational roots of the Germanic immigrants: it did not matter one bit linguistically that the Germanic speakers of the Rhineland went by the name of Franks and that those of northern Italy prided themselves on their first-century Langobardian roots along the Lower Elbe. Apparently, the Rhineland way of pronouncing Germanic was bound to arise whenever and wherever speakers of Late Latin shifted to Germanic under comparable socio-political conditions.

The best clues we have about those socio-political conditions are given by the law codes: the Langobardian Edict of Rotharius and the Franconian *Lex Salica*.[22] Both codes mainly deal with the very Germanic issue of feuds. The fact that honour played a prominent role in Germanic society and that barbarians in contradistinction to Romans carried arms made it imperative that massive bloodshed was avoided and violence curtailed by law. Although written in Latin, both codes contain traditional Germanic legal vocabulary and concepts. Neither code has much to say about the Roman population of the areas covered by the laws. Both were concerned with the traditions of their own people. Rotharius expressed this in the epilogue to the edict:

> We have sought out . . . the ancient laws of our ancestors which were not written and, with the equal counsel . . . of our . . . leading judges, and all our most happy army assisting, we . . . have ordered them to be written onto this parchment, so that we should include in the edict what we could ourselves or through the old men of the people [*gentis*] recover of the ancient law of the Langobardians.[23]

The so-called Shorter Prologue to the *Lex Salica* states:

> It has been accepted and agreed among the Franks and their leaders that for the sake of keeping peace among themselves, all intensified dispute should be curtailed, so that just as they stand out among their neighbours for the strength of their arm, so they may also excel in

the authority of law, and thus put an end to criminal behaviour. . . .
Hence, there came forward among them, chosen from many, four men
by name Wisogast, Arogast, Salegast and Widogast who, assembling
in three courts and carefully debating the sources of litigation gave
judgement on each.[24]

So it would seem that these were barbarian laws that were merely imported
into a sub-Roman setting by barbarian rulers. Yet first appearances are
deceptive. The mere fact that these laws were written down and were written in Latin implies that the barbarian rulers made use of the good services
of men who were trained in the techniques of Roman law and legislation.
The prologue of the Edict is careful to point out that the code allows 'each
man to live quietly in secure law and justice', which is 'more like what
a sub-Roman society expected of its lawmakers'.[25] In Patrick Wormald's
words, the Edict was 'an attempt to write the Lombards [i.e. Langobardians]
into the still lively legal culture of post-Roman Italy'.[26] The Edict probably
supplemented the Roman law that was still in place for most of Rotharius'
subjects.

Where it deals with compensations to be paid for killing, the Franconian
Lex Salica distinguishes between a 'free (Latin *ingenuus*) Frank or barbarian
who lives by Salic law' and a 'Roman man, a landholder'. The former is entitled to double the compensation awarded to the latter, except if the Roman
is a 'guest of the king', in which case he is entitled to more than the free
Frank. According to other clauses, the compensation allotted to a Roman
is identical to that allotted to a so-called *letus*, which is remarkable because
letus or *laetus* is the Latin term for a barbarian soldier-farmer who had
settled down in the Empire to work a plot of land: apparently the *Lex* identified him with a Roman rather than with a Frank or a barbarian living under
Salic law. In Wormald's interpretation, these regulations imply both a process of ethnic engineering and upward social mobility: 'anyone not already
laying claim to Frankish ethnicity would find that his (or her) legal position
became up to twice as secure if they proceeded to do so'.[27] This is exactly
the kind of social mechanism that would produce the HGCS in the German
of the Rhenish Fan and in Langobardian: the desire for a secure legal status
under barbarian law would drive Latin-speaking Romans to assimilate to
their Germanic-speaking neighbours, both socially and linguistically. Those
Romans would speak Germanic with a Latin accent, which expressed itself
as the HGCS. At the same time, their Germanic countrymen must have been
willing to fully accept the assimilated Romans in their midst, for only in this
way can we explain that they tolerated and even emulated a Latin accent in
Germanic, which resulted in the spread of the HGCS throughout Rhineland
German and Langobardian.

Since the *Lex Salica* is usually ascribed to Clovis' reign, the area in which
this mechanism of social engineering must have operated was much larger than
the Rhineland and comprised present-day Belgium, the southern part of the

Netherlands, and the northern half of France. Hence varieties of Germanic with a Rhenish Fan type of HGCS must have sprung up well beyond the Rhineland. We get a glimpse of one in the Old High German *Pariser Gespräche*, a Latin-German conversation manual which probably reflects an archaic Rhenish Fan type of dialect that was spoken somewhere in northern France (Gusmani 1996). Those varieties of German that were spoken deeply into France and Belgium ultimately succumbed to the pressure of the massive Gallo-Romance-speaking population, just as Langobardian gradually gave way to Italian in Italy.

6. EXPLAINING THE HGCS IN GENERAL

Up to this point, the explanation of the HGCS has centred on German dialects of types III–V (Rhineland Franconian) and on Langobardian, which have the most asymmetrical HGCS of all German dialects. Its essential ingredients can be summarized as follows:

- The dialects involved were spoken in a certified contact zone of Germanic and Latin in late Antiquity and the early medieval period
- The positions in the word in which the HGCS operated in Rhineland Franconian and (probably) Langobardian are mirrored exactly by the positions in the word in which affricates appeared in Late Latin.
- The first stage of the HGCS turns the voiceless aspirated plosives [pʰ, tʰ, kʰ] into the affricates [pf, ts, kx]; there is evidence in Late Latin and in Germanic that Germanic voiceless aspirated plosives were readily associated with Late Latin affricates.

The most plausible scenario that can be concocted from those ingredients is that speakers of Late Latin who learned Germanic replaced its 'foreign' aspirated voiceless plosives [pʰ, tʰ, kʰ] with 'native' voiceless affricates [pfⁱ, tsⁱ, kxⁱ] *but only in those positions in the word in which these affricates occurred in Late Latin*. This Latinate type of Germanic survived to become Rhineland Franconian and Langobardian.

The type of HGCS that has not yet been accounted for is the simplest system, which is found in type I and II[28] dialects, where the HGCS was applied to all positions in the word in which voiceless plosives occurred:

Type I and original type II

Proto-Germanic	/#_	/V_V	/V_#	/VL_	/VN_	geminate
*t	/ts/ehn	la/ss/en	da/s/	bol/ts/en	pflan/ts/e	ka/ts/e
*p	/pf/anne	kau/ff/en	au/f/	hel/f/en	dam/pf/	a/pf/el
*k	/kx/alt	ma/xx/en	i/x/	mer/(k)x/en	trin/kx/en	a/kx/er

The obvious question arises how these simple types I and II relate to the complex types III–V of Rhineland Franconian. Most traditional accounts of the HGCS have the development start as a full-flung shift in types I–II and then spread north, gradually petering out across types III, IV, and V. That cannot be correct because we have seen that types III–IV in no sense of the word represent a petering out. But it is still possible to entertain the idea that the HGCS started in type I–II dialects, then spread northwards to types III–IV and southwards to Langobardian, where contact with Late Latin and its asymmetrical system of affricates limited the application of the HGCS to those positions in the word where affricates occurred in Late Latin. What disfavours this scenario, however, is that it is uneconomical in the sense that it requires two origins for the affricates: one in the type I–II dialects that set the HGCS in motion and the other in the Late Latin dialects in the Rhineland and in northern Italy. Another counterargument which has frequently been canvassed is that dialect features tend to spread from centres of political, social, and economic power to the periphery. In early medieval Europe, there were no centres in zones I and II that could have propelled the HGCS northwards and southwards. Rather, the situation was the reverse: the Langobardian and especially the powerful Franconian Rhineland centres should have carried linguistic changes into zones I and II.[29]

So we are left with a more economical and more plausible alternative: that the HGCS started in the Rhineland and in Langobardian Italy as a Latin accent and that zones I and II acquired their version of the HGCS in the wake of the Franconian takeover of those areas. If the Franks continued to apply their policy of social mobility and ethnic engineering to extending their power over the Alemannians and Bavarians down south, this might have given the latter a strong incentive to 'speak like a Frank'. That meant replacing one's native aspirated plosives with affricates. But the further away people lived from the Rhineland model, the less accurate was the copying process. Apparently, the mountain men of the Alpine south went the whole hog and replaced each and every [pʰ, tʰ, kʰ] with [pf, ts, kx].

7. GERMANIC AND LATIN UP NORTH

All of this means, of course, that High German (that is, German dialects of types I to V) can be characterized as Germanic with a Late Latin accent. But there are other ways in which Late Latin could interfere with Germanic. One could say that speakers of Late Latin in zones III–V at least acknowledged that the voiceless aspirated [pʰ, tʰ, kʰ] of Germanic were different from their own voiceless unaspirated [p, t, k] and that they made an effort to render the aspirates as closely as they could within the confines of their own sound system. If an early medieval merchant had sailed the Rhine downstream beyond Cologne and Wermelskirchen, however, he would have met speakers of Germanic dialects who had not even bothered to do that: they had simply replaced Germanic [pʰ, tʰ, kʰ] with Late Latin [p, t, k], much as modern French, Spanish, or Italian speakers do when they learn German or English. These people are the earliest speakers of Dutch.

IV. The Origins of Dutch

1. NON-ASPIRATION OF p, t, k

Together with English dialects in Scotland, Westphalian dialects of German, and Swedish dialects in Finland, the Dutch language has lost the aspiration of Proto-Germanic [p^h, t^h, k^h]. No doubt the loss of aspiration in those dialects occurred independently of one another: they belong to different branches of the Germanic family tree, and all of the closest relatives of unaspirated dialects do have aspiration. If the loss of aspiration was independent, it may well have been caused by different factors that are specific to each unaspirated dialect. In the case of Swedish in Finland, aspiration loss is bound to be connected with language contact. Swedish in Finland arose in a bilingual setting: Swedish originally had aspiration, and Finnish did not. The loss of aspiration is therefore probably due to the influence of Finnish speakers who became bilingual. The case of Dutch may be similar, but the language contact situation that may have caused the loss of aspiration – Germanic and Latin in the early Middle Ages – is more remote in time and requires intricate reconstruction before it can be taken seriously as an explanation. That reconstruction is the theme of the present chapter.

At this point of the argument, three reasons can be produced that support the idea that the loss of aspiration in Dutch was caused by early contact with Latin. The first is that studies of the phonology of Modern Dutch plosives (p, t, k, b, d) reveal that Dutch sides with Romance languages such as French and Spanish rather than with its closest relatives, German and English (Kager 2007). The second reason is one of geography: Flemish as well as southern and central Dutch dialects lack aspiration of p, t, k, but those of the Dutch northeast preserve it. That is, aspiration is preserved only in the dialects that are removed furthest from French. The final reason to think that contact with Romance may have been responsible for the loss of aspiration in Dutch is that the previous chapter has placed lost varieties of Romance in the present-day Dutch-speaking areas of Dutch and Belgian Limburg as well as in the Rhineland as far north as Cologne, i.e. well north of the present-day linguistic border between French and Dutch.

There are two potential obstacles to embracing the idea that loss of aspiration in Dutch is due to contact with Romance in the early medieval period.

First of all, it is unclear when Dutch lost aspiration. The absence or presence of aspiration in Dutch *p*, *t*, *k* is not indicated in spelling, nor has it ever been. We know about non-aspiration only by listening to present-day spoken Dutch and by studying modern dialect descriptions that care to mention this feature, which do not go back in time beyond the twentieth century. As a consequence, loss of aspiration may be attributed to any period between, say, the first and the nineteenth century. That makes it very difficult to be confident about connecting the phenomenon to any specific historical scenario. Who is to say whether loss of aspiration in Dutch is due to contact with Late Latin speakers in the early Middle Ages rather than to, say, the well-known influence of French language and culture on the upper-class Dutch of the eighteenth and nineteenth centuries?

The second obstacle to attributing aspiration loss to early medieval contact with Romance is that there may have been another vehicle for the same process. We saw earlier that Westphalian German dialects lack aspiration and that German dialects along the Lower Rhine around Cologne do too. In the sixteenth and seventeenth centuries, the towns of Holland were population sinks which attracted large numbers of immigrants from other parts of the Netherlands as well as from neighbouring Germany. In as far as those German immigrants came from Westphalia and the Rhineland, they may well have introduced non-aspiration into the Netherlands, which subsequently spread to the countryside surrounding the Dutch towns. Yet a closer investigation gives a twist to this matter: non-aspirating dialects in Westphalia happen to be dialects spoken to the south and west of the town of Münster,[1] which are adjacent to the Netherlands and to the Lower Rhine dialects that lack aspiration. So we are confronted with a united region of non-aspiration, encompassing a large Dutch and an adjacent, small German area (remember that this is a dialect continuum and that there are no sharp linguistic boundaries). Since this is a single region, aspiration loss in it probably had one and the same cause. If non-aspiration in Dutch spread from the German Lower Rhine and adjacent Westphalia, this brings us back to contact with Romance anyway, because Romance influence on Rhineland German has already been established in chapter III.

Given such complications, attributing non-aspiration of *p*, *t*, *k* in Dutch to early medieval contact with Romance is just an attractive guess. In order to turn it into something more substantial, we need to find out whether medieval Romance influence on Dutch betrays itself elsewhere in the Dutch language. If Romance influence can be shown more clearly for other aspects of Dutch, non-aspiration can hitch a ride with them.

2. *i*-UMLAUT IN EASTERN AND WESTERN DUTCH

A phenomenon that characterizes all medieval and modern Germanic languages is *i*-umlaut: a vowel in the stressed syllable of the word, which is usually the first syllable, is changed under the influence of an original *$*i$ or *$*j$ in the following syllable. An example is the Proto-Germanic verb for 'to put, to set', *$*satjan$: its stressed vowel, *$*-a-$, is affected by the *$*-j-$ in the second syllable, as a result of which *-a-* becomes *-e-*: **setjan*. Other changes affect this word, which ends up in the various medieval Germanic languages as follows:

*satjan > **setjan* >	Old English *settan* > *set*
	Old Frisian *setta*
	Old Norse *setja*
	Old Saxon *settian*
	Old High German *sezzen* > *setzen*
	Old Dutch *settan* > *zetten*

The process of *i*-umlaut belongs to the early medieval period. Hence the original, unaffected vowel is preserved in the fourth-century Germanic language called Gothic, where the verb is *satjan*. Although all Germanic languages – apart from Gothic – undergo *i*-umlaut, the exact rules that govern its operation are different for each individual language. For instance, a short **i* was lost so early in Dutch and German that it failed to produce *i*-umlaut, as in **gastiz* > Old High German *gast*, Middle Dutch *gast* 'guest'. In other Germanic languages, however, this word did undergo *i*-umlaut, e.g. in Old Norse *gestr*, Old English *giest*, because their rules for *i*-umlaut were slightly different. In general, Dutch and German stick very closely to one another: their rules are practically identical, all vowels are affected, and all are affected in the same way. This can be illustrated by the following list of words from the Modern Dutch dialect of Tilburg (Dutch Brabant)[2] and their Modern High German counterparts.

i-Umlaut in Dutch and German

original vowel	*i*-umlaut?	Proto-Germanic form before *i*-umlaut	Dutch (Tilburg)	German	English cognate or meaning
*a	yes	**mari*	[mer]	*Meer*	*mere*
	no	**dagaz*	[dax]	*Tag*	*day*
*u	yes	**hrugjaz*	[rɘx][3]	*Rücken*	*ridge*
	no	**wulfaz*	[wʊləf]	*Wolf*	*wolf*
*ǣ	yes	**skǣri-*	[sxɛːr]	*Schere*	*shears*
	no	**slǣpanan*	[slɔːpə]	*schlafen*	*to sleep*
*ō	yes	**fōljanan*	[vylə]	*fühlen*	*to feel*
	no	**blōmān*	[blum]	*Blume*	*bloom*
*au	yes	**raukjanan*	[rɘːkə]	*räuchern*	(to smoke, e.g. fish)
	no	**hlaupanan*	[lʊːpə]	*laufen*	*to leap*

The vowels that are affected by *i*-umlaut are so-called central and back vowels, which are produced by leaving the tongue in its neutral position (i.e. not doing anything special with it, as in the case of *a*, a central vowel) or by retracting the tongue backwards from its neutral position (as in the case of *o*, *u*, hence the term back vowels). Original front vowels, which are produced by slightly protracting the tongue, as in the case of *i, e*, are generally not affected by *i*-umlaut. What *i*-umlaut does is turn central and back vowels into front vowels whenever they are followed by the front vowel *i* or the front consonant *j* in the next syllable. So original **mari* 'lake' has a central vowel *a* in the first syllable and a front vowel *i* in the second syllable. *i*-Umlaut turns the central vowel *a* into the front vowel *e*, and the result is **meri*. After some time and a number of other sound changes, **meri* turns into Tilburg Dutch [mer], standard Dutch *meer*, German *Meer*, and English *mere*. Similarly, Proto-Germanic **fōljanan* 'feel' has a long back vowel **ō* in the first syllable and a front consonant **j* in the second. Here *i*-umlaut turns the long back vowel into its front counterpart **ø̄* (as in French *feu*), so that **fōljanan* becomes **føljan*. Here, too, many subsequent changes affect the word, which ends up as Tilburg Dutch [vylə], German *fühlen*,[4] and, with the loss of lip rounding that is typical of English, *feel*. What all offspring of **fōljanan* have in common is a front vowel in the first syllable which arose as a result of *i*-umlaut.

There is a striking limitation to the close correspondence between German and Dutch, however: it occurs only in the Dutch dialects of the eastern half of the Netherlands and Flanders. In the west, those dialects are flanked by a bundle of dialect boundaries, so-called isoglosses, that run from the southern coast of the IJsselmeer near Amersfoort in a southwesterly direction until they hit the linguistic boundary between Dutch and French near Geraardsbergen (Flanders). West of that bundle, dialects used to be spoken that are unique among the Germanic languages: they underwent *i*-umlaut only of originally short *a*, and just possibly also of short *u*, but definitely not of the other vowels. These are the dialects of Western Dutch, which are of special importance because the Modern Dutch standard language is largely based on them. Let us reproduce the diagram above and replace the German forms with their Western Dutch (i.e. standard Modern Dutch) forms:

i-Umlaut in Western and Eastern Dutch

original vowel	*i*-umlaut?	Proto-Germanic form before *i*-umlaut	Eastern Dutch (Tilburg)	Western Dutch (standard)	English cognate or meaning
*a	yes	**mari*	[mer]	*meer* [e]	*mere*
	no	**dagaz*	[dax]	*dag* [ɑ]	*day*
*u	yes	**hrugjaz*	[rɵx]	*rug* [ɵ̈]	*ridge*
	no	**wulfaz*	[wʊləf]	*wolf* [ɔ]	*wolf*
*ǣ	yes	**skǣri-*	[sxɛːr]	*schaar* [a]	*shears*
	no	**slǣpanan*	[slɔːpə]	*slapen* [a]	*to sleep*
*ō	yes	**fōljanan*	[vylə]	*voelen* [u]	*to feel*
	no	**blōmān*	[blum]	*bloem* [u]	*bloom*
*au	yes	**raukjanan*	[rɵ̈ːkə]	*roken* [o]	(to smoke, e.g. fish)
	no	**hlaupanan*	[lʊːpə]	*lopen* [o]	*to leap*

The examples illustrate that in Western Dutch *a and *u each have two different outcomes, one front and one central/back, according to whether they underwent *i*-umlaut or not. As we will see later on, the status of *i*-umlaut of *u is problematic, but apart from that complication the situation in Western Dutch agrees with Eastern Dutch, German, and the rest of Germanic. Following Goossens (1980), we call this primary *i*-umlaut because it appears to be the oldest stage of umlaut. But *ā, *ō, and *au each have just one outcome, which is a central or back vowel that did not undergo *i*-umlaut, even though it should have undergone *i*-umlaut where an *i or *j was present in the second syllable. *i*-Umlaut of *ā, *ō, *au, and other vowels (including *u) is called secondary *i*-umlaut. Secondary *i*-umlaut did not affect Western Dutch. The fact that Western Dutch is the only type of Germanic to behave in this way is what makes it so special. Since it sticks out among the Germanic languages, it calls for an explanation.

3. WESTERN DUTCH

The Western Dutch area comprises the Belgian provinces of West and East Flanders, the extreme west of the Belgian provinces of Brabant and Antwerp, and the extreme west of the Dutch provinces of North Brabant and Utrecht, as well as the entirety of the Dutch provinces of Zeeland, South Holland, and North Holland. The total area is relatively small (approximately 1000 square kilometres). Before the large-scale land reclamations and the construction of dikes, which started by the eleventh century, the inhabitable area was considerably smaller than it is nowadays and very sparsely populated. Most of the land was too wet and boggy to be hospitable to long-term settlement, being little more than a large estuary formed by the Rhine, Maas, and Schelt and consequently prey to periodic inundations by the rivers and the sea. The first large-scale reclamations were followed by urbanization, first of all in Flanders, where towns expanded greatly between the eleventh and thirteenth centuries. Examples are Gent, Brugge, Aalst, and Ypres. In Holland, the process started with the towns of Utrecht and Dordrecht, but here massive urbanization took off only in the fifteenth century. Medieval towns were population sinks. The average life expectancy of medieval man ranged between thirty and forty years,[5] but in towns disease and unhealthy living conditions shortened the life spans of their inhabitants even further. As a consequence, towns generated a constant flow of immigration, which was required to sustain them.

So large-scale land reclamation and the successful development of towns entailed that people moved into the Western Dutch area from outside. This population influx must have originated primarily from the higher ground and more densely populated areas that lay to the east of Holland and Zeeland and to the east and south of Flanders. The linguistic map of Western Dutch can be expected to reflect this. First of all, we expect that Western

Dutch is linguistically a composite: the dialects of the early medieval natives came into contact with a variety of dialects spoken by immigrants. This phenomenon is well attested for Holland from the late medieval period onwards,[6] but it must have had predecessors stretching back to the early medieval period. Second, as immigrants moved into the Western Dutch area from the east and south, their dialects followed them. The result is that ancient dialectal boundaries may have moved in the same direction. For example, based on data from nineteenth- and twentieth-century dialectological research, the western boundary of secondary *i*-umlaut runs from approximately Hilversum (Utrecht) in the north to Geraardsbergen (East Flanders) in the south. Goossens demonstrated that this was more or less its position during the later medieval period.[7] If we were to speculate on its position during the early medieval period, the demographic history of the Western Dutch area would lead us to assume that it ran approximately at the same position as today or, if not the same, then more eastwards rather than westwards.

The expectations that the Western Dutch area is dialectally mixed in origin and shows native features as well as features that derive from the east and south are borne out by the investigations of many generations of researchers. Yet the data are more complex than those expectations would lead us to assume, and they leave a number of knotty problems, which will be addressed subsequently. These problems come under two general headings: Coastal Dutch and spontaneous vowel fronting.

4. COASTAL DUTCH

The Western Dutch area contains the debris of a lost variety of Germanic that was probably native to the area in the early medieval period, before large-scale land reclamation and urbanization injected immigrants into the area from the south and east. This variety was more akin to Frisian and English than to Eastern Dutch, which, as we saw earlier, sides with German in as far as *i*-umlaut is concerned. It will be labelled Coastal Dutch.[8] Coastal Dutch survives in the form of individual words and names in Western Dutch, some of which continue in the Modern Dutch standard language. Its most striking feature is that Coastal Dutch—unlike Western Dutch—underwent full-flung *i*-umlaut and that it did so in the manner of English and Frisian. Here are a number of examples of typically Coastal Dutch *i*-umlaut:[9]

(1) $*\bar{u} > *\bar{y} > \bar{\imath}$ in $*h\bar{u}djan > *h\bar{y}djan >$ Middle Coastal Dutch *hīden* 'to hide'; also in place names ending in *-hīde*, where it means 'harbour', as in *Coxhyde* (West Flanders, 1270), present-day *Coxijde*, locally pronounced as [kɔksidə]; and *Palvoetzide* (Zeeland, 1351).

This contrasts with 'normal' Middle Dutch *hūden* 'to hide' but agrees with Old English *hȳdan > hīdan >* Modern English *hide* and with place names such as *Rother-hide*. Its Old Frisian cognate *hēda* 'to hide' shows *i*-umlaut as well but has *ē* rather than *ī*.

Other examples are Middle Coastal Dutch *hyr-lant* (1187; *y* = probably [ī]) 'hired land', from **hūr-i-* 'hire', which also survives in Old Frisian *hēre* and Old English *hȳr* > Modern English *hire*; and Modern Dutch *kies* 'molar' from **kūs-i-* as in Old Frisian *kēse*, beside Middle Western Dutch *kuyse*, which did not undergo *i*-umlaut.

(2) **ō* > **ø̄* > **ē* > *ie* in **ga-dōb-i-* 'fitting' > **gadø̄bi-* > **gadēb* > Middle Coastal Dutch *on-ghedieve* 'unfitting' (with *on-* = English *un-*), with a development of the vowel much as in Old Frisian *unidēve* 'improper'.

This contrasts with Middle Western Dutch *onghedoeve*, which has written <oe> for what phonetically was approximately [ō], so without (secondary) *i*-umlaut.[10]

(3) **ǣ* > **ē* > *ie* as in **lǣkijaz* 'leech' > **lēki* > Middle Coastal Dutch *lieke* and *lēke*, corresponding to English *leech* rather than Middle Western Dutch *lāke*, where *i*-umlaut is regularly absent. Similarly **mǣljan* 'to paint' > Middle Coastal Dutch *mielen*, which contrasts with Middle Dutch *mālen*, Old High German *mālōn*.

The **ǣ* that stands at the beginning of this development is a typically Coastal Dutch sound, with correspondences in Old English and Old Frisian. Its counterpart in all other medieval Germanic languages, including Dutch, is *ā*. The *ǣ/ā* split is an ancient dialectal split which has nothing to do with *i*-umlaut. Its Proto-Germanic source is **ǣ*, which shows that Germanic languages such as Coastal Dutch that have *ǣ* preserved (or reverted to) an ancestral state. An example of a word containing this vowel is Modern Zeeland Dutch dialect [sxæp] 'sheep', which reflects the Coastal Dutch form and corresponds to Old English *scēap*, Old Frisian *skēp*. It contrasts with Old High German *scāf*, Old Saxon *skāp*, and Dutch *schaap*.

(4) **au* > **ā* > **ē* > *ie* as in **staumjan* 'to steam' > Modern Dutch (North Holland dialect) *stiemen* 'to steam', which agrees with Old English *stīeman* 'to steam' rather than with Modern Western Dutch *stomen*, which lacks *i*-umlaut.

The first stage in the development of **au* (4) is the monophthongization of **au* to **ā*. This has nothing to do with *i*-umlaut, representing an early development typical of Coastal Dutch, Frisian, and part of Old Saxon. It occurs in a number of early Coastal Dutch place names, e.g. *Vronan-slat* (1125–1150, South Holland) < **-slauta-* 'ditch, canal' and *Datnesta* (820–822, copy 941; East Flanders) < **daud-* 'dead'. The same development occurs in common nouns such as Middle Dutch *bāken* 'beacon' < **baukna-* and *sāde* 'sod' < **sauθō*. The normal Middle Western Dutch equivalents of those words show **au* > *ō*: *slōt* 'ditch', *dōt* 'dead', *bōken* 'beacon', *sōde* 'sod'.

Similarly, old **ai* became *ā* in Coastal Dutch, just as it did in Frisian and English: Modern Dutch *ladder* 'ladder' originated from Coastal Dutch **lādder*, which itself goes back to **hlaidra-*. Its cognates are Old English *hlædder*, Modern English *ladder*, and Old Frisian *hladder*, which show the same development as Coastal Dutch.[11] In other Dutch dialects, **hlaidra-* developed into *lēder > leer*. So the development of **ai* and **au* to **ā* in Coastal Dutch confirms the idea that it joined Frisian rather than Dutch and German as far as *i*-umlaut is concerned.

As is shown by examples such as *hīden < *hȳdjan* and *onghedieve < *gadōbi-*, Coastal Dutch eliminated the rounded front vowels *ȳ* and *ø̄* by unrounding them to *ī* and *ē* (which later became *ie*, a diphthong, in Middle Dutch and long [iː] in some modern western dialects). It agrees in this with later Old English and Old Frisian. Unrounding also affected the short **y* that resulted from *i*-umlaut of short **u*:

> Coastal Dutch *pit* and *pet* 'pit' < **pyt* < **putjaz*
> Coastal Dutch *brig* and *breg* 'bridge' < **brygg* < **brugjō*

The English translations are cognates. They show that English underwent the same development, and so did Frisian. Dutch and German, on the other hand, in general retained the rounded front vowel: Dutch *put* [pɵt], German *Pfütze* [pfʏtsə], and Dutch *brug* [brɵx], German *Brücke* [brʏkə].

It is generally agreed that all these similarities between Coastal Dutch, Frisian, and English date from the early medieval period and that they are connected with the same population movements that brought the Anglo-Saxons to Britain. In the later Roman period, the North Sea and Channel coasts were frequently raided by pirates from the north. The general Roman term for those raiders was *Saxones*, Saxons, a name that no doubt covered various ethnic groups. From the early fifth century onwards, when Roman control of the area was completely given up, raiding was accompanied by settlement. Between the fifth and eighth centuries, a common culture joined the English and Continental sides of the North Sea and the Channel. In the estuaries of the Rhine, Maas, and Schelt, this culture is connected with the name of the Frisians. The Frisians controlled the estuaries and there-fore also the trade routes along the coast and with Britain. Where the land was threatened by periodic inundations, people threw up artificial mounds, called *terpen* or *wierden*, on which they built their farmsteads. Excavations in present-day Frisia have revealed the wealth that the inhabitants of this region were capable of accumulating.

The Frisians' main trading centre was the town of Dorestad, which lay southeast of Utrecht at the junction of the Rhine and the Lek near the remnants of an old Roman fort along a stretch of the old *limes* that had passed out of Roman control as early as the middle of the third century. Whether there was a trickle of population continuity between the Roman and the early medieval period is unclear. We do know that the town flourished already during the first half of the sixth century, when a mint master called Madelinus, who came from Maastricht, set up shop here. By the late seventh century, the Franks, who controlled centres of power along the Maas in eastern Belgium and in the German Rhineland, had gained control over their western neighbours and began casting their eyes towards the northwest. Sometime around 689, the Franconian ruler Pippin gained a victory over the Frisians under Redbad in the Battle of Dorestad. In 695–696, Pippin appointed the Anglo-Saxon Willibrord as bishop in Utrecht with the specific assignment to convert the heathen Frisians to Christianity. As usual in those days, Franconian power plays and missionary activities went hand in hand. Although it took the best part of the eighth century to subdue and convert the Frisians, the combined approach was so successful that Franconian power in the Low Countries was there to stay.[12]

These historical data are mirrored by linguistic history. Coastal Dutch is the language of the 'Saxon' pirate-settlers of late Antiquity and the early medieval period. It is an early form of Frisian. One might object to using the label Frisian for Coastal Dutch in Flanders, because as far as we know Flanders was never part of the realm of the Frisians, which did include North and South Holland and Zeeland. As so often in similar cases, however, historians and linguists use the term *Frisian* with different meanings. For a historian, Frisians are persons who lived in Frisia and took part in aspects of its culture to such an extent that this shaped a common identity. To linguists, Frisians are people who spoke Frisian. The two do not always match.

Coastal Dutch—Frisian in the linguistic sense of the word—was gradually replaced by Western Dutch, first of all in Flanders, followed by Holland, then Zeeland, and finally the north of North Holland, where Frisian may still have been spoken in the seventeenth century. It survives in the modern province of Friesland as well as in enclaves further east in northwestern Germany. The gradual replacement of Coastal Dutch is usually connected with the growing influence of eastern and southern Dutch dialects, which followed the Franconian march towards the west that started in the late seventh century. The land reclamations and urbanization of later centuries intensified the Franconian influx and put additional pressure on Coastal Dutch.

Through the excavation of Coastal Dutch and some of its linguistic features from Western Dutch soil, linguists have identified the native element in the Western Dutch area. But this is not to say that Coastal Dutch was the only language present in the early medieval Western Dutch area. Since Coastal Dutch, like English, is an immigrant language, one wonders what the natives of the Western Dutch area spoke in the fifth century. As in the case of Britain, Celtic and Latin are the best contenders,[13] but preciously little is known about this.

5. SPONTANEOUS VOWEL FRONTING

We have seen that Coastal Dutch has fully developed *i*-umlaut of the type that is also attested in Frisian and English, and that Eastern Dutch has fully developed *i*-umlaut, too, although of a different type which is also found in German. Western Dutch, on the other hand, underwent only so-called primary *i*-umlaut, which affected short **a* and possibly **u*, whilst long vowels and diphthongs remained unaffected. Even though complex enough, this is not the entire story, for Western Dutch contains a number of words which look as if they underwent *i*-umlaut but actually did not. Such words have undergone what is known as 'spontaneous fronting'. Here are a number of Western Dutch examples, together with reconstructions and cognates in English and Eastern Dutch.

Spontaneous fronting in Dutch

original vowel	reconstructed example	medieval Western Dutch	modern Western Dutch	English cognate	Eastern Dutch cognate
*a	**stappaz*	**step*	*step* [stɛp]	*step*	*stap* [stɑp]
*u	**fullaz*	**fyll*[14]	*vul* [vəl]	*full*	*vol* [vɔl]
	*suguz	**sygu*	*zeug* [zøx]	*sow*	*zoog* [zox]
*ū	**hūsan*	**hȳs*	*huus* [hys]	*house*	*hoes* [hus]
*ō	**brōθēr*	**brōder*	*bruur* [bryr] *breur* [brør]	*brother*	*broer* [brur]
*au	**augōn*	**ōga*	*uug* [ȳ(ə)x]	*eye*	*oog* [ox]

As the reconstructions in the second column show, there was neither an **i* nor a **j* in the second syllable of these words that could have caused *i*-umlaut. Yet in Western Dutch all words developed as if there was: short **a* became **e*, and the rounded vowels and diphthong all become rounded front vowels, exactly as they would if they had undergone *i*-umlaut. This is what is called spontaneous fronting: a mid or rounded back vowel becomes a front vowel without apparent cause.

What the diagram does not show is one of the well-known banes of Dutch dialectologists: these spontaneous frontings have a widely different distribution across the dialect map and across the lexicon.

(1) **a* > *e* occurs in isolated words in Middle and Modern Dutch dialects.[15] Examples comprise *step* 'step', *dek* 'roof', *strek* 'tight', *tem* 'tame', *tek* 'branch', and *bled* 'leaf', all of which have -*a*- in standard Dutch. In each word, the distribution of forms with -*e*- and -*a*- is different, but the preponderance of -*e*- along the coast and up the rivers is clear. Since Frisian (and

English) underwent a similar development, this may be a feature of Coastal Dutch that managed to be transferred to Western Dutch. Recall that its long counterpart *$\bar{a}$ shared a similar fate: it was fronted to *$\bar{æ}$ in Coastal Dutch (whence it could enter Western Dutch), Frisian, and English.

(2) *$\bar{o}$ was retained as a closed *$\bar{o}$ along the coast and in the extreme east. Medieval Flanders (that is to say in the south of the Western Dutch area, which is well represented in medieval literary sources) appears to belong to this area but shows special developments: *$\bar{o}$ became *ou* before labial and velar consonant (e.g. *roupen* 'call' < *$hr\bar{o}p$-, *bouk* 'book' < *$b\bar{o}k$-) and $\bar{o}$ on its way to $\bar{u}$, spelled <oe>, before a dental (e.g. *groen* 'green' < *$gr\bar{o}n$-, *voet* 'foot' < *$f\bar{o}t$-). In a wide band between this western area and the extreme east of the Dutch-speaking area, however, *$\bar{o}$ became *uo* and then $\bar{u}$, which in Middle and Modern Dutch was spelled as a rule as <oe>.

In this landscape, with closed *$\bar{o}$ in the west and the extreme east, and *uo* in the centre, spontaneous fronting occurred incidentally in a small number of words, as a result of which *$\bar{o}$ became *$\bar{ø}$, and *uo* became *yø* and thence *$\bar{y}$. Because this fronting has not received as much coverage in the secondary literature on Dutch as the other frontings, a detailed treatment is in order (disheartened readers may wish to continue at (3) below). In Middle Dutch, the only unambiguous spellings of this front vowel are <ue> and <u>, but they are unambiguous only in the west.[16] Berteloot (1984) provides a number of maps on the distribution of such <ue> spellings across Middle Dutch scriptoria in the thirteenth century. His map 111, *$m\bar{o}d\bar{e}r$* 'mother', shows <mueder> only in Brussels.[17] Map 112, *$br\bar{o}\theta\bar{e}r$* 'brother', on the other hand, has <ue> and <u> spellings in the southwest of Belgian Brabant and in Dutch Brabant as well as in Houten (Utrecht) and Wateringen (South Holland). This strongly resembles the pattern on map 114 of the spellings <gued, gud> of *$g\bar{o}daz$* 'good'. The fronting of these two words is confirmed by modern dialect data. Modern Dutch *bryr* 'brother' is widespread in Belgian Brabant and Belgian Limburg as well as in Dutch North Brabant and the river area of Gelderland.[18] Fronted /γyt/ 'good' and the like are attested in Belgian Brabant.[19] The word for 'mother' is generally *moeder* [mudər] or the like, so without fronting, but the affectionately shortened form *$m\bar{o}d$*- > *$m\bar{o}j$*- comes out as fronted *møj* in Zeeland, Utrecht, and western Gelderland (standard Dutch has *moei* /mui/, so lacks fronting).[20] The verb *duun* [dyn] 'to do' is widespread in the Gelderland river area (Betuwe), to which other dialects and the standard language correspond with unfronted *doen* [dun]. Place-name evidence marks incidental dots in the original area of distribution of fronting: *Vleuten* < *$fl\bar{o}t$*- 'flood' and *Breukelen* < *$br\bar{o}k$*- 'periodically inundated land, marsh' (standard Dutch *broek* [bruk], cognate with English *brook*) just west of the town of Utrecht, *Bruchem* < *$Br\bar{o}ka$*-*haima*- in westernmost Gelderland, and *Brussel*, the town of Brussels, < *$Br\bar{o}ka$*-*sal*- all show spontaneous fronting. The Middle Dutch spelling *bruek* of the common noun *broek* 'swamp' probably does, too.[21] Most instances of spontaneous fronting of *ō have been lost in the modern dialects. A precious instance is the word for Wednesday, Proto-Germanic *Wōdanasa dagaz, literally, 'Woden's day'. This is *woensdag* [wunsdax] in Modern Dutch, so without fronting. But the data of a dialect study undertaken in 1879 reveal widespread *weun(e)sdag* [wøn(ə)sdax] in Frisian towns, North and South Holland, and Zeeland, as well as the archaic form *wuunsdag* [wynsdax] in the towns of Den Bosch and Tilburg in Dutch North Brabant. By the middle of the twentieth century, these forms had all but disappeared.[22]

(3) *au normally became ō in Dutch, which turns up in southern Modern Dutch dialects as a diphthong *oə* or *uə*. In East Flanders and Southwest Brabant around Brussels, modern dialects show spontaneous fronting to *y* or *yə*.[23] Examples are [byəm] 'tree' < *bauma- (English *beam*, Dutch *boom*) and [bryət] 'bread' < *brauda- (Dutch *brood*). There is no indication how old the diphthongization to *oə*, *uə* is,[24] nor when fronting to *y(ə)* occurred. Middle Dutch spellings with <ue> or <u>, which would indicate approximately [y(ə)], appear to be lacking, and this might point to the conclusion that fronting had not yet occurred or that dialects that had [y(ə)] happen not to be represented in the written language of the time. There are indications that Flanders showed a particularly close pronunciation of *au > ō, which verged upon [ū]: the place names *Roeselaar* (near Aalst, East Flanders) and *Roeselare* (central West Flanders) contain the old word for 'reed', *raus-, which had become *rōs- as elsewhere and then was closed to *rūs-, spelled <roes>.[25] It is this *ū* that was fronted to *y(ə)*.

(4) *u > *y is one of the most enigmatic developments in the history of Dutch, for each affected word seems to have its own distribution across the map. Again a preponderance along the coast is overwhelmingly clear, but in some words *y also occurs in the northeast of the Netherlands and neighbouring parts of Germany (*zeun* < *syn < *sunuz 'son', standard Dutch *zoon*, German *Sohn*; *veugel* < *fygl < *fuglaz 'bird', standard Dutch *vogel*, German *Vogel*), and in other words in Belgian Brabant (*weunen, wunen* 'to live, inhabit' < *wyn- < *wun-, standard Dutch *wonen*, German *wohnen*).[26]

An important aspect of the problem is the input of the rule *u > y. Proto-Germanic had only *u, not *o. In West Germanic, *u became *o as a result of so-called *a*-umlaut: *fuglaz became *foglaz because of *a (or *ō) in the second syllable, while *sunuz retained its *u. But the *a*-umlaut rule was blocked in English, Frisian, and Coastal Dutch if *u was flanked by a labial sound (*f*, *b, *m, *p, *w) or by a nasal (*n, *m).[27] So in Coastal Dutch *fuglaz retained its *u, and so did *wullō 'wool'; both underwent fronting: *fygl, *wylla, whence Dutch (dialectal) *veugel, wul*. Eastern Dutch had *fogl, *wolla, which could not undergo fronting because they had *o rather than *u and therefore the incorrect input for the fronting rule (just like Old High German *fogal, wolla*). Retained *u*-forms of the type *fugl also existed in Old Saxon, which may explain why the input for the fronting of *u to *y also existed in the northeast of the Netherlands (Old Saxon *fugl* 'bird', northeastern Modern Dutch *veugel*).

Later on in the history of Dutch, any remaining short *u was opened towards *o (as in *sunuz* 'son' > *sone > Modern Dutch *zoon* [zōn] and *sumraz > *somr > Modern Dutch *zomer* [zōmər]). Again, Eastern Dutch developed in concert with German: Old High German *sunu*, *sumar* became Modern German *Sohn*, *Sommer*. This opening of *u to *o reduced the number of potential candidates for fronting to zero. So it is possible that the spontaneous fronting of *u to *y occurred wherever the input *u was preserved long enough for the rule to affect it: most in the west and possibly northeast, least in the east of the Dutch-speaking area.

This analysis of the data and the fact that fronting of *u is so widespread outside the extreme west undermine the idea that spontaneous fronting of *u is a Coastal Dutch development, as has sometimes been maintained.[28] Another counterargument to that idea is that English and Frisian do not show fronting of *u.[29]

A different consideration might speak in favour of a connection with Coastal Dutch, however: as we saw earlier, the *u that became *y as a result of *i*-umlaut in Coastal Dutch was unrounded to *e* or *i* (remember the example *brugjō > *brygjō > *brygg > brig*, *breg* 'bridge'). There are two ways of connecting this Coastal Dutch unrounding to the spontaneous fronting of *u to *y. Either the *u becoming *y by spontaneous fronting pushed the other *y (the result of *i*-umlaut) away lest they merge (a so-called push chain),[30] or the *y produced through *i*-umlaut had moved out of the way towards *e* or *i*, thus creating space in the vowel system for *u to spontaneously front to *y (a so-called pull chain):

---

i   ←   *y*   ←   *u*

e   ←

The problem with this account is that it is just a possibility to be believed or disbelieved. Frisian and English underwent unrounding of the *y that arose by *i*-umlaut to *i* or *e* but had no spontaneous fronting of *u, so the impression that both developments are somehow naturally linked is incorrect. Hence the development *u > *y probably has no relation to Coastal Dutch.

(5) The idea that the spontaneous fronting of *u to *y should not be connected with Coastal Dutch is strengthened by the fact that its counterpart, the spontaneous fronting of long *ū to *ȳ, quite clearly is not native to Coastal Dutch. Although nowadays the west coast has fronting, a number of common nouns and western place names preserve old *ū, which nowadays is [u], spelled <oe>. Examples comprise Scheveningen (South Holland) dialect form *zoer* [zur] < *sūra- 'sour' and the Zeeland place names *Soeburg < *Sūθ-burg-* 'south town' and *Armoederhoek < *-mūθ-* 'mouth (also of a river)'.[31]

Fronting of $*\bar{u}$ to $*\bar{y}$ characterizes the standard language, where it developed into a modern diphthong [ʌə̈]. Fronting was originally at home in the west and centre of the Dutch-speaking area, and it stretches further east along the rivers, reaching northwards along the Guelder IJssel. Only the extreme northeast and southeast preserve unfronted $*\bar{u}$.

In Belgium, the line that separates western fronted $*\bar{y}$ from eastern unfronted $*\bar{u}$ is continued across the linguistic boundary with French, where it separates West Walloon *y* from East Walloon *u* (as in the verb 'to kill', western *tuer* [tye], eastern *touer* [tue]). This significant fact has given rise to the idea that the fronting of $*\bar{u}$ to $*\bar{y}$ in Dutch and French are causally linked. The usual interpretation is that fronting was caused by contact with French.[32] However that may be, the fact that the $*\bar{y}/*\bar{u}$ line is not deflected by the linguistic boundary between Dutch and French points to it being something old, just like the line separating word-final $*$-*k* from $*$-*x*/$*$-*ʃ* that was discussed earlier, which happens to run only thirty kilometres to the west (III.4.1). We have argued that the $*$-*k*/$*$-*x* line probably originated in Old French and that its continuation in Dutch and German reflects an early medieval francophone population that subsequently switched to Germanic whilst holding on to their native pronunciation of word-final $*$-*k* in the west and $*$-*x* in the east. The continuation of the $*\bar{y}/*\bar{u}$ line in Dutch probably has the same background. This will be one of the cornerstones in the main argumentation of this chapter, to which we will return in section IV.12.

6. COASTAL DUTCH, WESTERN DUTCH, CENTRAL DUTCH, AND EASTERN DUTCH

Before attempting an explanation of the complex linguistic situation of Western Dutch, it is useful to take stock of the relevant data that were discussed earlier.

Along the Dutch and Flemish coast, **Coastal Dutch** was spoken, which to all intents and purposes is an early form of Frisian. Coastal Dutch had full-flung *i*-umlaut, which gave rise to the rounded front vowels $*y$, $*\bar{y}$, and $*\bar{ø}$ (from $*u$, $*\bar{u}$, and $*\bar{o}$, respectively). These lost rounding and became *i*/*e*, *ī*, and *ē*, respectively, probably well before AD 1000. Coastal Dutch disappeared. Vestiges survive in Western Dutch, which replaced it.

Western Dutch is found between the coastal strip and the westernmost boundary of secondary *i*-umlaut. Western Dutch underwent *i*-umlaut of short $*a$ to $*e$ (primary *i*-umlaut) but not of $*\bar{a}$, $*\bar{o}$, $*\bar{u}$, and $*au$ (secondary *i*-umlaut). Whether it underwent *i*-umlaut of short $*u$ is unclear: the *eu* [ø] in words like *sleutel* 'key' (German *Schlüssel* < $*slutilaz$) may be the result of *i*-umlaut or of spontaneous fronting, an issue that has continued to unsettle Dutch historical linguists.[33] The matter may be settled on the basis of Western Dutch words like *slotel* < $*slutilaz$, which is confined to local western dialects, and *molen* 'mill' < $*mulīn$ < Latin *molīna* and *koning* 'king' < *kuningaz, which entered the standard language. If Western Dutch had undergone *i*-umlaut of **u*, these forms, which contain an **i* in the second syllable but patently lack the effect of *i*-umlaut, should not have existed, but they do. The only way we can explain such forms is by supposing that *i*-umlaut did not affect **u* in Western Dutch and that fronting in words like *brug* [brᵊɣ] < **brygg* < **brugjō* was caused by spontaneous fronting (which did affect Western Dutch) rather than *i*-umlaut. As fronting was an erratic process, some words show it (e.g. *brug*), and others do not (e.g. *molen*, *koning*), and again others show it in some dialects but not in others (e.g. fronted *vul* as opposed to unfronted *vol* 'full' < **fullaz*). So Western Dutch developed rounded front vowels, but it did so as a result of spontaneous fronting rather than *i*-umlaut.

To the east of Western Dutch, in a wide band in the centre of the Netherlands and Belgium, lie dialects that were within reach of secondary *i*-umlaut (which connects them to Eastern Dutch) but also underwent spontaneous fronting to varying degrees (which connects them to Western Dutch). This intermediate zone will be called **Central Dutch**.

Because of their complexity it is useful to summarize the data concerning spontaneous fronting in Western and Central Dutch.

- Spontaneous fronting of **ū* to **ȳ* was originally widespread except along the coast (remnants of Coastal Dutch) and in Eastern Dutch. It is found in Western and Central Dutch. It links up with a similar development in Walloon French and was ultimately so successful that it made its way into the modern standard language.
- Spontaneous fronting of **ō* to **ø̄* (west) or **yø* (east) was originally widespread in the Western Dutch of Holland and Zeeland (but not in Flanders) and in Central Dutch, it seems. For reasons as yet unknown, it was not as successful in the long run, did not make it into the standard language, and survives only as traces in dialects that originally had it.
- Spontaneous fronting of short **u* to **y* shows an erratic distribution across the map, with a focus in Western Dutch, but it also occurs in Central Dutch, although it seems not to have penetrated as far east as fronting of **ū* and **ō*. The reason for that may be that the input of the rule, **u*, was a much rarer sound in the east than in the west. Examples of fronting did not penetrate the standard language apart from a few exceptions (such as *zeug* 'sow' < **sugō*).
- Spontaneous fronting of **au* > **ō* to *y(ə)* is limited to East Flanders and adjacent Southwest Brabant and never made an advance on the medieval or modern written language. Its age is unclear.

Finally, **Eastern Dutch**, which was spoken in the easternmost regions of the Netherlands and Belgium, underwent full-flung *i*-umlaut and preserved the rounded front vowels (*y*, ø) which had arisen as a result. It did not undergo spontaneous fronting. In terms of the development of its vowel system, Eastern Dutch is the same as German. Since they are so aberrant within the Germanic-speaking world, the absence in Western Dutch of secondary *i*-umlaut and the presence of spontaneous fronting in Western and Central Dutch, including its erratic nature, require an explanation.

7. WESTERN DUTCH AS AN INTERNALLY MOTIVATED SYSTEM

It has been a well-known fact among historical linguists of Dutch that the absence of secondary *i*-umlaut and the presence of spontaneous fronting define the profile of Western Dutch. One approach to explaining these characteristics is to be satisfied with the bland ascertainment that it simply underwent different sound laws than all other Germanic languages. To the extent that no two related languages ever have the exact same set of sound changes – otherwise they would be one and the same language – this is correct but also trivial and uninformative. Goossens (1980: 198–199) offers a subtler variant of this approach by stating that spontaneous fronting and *i*-umlaut interfered with each other, and as a result the *i*-umlaut rule was destroyed. The point can be illustrated by the examples *fullaz* 'full' and *slutilaz* 'key'. In Eastern Dutch and in Coastal Dutch, according to Goossens, these developed into *full* (no *i*-umlaut) and *slytil* (*i*-umlaut). The vowels in the first syllable became sufficiently distinct in quality that they remained distinct (the distinction was increased in Coastal Dutch by the unrounding of the type *slytil* to *slitil*, *sletil*). In Western Dutch, however, *fullaz* developed into something like *föll* by spontaneous fronting, Goossens proposes. Supposing that *slutilaz* originally underwent secondary *i*-umlaut in Western Dutch as well, it would become *slytil*. Now *ö* and *y* were different vowels as well but only subtly so: *ö* is a rounded central vowel, while *y* is a rounded front vowel.[34] One could therefore imagine that they were insufficiently different from one another and therefore merged: *fyll*, *slytil*, which later became *vul*, *sleutel*. Dialects within Western Dutch that did not have spontaneous fronting (remember that this was an erratic process, for whatever reason) would have had *full* (no fronting) as opposed to *slytil* (*i*-umlaut), just like Eastern Dutch. Such dialects might have reacted to dialects that had *fyll*, *slytil* by reasoning: 'where you say *fyll*, we say *full*, so where you say *slytil*, we'd better say *slutil*.' Accordingly, the latter is to be considered a hyperdialectism, which served to create a linguistic identity that was different from that of their neighbours, who said *fyll* and *slytil*. Finally, *full* and *slutil* developed into modern *vol*, *slotel*, respectively. Whatever the details, it was the phonetic proximity of the effects of spontaneous fronting and *i*-umlaut that obscured the effects of *i*-umlaut in Western Dutch and ultimately led to its demise.

A weak spot in the argument is that it is very difficult to lift this scenario beyond the status of a purely theoretical possibility: it is possible that this is what happened, but there is no indication that it actually did. Another weak spot is that the theory does nothing to explain why spontaneous fronting occurred at all. Neither does it account for Central Dutch, which had both secondary *i*-umlaut and spontaneous fronting, showing that the one does not exclude the other at all. Goossens himself qualifies his proposal as vague and strongly speculative (1980: 199).

8. WESTERN DUTCH AS THE PRODUCT OF CONTACT BETWEEN COASTAL DUTCH AND EASTERN DUTCH

A different approach to Western Dutch is based on the reasonable supposition, supported by history, that the Western Dutch area witnessed a confrontation between Frisians, who spoke Coastal Dutch, and Franks, who spoke Eastern Dutch, after about AD 700, when power gradually devolved from the Frisians to the Franks, and that Western Dutch is the product of this confrontation. In a broad sense, this approach has been popular among linguists of Dutch for many decades now (e.g. Heeroma 1951). With respect to *i*-umlaut, it has been updated and elaborated by Anthony Buccini (1988, 2010).

At first sight it seems rather surprising to attempt to explain the absence of secondary *i*-umlaut in Western Dutch as the consequence of contact between Coastal Dutch and Eastern Dutch, for both of those are characterized by the fact that they did have full-flung *i*-umlaut. The crucial point, however, is that Coastal Dutch (Frisian) and English had a different chronology of events from Eastern Dutch and German, which entailed that speakers of both dialect groups would have found it difficult to speak one another's language. By about AD 700 and for a number of centuries after that, secondary *i*-umlaut in Eastern Dutch and German was still in its initial stages. Proto-Germanic **hrugjaz* 'back' had become **hruggi*, which tended to become **hryggi* by *i*-umlaut. Old High German spells it *rucki*, as if *i*-umlaut had not occurred at all. It could do this because secondary *i*-umlaut was still an automatic rule which stated that any **u* followed by **i* in the next syllable became **y*. Consequently, the fronting of **u* to **y* in **hruggi* automatically ensued because there was an **i* in the second syllable. In formal terms this means that the phonological form (i.e. the mental form of the word for speakers at the time) was /hruggi/ and that there was an automatic rule of *i*-umlaut that operated on this mental form, turning it into the phonetic (pronounced) form [hryggi].

In Coastal Dutch (Frisian) and English, by contrast, secondary *i*-umlaut had already been completed by the seventh century at the latest, and the **i* and **j* that caused it had been lost by that time as a result of early simplifications that affected non-initial, unaccented syllables. So when the Frisians came into intensive contact with the Franks after 700, **hrugjaz* 'back, ridge' had already become Frisian **hrygg* (as in Old English *hrycg*): **u* had become

*y, and the **j* that was responsible had already been lost. That means that *i*-umlaut was no longer a rule that speakers could automatically apply given the appropriate phonetic context. In other words, *i*-umlaut had been phonemicized, and **/hrygg/* was the phonological (mental) form of the word, which was pronounced as **[hrygg]*. Probably in the course of the eighth century, **/hrygg/* was unrounded to **/hrigg/* or **/hregg/*, depending on the dialect within the Coastal Dutch area.[35]

So by the eighth to tenth centuries, the word for 'back' would be approximately **/hrigg/* or **/hregg/*, pronounced **[hrigg]* or **[hregg]*, in Coastal Dutch (Frisian), but it would be **/hruggi/*, pronounced [hryggi], in Eastern Dutch (Franconian). Coastal Dutch had phonemicized *i*-umlaut, so that the underlying rule had become obscure to its speakers, while Eastern Dutch still preserved the phonetic rule of *i*-umlaut, which automatically turned the phoneme /u/ into the sound [y] because of the /i/ in the second syllable. In order to bring out the differences between Coastal Dutch and Eastern Dutch on a wider front, a larger list of reconstructions is useful which also incorporates other changes typical of the two dialects at the time.

Coastal Dutch and Eastern Dutch

original vowel	*i*-umlaut?	original form before *i*-umlaut	Eastern Dutch (eighth–tenth centuries)	Coastal Dutch (eighth–tenth centuries)	English cognate or meaning
*a	yes	**mari*	/meri/	/mere/	*mere*
	no	**dagaz*	/dag/	/dæg/	*day*
*u	yes	**hruggjaz*	/hruggi/ [hryggi]	/hrigg/	*ridge*
	no	**wulfaz*	/wolf/	/wulf/	*wolf*
*ā	yes	**skāri-*	/skāri/ [skǣri]	/skēr/	*shears*
	no	**slāpan*	/slāpan/	/slǣpan/	*to sleep*
*ō	yes	**fōtiz*	/fuoti/ [fyøti]	/fēt/	*feet*
	no	**fōtz*	/fuot/	/fōt/	*foot*
*ū	yes	**hūdjan*	/hūdjan/ [hȳdjan]	/hīdan/	*to hide*
	no	**hūsan*	/hūs/	/hūs/	*house*
*ai	yes	**haiθī*	/heiθi/	/hēθe/	*heath*
	no	**haimaz*	/hēm/	/hām/	*home*
*au	yes	**raukjan*	/rōkjan/ [rȫkjan]	/rēkan/	(to smoke, e.g. fish)
	no	**hlaupan*	/hlōpan/	/hlāpan/	*to leap*

It can be observed that the consonants in both dialects are identical but the vowels are different in almost all forms. Most important, as we saw, Eastern Dutch still possessed a productive, automatic rule of *i*-umlaut that dictated that e.g. /fuoti/ should be pronounced /fyøti/, which was alien to Coastal Dutch. Closely connected with this difference is the fact that Coastal Dutch had changed *i and *j as well as a number of other vowels in unstressed (second) syllables while Eastern Dutch still preserved them.

Buccini's idea starts from the obvious assumption that speakers of Western Dutch who wanted to speak Eastern Dutch, which was becoming the dominant language, were confronted with those differences and had to find a way to deal with them. He suggests that the Eastern Dutch rule of *i*-umlaut, like any abstract phonological rule, was difficult to acquire for speakers whose first language was Coastal Dutch, and that Coastal Dutch speakers had difficulty acquiring the difference between *i and *e in unstressed syllables because this had been lost in Coastal Dutch in favour of *e. This confused state then led to much variation and simplification in the variety of Eastern Dutch spoken by people whose mother tongue was Coastal Dutch. Thus, failure to grasp the *i*-umlaut rule behind Eastern Dutch singular *[fuot] – plural *[fyøti] 'foot – feet' and difficulty in pronouncing unstressed final [i] in the plural of that word would have led Coastal Dutch learners of Eastern Dutch to simplify this pair to something like either *[fuot] – *[fuote] or *[fyøt] – *[fyøte] 'foot – feet', where [uo] and [yø] could end up in the wrong place – wrong, that is, from the perspective of a speaker of Eastern Dutch. Usually, it was the non-umlauted variant ([fuot] in the example) that ultimately prevailed because that was closer to one of the native Coastal Dutch forms (viz. the singular [fōt]) and because [fyøt], with its unfamiliar rounded front vowels, was alien to Coastal Dutch.

One would think that Coastal Dutch speakers might have wanted to avoid the rounded front vowels of the type [y, ø] in Eastern Dutch altogether because those were alien to Coastal Dutch and therefore difficult for them to pronounce. This would help explain why Eastern Dutch forms like /fuoljan/, which was pronounced [fyøljan], reverted to [fuol]- (or [fōl]-) in the mouths of speakers of Coastal Dutch, the effect being absence of *i*-umlaut in such forms. Yet what we find is more complicated than this, for Western Dutch is full of rounded front vowels: after all, it underwent spontaneous fronting. So how did Coastal Dutch speakers who wanted to speak Eastern Dutch acquire the rounded front vowels that were so alien to Coastal Dutch? In order to get a handle on this issue one might suggest that Coastal Dutch speakers considered rounded front vowels as flags of Frankishness and in a bid to identify with the dominant Franconian-speaking population exaggerated their use of them. This mechanism explains spontaneous fronting as a hyper-Franconianism used by people who wanted to assimilate to Frankish society but got this aspect slightly wrong.

The great advantage of Buccini's ideas is that they have the potential to create enough linguistic chaos to explain the situation that is attested in Western Dutch: unfamiliarity amongst speakers of Coastal Dutch with the living *i*-umlaut rule and with the rounded front vowels of Eastern Dutch gave rise to varieties without *i*-umlaut and without rounded front vowels, while the imperfect acquisition of where and when rounded front vowels should occur in Eastern Dutch gave rise to varieties with spontaneous fronting. Add a couple of centuries of dialect mixture to confuse the dialectal map even further and out pops Western Dutch.

A disadvantage is that the scenario is fairly coarse. It does not explain why spontaneous fronting of *ō, as in *brōθēr > Middle Dutch *brueder* 'brother', is found both west and east of the umlaut boundaries, with a particular focus on Brabant, while spontaneous fronting of short *u, as in *sunuz > *zeun* 'son', has its epicentre in the west. Nor does it account for the fact that spontaneous fronting of *ū prevailed both east and west of the umlaut boundaries, while that of *ō was gradually eliminated, even in cases where Eastern Dutch supported the rounded front vowel, as in *fōljan > *fyøljan 'to feel' (Eastern Dutch *vulen* [y], *veulen* [ø], Western Dutch *voelen* [u]).

Weighing the pros and cons of Buccini's proposal is not so much a matter of trying to decide whether it is right or wrong on its own merits but rather one of considering whether an alternative proposal can be suggested that shares its advantages but not its disadvantages and that offers a more exact explanation of the extraordinary features of Western Dutch. Such a proposal is indeed at hand.[36] It involves the presence of a contact language that has hitherto remained in the shadows: medieval spoken Latin of the Old French type.

9. SPOKEN LATIN IN THE LOW COUNTRIES

On the basis of tribal and personal names, it is possible to determine that when Caesar conquered Gaul between 58 and 51 BC and subjugated the tribes that were living in present-day Belgium and the Netherlands, he met with speakers of Germanic and Celtic. It is often difficult to decide whether individual names are Celtic or Germanic, but by and large the evidence suggests that in Belgium and the southern part of the Netherlands up to the estuary of the Rhine and the Maas predominantly Celtic was spoken, while further north it was mainly Germanic. During the following half century, tribes which originated in present-day Hessen (Germany) moved into the area of the Lower Rhine and Maas, which was already inhabited by the Menapii in the west (Flanders, Zeeland) and the Eburones to their east (North Brabant, Limburg, and the Guelder river area in the Netherlands and the adjacent Belgian provinces of Antwerp and Limburg). In this linguistically mixed Germanic and Celtic area, the tribe of the Batavi played a prominent role as defenders of Roman power and as a recruiting ground for Roman soldiers.[37] The Batavians continued to do so for the best part of three centuries, until they became submerged in the wars and political chaos of the second half of the third century.

The boundaries of the Roman Empire stabilized in the form of the fortresses of the *limes* on the Lower Rhine. The area was heavily militarized, and therefore Roman influence must have been intense and would have led to widespread Celtic-Latin and Germanic-Latin bilingualism. Important evidence to support this scenario comes from the Batavian lands of Gelderland and North Brabant, a densely settled, predominantly rural zone during the first and second centuries AD. Rural settlements consisted of traditional farmsteads, which showed few outward signs of Romanization. What is special about these settlements is the large amount of so-called seal boxes that have been found in them. Seal boxes are small copper boxes which contained a waxed imprint that was used to seal written documents. Those documents probably were private letters that were exchanged between Batavian soldiers, who served in auxiliary units all over the Empire, and their family and friends at home. It has been calculated that almost every single family had one or two of its members under arms. Their period of service was twenty-five years, and most veterans returned home afterwards, so there was every reason for them to keep in touch with the home front; letters offered the only practical means of doing so, and Latin was the only available medium in which to write them. The finds indicate that a large segment of the local rural population in the Batavian lands was capable of reading and writing Latin, and that this was a skill that people acquired in the army. This degree of linguistic Romanization of everyone directly or indirectly connected with the Roman army must have had profound effects on the everyday spoken language to the extent that people were probably actively bilingual. In the course of the three long centuries between Caesar's conquest of the Low Countries and the collapse of Roman power in the area around 250, the native language may well have been replaced by Latin.[38]

What is not clear is whether the spoken Latin of the Batavian area survived the disappearance of Batavian identity during the troubles of the late third century. Derks and Roymans (2002: 103) stress the 'strong discontinuity in habitation in late-Roman times and the Migration period, combined with the massive influx of new Germanic-speaking groups', which 'brought about a clean break in the Latin linguistic heritage in the region, which ultimately prevented it from being transmitted to the Middle Ages'. Those newcomers are associated with the name of the Franks in Roman sources. What is certain is that the Roman *limes* never recovered. In their stead came fortifications further south, along the Roman road that connected Cologne via Maastricht and Tongeren with Bavai on towards Boulogne-sur-Mer. North of the road, periodic military altercations between Rome and the immigrants lasted throughout the fourth century. Gradually the Franks formed a buffer state that protected the Empire against renewed immigrations and attacks from the north until well into the fifth century. This far north, Roman activity became ever more limited, and the Franconian buffer state gradually took over Roman strongholds. South of the fortified road Roman life resumed and even flourished until the early fifth century. It is significant that the road more or less corresponds to the modern linguistic boundary between Dutch and French.

During the fifth century, as Roman power waned and Franconian pressure grew, various small kingdoms under Franconian rulers were established in the present-day Netherlands, Belgium, and northern France. This area was inhabited by a mixed Latin- (Romance-) and Germanic-speaking population. Bilingualism must have been widespread. In the south, Romance speakers probably greatly outnumbered Germanic speakers, so that in the course of the medieval and early modern period Germanic gradually disappeared. In the north, Germanic dominated and Romance disappeared. There is a wealth of toponymic evidence that supports the survival of Germanic pockets south of the modern linguistic boundary and Romance pockets north of it.[39] Interesting outliers that demonstrate that Romance survived well into the medieval period in areas that later on were solidly Dutch can be found in Flanders. Gysseling (1981: 114) draws attention to the name pairs Dutch *Temse*—French *Tamise* (southwest of Antwerp) and *Drongen*— *Tronchiennes* (west of Gent): the former are the ancient Germanic and the latter the ancient Romance versions of the same names. *Walem*, near Mechelen (province of Antwerp), goes back to an early medieval Germanic *Walha-haim* 'village of *Walhōs*', that is, of speakers of Romance. The same element is found much further north, in *Waalwijk* (North Brabant, near the Maas; unless it contains the word *waal* 'pool') and in a ninth-century place name *Walahheim* somewhere in Frisia (that is, somewhere near the estuary of the Rhine and the Maas), which clearly reflects *Walha-haim*.[40] Such names would make sense only in an environment that was predominantly Germanic-speaking.

Such northern outposts of Romance speech offer no more than tantalizing glimpses of a lost linguistic landscape and raise more questions than they can answer. How many Romance speakers were there so far north, and what percentage of the entire population did they form? Did they descend from Latin-speaking Batavians who survived the collapse of the third century? Or were they the linguistic remnants of the Romanized Franconian buffer state of the fourth and fifth centuries, which saw the prominent Franks Bauto and Arbogast rise to the highest military ranks the Roman Empire had on offer? Or does their origin lie later still, when Romance speakers moved north as part of a reflux during the Merovingian period? Such questions cannot at present be answered. For all that, it is important to stress what we do know: that Romance speakers did indeed live far north of the present linguistic boundary during the early medieval period. This is the narrow basis on which a much stronger linguistic argument can be built.

10. NORTHERN OLD FRENCH VOWEL SYSTEMS

The Late Latin of the northwestern Roman Empire that survived and presently forms the northern fringe of the French language bordering on the Dutch-speaking area developed into two major dialects: Picardian in the west and Walloon in the east. Picardian and Walloon were already different from one another during the early Middle Ages. In order to understand the history of Dutch, it will be necessary to pay attention to the development of the vowel system in those two Old French dialects.

The starting point is the Late Latin (Early Romance) vowel system as it had developed by the fifth century in the Roman west:

A		
i		*u*
e		*o*
ɛ		*ɔ*
	a	

This system forms the basic system of Romance languages such as Spanish, Catalan-Provençal, Rhaeto-Romance, French, and most varieties of Italian. Vowels could be long or short depending on two factors:

- stress
- the structure of the syllable.

With a few well-defined exceptions, stressed vowels in open syllables (i.e. vowels that were word-final or followed by a single consonant plus a vowel) were long, and all others were short.

Since the difference between long and short vowels was governed by transparent rules, vowel quantity (i.e. length or shortness) was not phonemic. This changed when, on the way to Old French, the quality of the long vowels became more and more different from the quality of short vowels. The basic system that underlies French reflects the initial stage of this change, showing that the long mid vowels (*$*\bar{e}$, *$*\bar{\varepsilon}$, *$*\bar{o}$, *$*\bar{ɔ}$) had become diphthongs (*$*ei$, *$*i\varepsilon$, *$*ou$, *$*uɔ$, respectively):

B	long vowels		short vowels	
	ī	*ū*	*ĭ*	*ŭ*
	ei	*ou*	*e*	*o*
	iɛ	*uɔ*	*ɛ*	*ɔ*
	ā		*a*	

At this point, dialectal differences began to materialize which drew the short and the long vowels still further apart. Before the tenth century, when the Old French written record sets in, the vowel system had developed in three different ways in what was to become Picardian and Walloon:

C3		C2		C1	
long vowels in Picardian		long vowels in West Walloon		long vowels in East Walloon	
ī	ȳ	ī	ȳ	ī	ū
ei	ou	ei	ou	ei	ou
īɛ	yø	īɛ	uɔ	iɛ	uɔ
	ā > ɛ̄		ā > ɛ̄		ā > ɛ̄
short vowels in Picardian		short vowels in West Walloon		short vowels in East Walloon	
ĭ	y̆	ĭ	y̆	ĭ	ŭ
ĕ	ŏ	ĕ	ŏ	ĕ	ŏ
ɛ̆	ɔ̆	ɛ̆	ɔ̆	ɛ̆	ɔ̆
	ă		ă		ă

The diagrams show that the back vowels *ū, *ŭ and the diphthong *uɔ could be fronted to *ȳ, *y̆, *yø, respectively. All three were fronted in Picardian, two in West Walloon, and none in East Walloon. Long *ā was fronted in all dialects of Old French. Examples that illustrate the developments can be found in the following diagram.

Vowel developments between Latin and Old French

Classical Latin	A	B	C1	C2	C3	Old French	meaning
rīpa	*rība	*rība	*rīve	*rīve	*rīve	rive	'bank'
scrīptum	*skrīpto	*skrīttu	*eskrīt	*eskrīt	*eskrīt	escrit	'written'
nĭvem	*nēve	*neive	*neif	*neif	*neif	neif	'snow'
sĭccum	*sĕkko	*sĕkku	*sĕk	*sĕk	*sĕk	sec	'dry'
vĕtus	*vĕtos	*viɛtus	*viɛts	*viɛts	*viɛts	viez	'old'
sĕptem	*sĕpte	*sɛtte	*sɛt	*sɛt	*sɛt	set	'seven'
făba	*fāva	*fāva	*fēve	*fēve	*fēve	feve	'bean'
grăssum	*grăsso	*grăssu	*grăs	*grăs	*grăs	gras	'fat'
bŏvem	*bɔ̆ve	*buɔve	*buɔf	*buɔf	*byøf	buef	'cow'
pŏrta	*pɔ̆rta	*pɔ̆rta	*pɔ̆rte	*pɔ̆rte	*pɔ̆rte	porte	'door'
flōrēs	*flōres	*floures	*flours	*flours	*flours	flours	'flowers'
multum	*mŏlto	*mŏlto	*mŏlt	*mŏlt	*mŏlt	molt	'much'
ūsum	*ūso	*ūso	*ūs	*ȳs	*ȳs	us	'use'
nūllum	*nūllo	*nūllo	*nūl	*nȳl	*nȳl	nul	'none'

A = Late Latin, B = Early Gallo-Romance, C1 = Old East Walloon, C2 = Old West Walloon, C3 = Old Picardian. For these languages, phonetic forms are given. Spontaneous fronting is indicated by shading. The Old French column contains spelled (not phonetic) forms in the Francian dialect, which was spoken around Paris.

All changes with respect to the original system B come under the heading of spontaneous fronting.

11. SPONTANEOUS FRONTING IN NORTHERN FRENCH AND IN DUTCH

Close inspection reveals that there is a relationship between the geography of spontaneous fronting of rounded back vowels in Walloon and Picardian and in adjacent Dutch dialects:

- East Walloon did not undergo any spontaneous fronting of rounded vowels; neither did its northern neighbours, the Eastern Dutch dialects of Dutch Limburg, eastern Belgian Limburg and eastern North Brabant.
- West Walloon underwent spontaneous fronting of *$\bar{u}$ and *$\breve{u}$; the neighbouring eastern Central Dutch dialects underwent fronting of *$\bar{u}$. They probably did not undergo fronting of short *$\breve{u}$ because that had been opened to *o before fronting could affect it (see sections IV.5, IV.6). The Walloon boundary between western *$\bar{y}$ and eastern *$\bar{u}$ is continued in Dutch (see section IV.5).
- Picardian underwent spontaneous fronting of *$\bar{u}$, *$\breve{u}$, and *$u\textschwa$; so did the neighbouring Central and Western Dutch dialects in a wide band between central Belgium/the Netherlands and the coast: *$\bar{u}$ was affected everywhere; *$\breve{u}$ where it had not become *o, thus more in the west than in the east. The diphthong *uo was affected, too, but the scanty remains of that development render a detailed geographical account impossible. What seems clear, however, is that in the Central Dutch dialects *uo had developed from earlier *$\bar{o}$, so that in this area words like Proto-Germanic *$g\bar{o}daz$ 'good' > *$guod$ > *$gy\o d$ > Middle Dutch *guet* were affected. In the Western Dutch dialect of Flanders, however, *$\bar{o}$ appears to have become *ou rather than *uo (see section IV.5 above). Here it was the product of the old diphthong *au that came closest to *uo, and it is this that became *$y\o$ > $y(\textschwa)$ in East Flanders (e.g. *$baumaz$ > *$boum$ > *$buom$ > *$by\o m$ > $by(\textschwa)m$ 'tree').

The correspondences between these neighbouring French and Dutch dialects are so exact that they cannot reasonably be ascribed to chance. What does not fit, however, is the behaviour of long *$\bar{a}$, which became *$\bar{\varepsilon}$ in all French dialects but not in their Dutch neighbours. It is conceivable that *$\bar{a}$ in Dutch had already become *$\bar{\jmath}$, as in almost all modern dialects except those of Holland, and that this was so different from French $*\bar{\varepsilon}$ that they could not be attracted to one another. Apart from this one failed correspondence, the match between early Dutch and French spontaneous fronting is near perfect.

The similarity between early medieval Dutch and French extends beyond the frontings to the entire vowel system, as a perusal of the following diagrams shows.[41] The effects of secondary *i*-umlaut on Dutch will be considered later, so they are not incorporated here.

Vowel systems in the first millennium (prior to secondary i-umlaut)

(1) Eastern Dutch (Limburg Dutch is taken as a model)

East Walloon	Limburg Dutch			East Walloon	Limburg Dutch		
Short Vowels				Long Vowels			
$\bar{\imath}$	$\breve{u}$	$\breve{\imath}$		$\bar{\imath}$	$\bar{u}$	$\bar{\imath}$	$\bar{u}$
$\breve{e}$	$\breve{o}$	$\breve{e}^1$	$\breve{o}^2$	*ei*	*ou*	*ei*[3]	*ou*[3]
$\breve{\varepsilon}$	$\mathfrak{o}$	$\breve{\varepsilon}^1$	$\mathfrak{z}^2$	*iɛ/ī*[6]	*uɔ/ū*[6]	*ie/ē*[4]	*uo/ō*[4]
	a		a	$\bar{a} > \bar{\varepsilon}$		$\bar{a} > \mathfrak{z}^5$	

[1] $*\breve{e}$ is the product of (primary) *i*-umlaut of $*\breve{a}$, which affected all medieval Germanic languages; it was initially distinct from $*\breve{\varepsilon}$ < Proto-Germanic $*e$ but later merged with it.

[2] Closed $*\breve{o}$ or [ʊ] is the product of Proto-Germanic $*\breve{u}$; open $*\mathfrak{z}$ arose from Proto-Germanic $*\breve{u}$ through *a*-umlaut and was reinforced by Latin loanwords containing $*\breve{o}$.

[3] Eastern Dutch agrees with the rest of Dutch in showing $*ei$, $*ou$ as continuations of Proto-Germanic $*ai$ and $*au$, respectively; later developments to $*ei/*\bar{e}$ and to $*ou/\bar{o}$ in Limburg are governed by *i*-umlaut and the nature of the following consonant (as in High German; see e.g. Van Loon 1986: 50).

[4] $*ie/\bar{e}$ is the product of Proto-Germanic closed $*\bar{e}$ (so-called $\bar{e}_2$) and of $*eo$ that had developed from $*eu$ as a result of *a*-umlaut; $*uo/\bar{o}$ reflects Proto-Germanic $*\bar{o}$. While Central Dutch dialects go along with German in showing $*ie$, $*uo$ instead of $*\bar{e}$, $*\bar{o}$, Eastern Dutch either preserved the long vowels or, like Walloon, turned the diphthongs into long vowels.

[5] $*\bar{a}$ developed from Proto-Germanic $*\ae$ (the latter was preserved in contemporary Coastal Dutch, Frisian, and Old English). This $*\bar{a}$ developed into $*\mathfrak{z}$ in most Dutch dialects.

[6] In Walloon, $*ie$ and $*uo$ developed into $*\bar{\imath}$, $*\bar{u}$, which nowadays are /ī, ū/ (Remacle 1948: 47–49, 60, 61, who dates the development to the twelfth century or earlier)

As the diagram bears out, Eastern Dutch, like Walloon, is first and foremost a conservative dialect, at least in the first millennium, which we are dealing with here. Since Eastern Dutch and Walloon changed so little, it is impossible to state that they developed in tandem. But things are different as we move towards the west.

(2) Eastern Central Dutch

West Walloon		eastern Central Dutch		West Walloon		eastern Central Dutch	
ī	ў	ī	(ў)¹	ī	ý	ī	ý
ě	ŏ	ě	(ŏ)¹	ei	ou	ei²	ou²
ɛ̃	ɔ	ɛ̃	ɔ̃	iɛ/ī	uɔ/ū	ie³	uo³
	a		a		ā > ɛ̃		ā > ɔ̃

[1] Both *ў and *ŏ go back to Proto-Germanic *ŭ. In the eastern Central Dutch dialects, fronting to ў is rare, and opening to *ŏ is more common.

[2] *ei < *ai; *ou < *au; they become ē (but by *i*-umlaut ei) and ō, respectively, during the later Middle Ages.

[3] *ie < *ē, *eo; *uo < *ō.

This model is representative of Dutch dialects in which originally only long *ū underwent spontaneous fronting, and just possibly also short *ŭ in as far as it had not become *ŏ (which it usually did in the east). This type of Dutch conforms exactly to the West Walloon vowel system, apart from *ā > *ɛ̃ (Walloon), *ɔ̃ (Dutch).

(3) Central Dutch

Picardian		Central Dutch		Picardian		Central Dutch	
ī	ў	ī	(ў)¹	ī	ý	ī	ý
ě	ŏ	ě	(ŏ)¹	ei	ou	ei²	ou²
ɛ̃	ɔ	ɛ̃	ɔ̃	iɛ	yø	ie³	yø³
	a		a		ā > ɛ̃		ā > ɔ̃

[1] Both *ў and *ŏ go back to Proto-Germanic *ŭ. In the Central Dutch dialects, fronting to ў is rare, and opening to *ŏ is more common.

[2] *ei < *ai; *ou < *au; they become ē (but by *i*-umlaut ei) and ō, respectively, during the later Middle Ages.

[3] *ie < *ē, *eo; *yø < *uo < *ō.

The third model represents the Central Dutch dialects of Belgian Brabant, Antwerp, and Dutch central and western Brabant as well as western Gelderland. They show spontaneous fronting of *ū to *ý; rarely of *ŭ to *ў because *ŭ had usually become *ŏ; and generally of *uo to *yø, although this survives only rarely in the later medieval and modern written record and in the modern dialect, a discrepancy to which we will return in section IV.13. This type of Dutch conforms exactly to the Picardian vowel system, apart from *ā > *ɛ̃ (Picardian), *ɔ̃ (Dutch).

(4) Western Dutch: Flemish

Picardian		Flemish		Picardian		Flemish	
ĭ	y̆	ĭ	(y̆)	ī	ȳ	ī	ȳ
ĕ	ŏ	ĕ	(ŏ)	ei	ou	ei	ou
ɛ̆	ɔ	ɛ̆	ɔ̃	iɛ	yø	ie	yø
	a		a		ā > ɛ̄		ā > ɔ̃

The Flemish system is identical to the Central Dutch system, but it has a different origin: Flemish *ou does not derive from *au, as elsewhere, but from *ō; and Flemish *yø < *uo does not derive from *ō but from *au (see section IV.5). In Flemish, the proportion of words that show spontaneous fronting *ŭ to *y̆ (rather than opening of *ŭ to *ŏ) increases as one moves further west. The resemblance of the Flemish vowel system of the first millennium to that of Picardian is striking.

12. ROMANCE FRONTING AND GERMANIC *i*-UMLAUT

The observed similarities are such that any attempt to explain the Old Dutch vowel system without reference to its Old French neighbour can be regarded as flawed, because any such attempt is based on the highly unlikely assumption that the similarities are accidental. What, then, can be the explanation for this extraordinary pair dance of French and Dutch?

Spontaneous fronting has a completely different status in French than in Dutch. In Germanic, fronting is normally a consequence of *i*-umlaut, which does not exist in Romance. Spontaneous fronting is typical of a number of Romance languages, and of none more so than French, while in Germanic it characterizes only a tiny portion of the Dutch–German continuum. So there can be little doubt that if spontaneous fronting in Dutch and French are connected phenomena, it is French rather than Dutch that started it.

If spontaneous fronting in Dutch stems from French, the question is how the transfer took place. There are two main scenarios that might be considered.

I. A group of bilingual speakers somewhere in the early medieval Dutch–French contact zone adapted the phonetics of their form of Old Dutch to Old French because Old French phonetics signalled a desirable socio-economic or socio-political status, which made people want to 'sound French'. Since in Old French fronting was a property of a particular set of vowels (*ū, *ŭ, *uɔ > *ȳ, *y̆, *yø spontaneously), while in Germanic fronting resulted from *i*-umlaut (any back vowel became a rounded front vowel before *i, *j in the following syllable), sounding

French meant abandoning the Germanic *i*-umlaut rule in favour of the French spontaneous fronting rule. This type of Gallo-Dutch became so popular that it spread among monolingual speakers of Dutch further north.

Given the right sociolinguistic setting, which rewarded people who sounded French with higher status and greater wealth and influence, scenario I could work with just a small bilingual community to start it off.

Although possible in theory, scenario I is unlikely to be correct in practice for the following reasons.

(1) In the early medieval period, the language of prestige in the area was Germanic rather than Romance. Ruling Frankish dynasts made a point of flagging their Germanic identity by religiously sticking to Germanic names, such as *Chlodovic*, *Chlothar*, *Chilperik*, and *Childebert*. The Franconian *Lex Salica* leaves no doubts about the importance of Germanic-Franconian traditions to this elite. Under those circumstances, one would expect to see speakers of Romance adopting a Germanic accent rather than the other way around.

(2) The prestige inherent in scenario I presupposes that a particular type of Old French was considered elitist or otherwise worth copying, not just any variety of Old French. Translated to a more modern setting, nineteenth-century speakers of Dutch who wished to associate with French culture for reasons of prestige chose Parisian French rather than Picardian, Walloon, or Burgundian French, because choosing any of the latter would not have had the desired sociolinguistic effect – quite the reverse, actually. Although we know next to nothing about the relative prestige of varieties of French during the early Middle Ages, it is a matter of common sense that they cannot all have conveyed the same degree of prestige. And although we may grant that the early medieval world operated on a smaller and less centralized scale than today's, the spread of Old French fronting in Dutch shows a disturbing absence of any centralization. The only structure we see is one of geography: the transfer of fronting from Old French to Dutch follows a distinct south-to-north pattern in no less than four distinct zones:
    - East Walloon–Eastern Dutch: no fronting
    - West Walloon–eastern Central Dutch: fronting of $*\bar{u}$ (perhaps also $*\breve{u}$)
    - Picardian–Central Dutch: fronting of $*\bar{u}$, $*\breve{u}$, $*uo$
    - Picardian–Western Dutch (Flemish): fronting of $*\bar{u}$, $*\breve{u}$, $*uo$, but Flemish $*uo$ has a different origin from Central Dutch $*uo$

A uniform Old French model that was copied into Dutch is therefore lacking. The south-to-north isoglosses that separate the four zones

suggest that different centres were active in spreading and adopting
Old French fronting in Dutch.

So it seems that spontaneous fronting in Dutch was probably not a result of
the adoption of prestigious Old French phonetics by a Germanic-speaking
population. We need a different scenario.

II. A Romance-speaking population that was present in the Low Coun-
     tries (see section IV.9) shifted to speaking Germanic when, sometime
     in the early medieval period, Germanic had become the language of
     the socio-political elite. This population replaced the Germanic rule
     of secondary *i*-umlaut, which was foreign to Romance, with the Old
     French rule of spontaneous fronting of $*\bar{u}$, $*\breve{u}$, and $*u\mathfrak{o}$. Spontane-
     ous fronting accordingly is an Old French substratum feature in
     Dutch.

Scenario II does not suffer from the disadvantages of scenario I. Language
shift favoured Germanic over Romance, which agrees with the elite status
of Germanic in the early medieval Franconian regions. The four distinct
zones, with isoglosses running from south to north across the linguistic
boundary of French and Dutch, suggest an ancient Romance dialect area
whose northern part, though overlaid by Germanic, preserved the Romance
isoglosses.

The Dutch area of spontaneous fronting formed a barrier to Germanic
secondary *i*-umlaut, which apparently moved in from the east in the later
first millennium. Where speakers of East Walloon shifted to Eastern Dutch,
no spontaneous fronting occurred, so *i*-umlaut could apply here in the same
way as further east, in German. Where speakers of West Walloon had shifted
to eastern Central Dutch, only $*\bar{u} > *\bar{y}$ was affected by spontaneous fronting with certainty. This did interfere with *i*-umlaut, but only in a limited
sense: all vowels could undergo it except $*\bar{y}$ because this already was a front
vowel. The interference was strongest where speakers of Picardian shifted to
Central Dutch and Flemish, for there $*\bar{u}$, $*\breve{u}$, $*uo$ had already been fronted
to $*\bar{y}$, $*\breve{y}$, $*y\o$, so that the only vowels that could be touched by *i*-umlaut
were Dutch short $*\breve{o}$, which was very rare; short $*\breve{a}$ in as far as this had
escaped earlier primary *i*-umlaut, which was rare as well; and $*ou$ (Central
Dutch) or $*\bar{o}$ (Flemish). Hence the further west one moves in Dutch, the
more spontaneous fronting had occurred, and the more *i*-umlaut peters out.
Not only are words affected by *i*-umlaut rarer in Central Dutch than in
Eastern Dutch, but the morphological status of *i*-umlaut is very different. It
is a well-known fact among dialectologists of Dutch that although Central
Dutch did undergo *i*-umlaut, it did not adopt the morphological role it had
in Eastern Dutch. In Eastern Dutch, for instance, *i*-umlaut was exploited
to distinguish singular from plural nouns (German *Fuss*, plural *Füsse* 'foot,
feet') and to distinguish the second and third person singular present of

certain verbs from other persons (German *ich fahre, du fährst, sie fährt* 'I drive, you drive, she drives'). This type of morphological *i*-umlaut is absent in Central Dutch, which suggests a more marginal role of *i*-umlaut here than in the east.

13. LANGUAGE AND HISTORY IN THE LOW COUNTRIES

The linguistic data suggest that the southern half of the Netherlands and the northern half of Belgium, which were linguistically Germanic at least from the later medieval period onwards, had witnessed a language shift from Romance to Germanic, the result being Central and Western Dutch. Spontaneous fronting in Dutch is the smoking gun that points to this shift. Eastern Dutch did not undergo spontaneous fronting, hence cannot be shown to have resulted from a language shift on this count. Nor, by the way, can it be shown not to have undergone a language shift: its southern neighbour, East Walloon, lacked spontaneous fronting, so if Limburg Dutch was the result of a shift, this cannot be argued on the basis of spontaneous fronting. But there are other features, which are attested in almost all of Dutch, including Eastern Dutch, that indeed suggest a Romance substratum.

- The development of word-final *-k* to *-x* in southeastern Dutch is one we met earlier (see III.4.1).
- So is the absence of aspiration of voiceless plosives that formed the beginning of our investigation (see IV.1).
- Dutch is the earliest among the Germanic languages to remodel its system of vowel quantity on Romance.

This requires a brief exposition. Classical Latin distinguished between phonemically long and short vowels. Latin *rīpa* 'river bank' had a long /ī/ and *vĭdet* 'sees' and *sĭccus* a short /ĭ/, and there was nothing in the phonetic context that predicted that this should be so: length and shortness were inherent qualities of the vowels /ī/ and /ĭ/. In Late Latin, this situation changed along the lines explained in IV.10 above: all vowels in stressed open syllables (i.e. word-finally or before single consonant plus vowel) became long, and all others became short. At the same time, slight phonetic differences in the quality of old long /ī/ and old short /ĭ/ became prominent: long /ī/ was close [i], while short /ĭ/ was a slightly more open [ɪ].[42] Accordingly, *rīpa* became Late Latin *r*[i:]*pa*, while *vĭdet* became **v*[ɪ:]*det* and *sĭccus* became **s*[ɪ]*ccus*. Similar changes affected all Latin vowels. A large number of languages that came into contact with Latin succumbed to a similar fate: Albanian, Slavic, British Celtic, and also Germanic. The British Celtic case, which involved a language shift, is discussed briefly in chapter II, section 5.1. All Germanic languages ultimately passed through a similar restructuring of their vowel system, but by far the first language to do so was Dutch: the earliest Middle Dutch sources of the twelfth century show its effects. How much older it is is unclear: it may go undetected in our scanty Old Dutch sources, whose orthography does not mark vowel length. We now have a possible answer to the question why this restructuring of the vowel system hit Dutch much earlier than the other Germanic languages: because the new vowel system was introduced into Dutch by a language shift from Old French to Germanic.

It is possible to be more specific about the time and place of the language shift of Old French to Dutch. As to date, the Dutch shift is evidently later than the language shift that was responsible for introducing the High German consonant shift into German. The latter involved a very early form of Romance which still distinguished the affricates *kxʲ, *tsʲ, *pfʲ and can be dated approximately to the fifth or sixth century. The Dutch shift involves a type of vowel system that is identical with the Picardian dialect as attested in tenth- and eleventh-century Old French written sources. It may well be that the Picardian vowel system is a few centuries older than that: we have no way of knowing this. A reasonable estimate of the date of the Romance-to-Dutch shift is therefore between the eighth and eleventh century. Although the date range is wide, it strongly suggests that the language shift was connected with the Carolingian power surge of the eighth and ninth centuries that led to the destruction of Frisian overlordship of the estuary of the Rhine and Maas.

The ancient Romance dialect boundaries that separated Picardian from Walloon, and East Walloon from West Walloon, survived the shift to Germanic. This suggests that a relatively stable, sedentary population shifted from Romance to Germanic: the language changed, but the people by and large did not. Whether it was a large or small population is hard to say, but that they were farmers rather than roving soldiers is more than likely.

The fertile soils along the Maas and Rhine in what is nowadays the Dutch province of Gelderland and the excellent transport possibilities which the rivers offered had always attracted farmers. Here the Romanized Batavians lived during the Roman period (see section IV.9), and the area must have regained its importance when the chaos of the late third century was over and the Romans and early Franks alternately held sway during the fourth and fifth centuries. This is a region where Central Dutch developed, from which we can now deduce that Late Latin was spoken here until well into the early medieval period. This assumption is supported by toponymic evidence. Blok (1981: 149–151) pointed out that place names in -*heem* < *haimaz* 'homestead' are typical of Franconian settlements dating between the sixth and tenth century. Such names are very frequent in the Low Countries, but they are very scarce in the Gelderland river area. At the same time, this is an area where many prehistoric and

Roman-age names survive, such as *Tricht* (Latin *trajectum* 'ford'), *Kesteren* (Latin *castra* 'army camp'), and *Wadenooien* (Latin *vada* 'fords'; Blok 1981: 144–145). The scarcity of *-heem* names and the good survival rate of Roman-age place names strongly suggest that the Gelderland river area shows a good deal of settlement continuity between Antiquity and the early Middle Ages, so much so that there was little land left to reclaim by the sixth century. At least a portion of this ancient farming population must have spoken Latin.

From the sixth century onwards, by far the most important settlement in the Dutch river area was the town of Dorestad (see IV.4). Its name fully illustrates the linguistic history of the region. Its most ancient form is a Latinized ablative *Dorestate* 'from Dorestad', which appears on Merovingian coins of the seventh and eighth centuries. It is probably a name of Celtic origin: **dworest-* 'gateway' (which underlies Old Irish *dorus*) + the inhabitant suffix *-atis*, plural **-atīs*.[43] Accordingly, the name of the town Dorestad is derived from a Celtic tribal name **Dworest-atīs* 'people who live at the gateway', i.e. at the point where the Rhine bifurcates into the Rhine and the Lek, giving access to the lowlands near the coast. It was the location of a Roman fort. Its modern form survives in the name of the nearby town *Wijk bij Duurstede*, literally 'settlement near Dorestad'. The form *Duurstede* shows phonological developments that can be explained only through an unbroken tradition that links Celtic, Late Latin, and Central Dutch. First of all, **Dworestat-*, etymologically Celtic, became **Dorestat-* while still Celtic. When Celtic was replaced by Latin, the name persisted. In Late Latin, **Dŏrest-* became **Dōrest-* by lengthening of the vowel in open syllables (see section IV.9), whence **Duɔrest-* and, with spontaneous fronting in the Picardian manner, **Dyørest-*. This name was retained when people switched from Old French to Central Dutch. During the later medieval period, **Dyørest-* became **Dȳrest-* > **Dȳrst-*, whence modern *Duurstede* (with *uu* representing [y]).

The persistent presence of Latin speakers in the Gelderland river area is remarkable because the area seems to have passed out of direct Roman control already by the middle of the third century. In the following centuries, Roman control was sometimes restored over brief periods of time, but by and large power seems to have devolved to local Franconian dynasts, who formed a buffer between the heartland of the Western Roman Empire around Trier and the barbarian north. Christianity penetrated these parts with difficulty. Under the Franconian king Dagobert I (632–639), a church was built in Utrecht, not far from Dorestad, but it lay in ruins when Willibrord made Utrecht the centre of his missionary activities amongst the Frisians towards the end of the seventh century. It may require an effort of the imagination to connect Latin speech with heathen, culturally completely Germanicized farmers whose ancestors had spent the best part of three centuries outside the direct control of the Roman Empire, but that is exactly what characterized the inhabitants of the Gelderland river area of the sixth and seventh centuries.

Yet there is some evidence, not unexpected, that the same area also harboured speakers of Germanic at the time. Blok (1974: 36–37) drew attention to two ancient Germanic items of geographical terminology. *Swifterbant*, literally meaning 'left or northern shire', denoted the area where the river IJssel split off from the Rhine, in the east of the river area. Its counterpart *Testerbant*, 'right or southern shire', was the name of the river area west of Tiel. Both terms are linguistically Germanic, but they are not Frisian or Franconian because they make no political sense from either point of view. The terms do make sense, however, from the point of view of a central area between them, which is exactly the fertile and eminently habitable Gelderland river area. No doubt there was some degree of Germanic-Romance bilingualism amongst the population.

The Germanic that overlay and gradually replaced Old French in the Central and Western Dutch area was to all intents and purposes identical to the Germanic of central and southern Germany, from which it differed in two respects that we can now understand.

- The German rule of secondary *i*-umlaut was replaced by the Old French rule of spontaneous fronting, as argued before.
- Dutch did not undergo the High German consonant shift but simply replaced the Germanic aspirated plosives [p^h, t^h, k^h] with their unaspirated Romance counterparts [p, t, k].

The High German consonant shift can be understood on the basis of a fifth- or sixth-century language shift from Late Latin to Germanic, in the sense that speakers of Late Latin replaced the Germanic voiceless aspirated plosives [p^h, t^h, k^h] with their closest Late Latin counterparts [pf^j, ts^j, kx^j], as argued in chapter III. It stands to reason that Eastern Dutch, like northern German, did not undergo the consonant shift because that dialect did not result from a shift from Late Latin to Germanic. But Central and Western Dutch did, according to the argument of this chapter. The shift of Old French speakers to Dutch probably occurred a few centuries later, when [pf^j] and [kx^j] may have no longer been available, but, more important, the sociolinguistic setting was completely different: the Late Latin speakers involved in the fifth- to sixth-century shift did their utmost to approach the Germanic model consonants with the means that Late Latin put at their disposal. This suggests they were driven by a desire to assimilate to the language, culture, and society of the Germanic elite of the time. Our Dutch speakers of Old French who shifted to Germanic, on the other hand, did almost nothing to make themselves sound Germanic. They spoke Germanic with Old French phonetics,[44] apparently because they acquired Germanic speech not out of a desire to assimilate to Germanic speakers but rather just to communicate with them. This presupposes a relatively high degree of cultural self-confidence.

By the time the Old French speakers switched to Germanic, the Germanic they acquired was no longer uniform in at least one respect: in Flanders, Proto-Germanic *au* had developed into something approaching Old French *uɔ* > *yø*, while Proto-Germanic *ō* had become similar to Old French *ou*. In the rest of Central and Western Dutch, the developments were reversed: *au* became *ou* > *ō*, and *ō* became *uo* > *yø*. It is possible to hazard the guess that this difference between Flemish and the rest had arisen as a result of the isolation of Flanders during the early medieval period. After Clovis' death in 511, the vast Franconian kingdom was divided amongst his sons. Flanders fell to the northwestern realm of Neustria, while the Central and Eastern Dutch areas up to the rivers formed part of Austrasia. Even though time and again a powerful king managed to rule both realms, subsequent divisions reinstated the boundary between Neustria and Austrasia.

14. TOWARDS MODERN DUTCH

An important issue that remains to be addressed concerns the subsequent history of Dutch after c. 1000, in particular the question why the spontaneous fronting of *ū* to *ȳ* was the only fronting that spread and ultimately came to dominate the standard language, whereas the fronting of *ŭ*, *uo*, and *au* remained local and did not enter the standard language except in isolated words, which sealed its fate as a recessive feature. It is important to remember that the land reclamations that had gained momentum by the seventh century greatly accelerated after 1000, particularly in West Flanders, Zeeland, and Holland. This was followed by urbanization, starting in Flanders and later in Holland. Land reclamation and urbanization attracted large numbers of people from outside, which is bound to have given rise to a dialectal melting pot in which Coastal Dutch and the different varieties of Western, Central, and Eastern Dutch came into contact. In such situations, new language varieties may arise which are supradialectal: speakers search for a common ground by reducing dialectal peculiarities that impair mutual comprehensibility and by highlighting existing commonalities and creating new ones. Such a hyperdialect is often termed a *koine*, after the Greek supradialectal variety that arose in the fourth century BC. Developments after AD 1000 gave rise to a Dutch *koine*. Against this background, it is easy to understand why spontaneous fronting of *ū* to *ȳ* became a feature of the *koine*: it was native to all dialects of Western and Central Dutch. By the same token, fronting of *uo* was not accepted into the *koine* because it occurred in the Western Dutch of Flanders in different words than in the rest of Western Dutch and in Central Dutch: where East Flemish said *byøm* 'tree', the rest said *bōm* (< Proto-Germanic *baumaz*), and where East Flemish said *brōder* 'brother', Central Dutch had *bryøder* (< Proto-Germanic *brōθēr*). The *koine* usually settled on non-fronting. An even more scattered pattern was found in the case of fronting of short *ŭ*: some dialects had fronted *symer* 'summer', while others had unfronted *somer* (< Proto-Germanic *sumraz*). In this case the usual procedure was to adopt the unfronted form (standard Dutch *zomer*) except in a number of instances where fronting was supported by Central Dutch *i*-umlaut (*slytel* 'key' by spontaneous fronting in Western Dutch and by *i*-umlaut in Central and Eastern Dutch, from Proto-Germanic *slutilaz*). It was this Dutch *koine* that encroached upon Coastal Dutch, rapidly in late medieval and early modern urbanized Flanders and Holland but at a much slower pace in rural parts and in Zeeland.

V. Beginnings

1. THE DAWN OF GERMANIC

In the preceding chapters, the foundational events that gave rise to the English, Dutch, and German languages have been found to be intimately connected with the assimilation of populations that originally spoke Celtic, Latin, or both. The linguistic demonstration of this assimilation presented in this book is new, but the idea that Germanic is, relatively speaking, a newcomer in Britain as well as in the Netherlands and Germany is not. Amongst historical linguists and archaeologists who have devoted attention to the issue, there is widespread agreement that the place where the Germanic branch of Indo-European originated is northern Europe, to be more precise, probably northernmost Germany, Denmark, and southern Sweden.[1] It is well known that the origin of English involved a population movement from that area because we happen to possess enough historical sources to that effect, as well as archaeological evidence that settlements in Denmark dwindled at a time when colonization events affected England. The coming of Germanic to the Netherlands and central and southern Germany is largely a matter of prehistory, which probably belongs to the last centuries BC. Movements further south continued off and on for many centuries until their culmination in the period of the Great Migrations of the third to sixth centuries AD. Where Germanic flowed into the later Roman Empire, the available data may suffice to reconstruct its disappearance or expansion, the latter usually at the expense of Latin or Celtic. In fact, knowing which languages were spoken by people who later came to adopt Germanic is invaluable for reconstructing the histories of English, Dutch, and German. That type of information is lacking for the other Germanic languages. The Germanic language first known to have come into intensive contact with the Roman Empire is Gothic, which was imported as a result of incursions and mass immigrations from the middle of the third century AD onwards. While the Gothic language is Germanic and ultimately comes from the northern Germanic homeland, those Goths who entered the Roman Empire came from the steppe area of eastern Europe (Ukraine, Rumania, Hungary). Their culture was very much a steppe culture, based on rapid mobility and good horsemanship. We know nothing about the ways in which life on the steppes shaped the Gothic language, simply because we know next to nothing about the languages with which it came into contact there. The further north we move, the greater becomes the distance to the Roman Empire and the graver the dearth of data about the linguistic situation before the Germanic expansion. That is why the origins of Frisian and Saxon are omitted from this book.

Given the originally southern Scandinavian homeland of Germanic, we might be excused for supposing that the Scandinavian branch of Germanic, which consists of the medieval and modern languages Swedish, Danish, Norwegian, Icelandic, and Faeroese, is the type of Germanic that stayed at home, as it were. If that were so, North Germanic—as the Scandinavian Germanic languages are known collectively—would show far fewer traces of language contact and shift than its southern sisters. This preconception may be correct for Danish and southern Swedish, but Norwegian and northern Swedish are definitely the result of a northern expansion whose beginnings we cannot date but which continued well into the modern period, with the gradual demise of the Saami languages in northern Scandinavia. Saami influence on Norwegian and Swedish dialects is considerable.[2] The population movements that resulted in Faeroese and Icelandic took place during the Viking period, during the last two centuries of the first millennium AD. We know that Iceland was uninhabited, apart from the odd Irish monk, when it was discovered in the ninth century; it was subsequently quickly settled by the Norse from Norway and the British Isles, so language contact may have played an insignificant role in shaping the ways in which Old Norse changed into Icelandic, although we do know that a significant proportion of the earliest settlers of Iceland came from Ireland and bore Irish names, suggesting they may have brought their language with them to Iceland.

As we delve down deeper, beyond the medieval period and the great migrations of late Antiquity, even beyond Caesar's conquest of Gaul around the middle of the first century BC, historical sources about the speakers of Germanic dry up completely. Yet this is the murky world that the present chapter addresses, dealing as it does with the origin of Germanic itself.

2. BALTO-FINNIC

The origins of the Germanic subfamily of Indo-European cannot be understood without acknowledging its interactions with a language group that has been its long-time neighbour: the Finnic subgroup of the Uralic language family. Indo-European and Uralic are linked to one another in two ways: they are probably related to one another in deep time—how deep is impossible to say[3]—and Indo-European has been a constant source from which words were borrowed into Uralic languages, from the fourth millennium BC up to the present day.[4] The section of the Uralic family that has always remained in close proximity to the Indo-European dialects which eventually turned into Germanic is Finnic. I use the term *Finnic* with a slightly idiosyncratic meaning : it covers the Finno-Saamic protolanguage and both of its children, Saami and Balto-Finnic. The Saamic or Lappish branch comprises about ten different modern languages that were traditionally spoken by hunter-gatherers and reindeer breeders of central and northern Scandinavia, Finland, and adjacent parts of Russia.[5] The other branch, Balto-Finnic, consists of the national languages Finnish and Estonian as well as four smaller languages: Livonian, Vote, Carelian, and Veps.

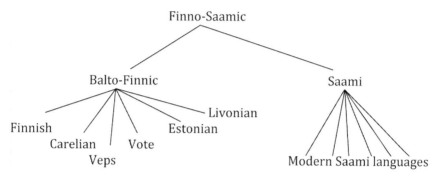

Figure 5.1   The Finnic family tree (simplified)

Historically, Saami was spoken throughout central and eastern Scandinavia, including southern Finland, while Balto-Finnic was at home in a wide arc spanning the southeastern Baltic, from the lakes Ladoga and Onega via St Petersburg to Estonia and Latvia. The early medieval expansions of Finnish into Finland and Karelia, and, presumably, the expansion of Germanic into western Scandinavia, have driven Saami further northwards.

Linguistically, the relationship between Indo-European and Uralic has always been asymmetrical. While hundreds of loanwords flowed into Uralic languages from Indo-European languages such as Germanic, Balto-Slavic, Iranian, and Proto-Indo-European itself, hardly any Uralic loanwords have entered the Indo-European languages (apart from a few relatively late dialectal loans into e.g. Russian and the Scandinavian languages). This strongly suggests that Uralic speakers have always been more receptive to ideas coming from Indo-European–speaking areas than the other way around. This inequality probably began when farming and the entire way of life that accompanies it reached Uralic-speaking territory via Indo-European–speaking territory, so that Uralic speakers, who traditionally were hunter-gatherers of the mixed and evergreen forest zone of northeastern Europe and gradually switched to an existence as sedentary farmers, were more likely to pick up ideas and the words that go with them from Indo-European than from anywhere else.

Farming requires a different mind-set from a hunter-gatherer existence. Farmers are generally sedentary, model the landscape, and have an agricultural calendar to determine their actions. Hunter-gatherers of the northern forest zone are generally nomadic, and rather than themselves modelling the natural environment they are modelled by it: their calendar depends on when and where a particular natural resource is available. Given such differences and seeing that farming allows the accumulation of wealth and the rise of social inequality unparallelled in northern hunter-gatherer societies, farmers who happened to speak Indo-European may well have looked upon hunter-gatherers who happened to speak Uralic as outsiders at best and inferior beings at worst, with the result that hunter-gatherers' ideas as well as the words they used for them were simply never embraced in farming communities. Another factor is that successful agriculture can feed a much larger population than a hunter-gatherer existence, so that hunter-gatherers will always be greatly outnumbered by farmers. If in northeastern Europe hunter-gatherers predominantly spoke Uralic while farmers predominantly spoke Indo-European, the demographic situation alone would render it much more likely that Uralic would adopt Indo-European linguistic features than the other way around.

All of this is no doubt a simplification of the thousands of years of associations between speakers of Uralic and speakers of Indo-European, but the loanword evidence strongly suggests that by and large relations between the two groups were highly unequal. The single direction in which loanwords flowed, and the mass of loanwords involved, can be compared with the relation between Latin and the vernacular languages in the Roman Empire, almost all of which disappeared in favour of Latin. It is therefore certain that groups of Uralic speakers switched to Indo-European. The question is whether we can trace those groups and, more particularly, whether Finnic speakers switching to Indo-European were involved in creating the Indo-European dialect we now know as Germanic.

Since there are good reasons to assume that language shifts from Uralic to Indo-European have indeed occurred, it is tempting to embrace that idea wholeheartedly and by so doing to prejudice the results of the investigation. For instance, if we were to observe that the sound structures of Finnic and Proto-Germanic became similar—which is indeed the case—it would be easy to imagine that what we are witnessing is speakers of Finnic shifting and importing a Finnic sound structure into Germanic. In this light it is a sobering thought that specialists in Uralic linguistics have consistently not accounted for Finnic and Germanic convergence in this way. What they have assumed is that Balto-Finnic speakers adopted a Germanic pronunciation of Finnic and thus took Indo-European influence one step further beyond the mere adoption of masses of Germanic loanwords, as previous generations of speakers had done. This would be the linguistic counterpart of the cultural split that divided the Finno-Saamic speech community into by and large Balto-Finnic farmers, who modelled their existence on their

Germanic-speaking neighbouring farmers, and Saami hunter-gatherers, who clung to the traditional Finno-Saamic way of life. By giving Balto-Finnic a Germanic pronunciation, Balto-Finnic speakers started on a slippery slope that might well have ended in wholesale adoption of Germanic and language death for Balto-Finnic, but this is clearly not what happened. What did happen, apparently, is that Finnic speakers had enough access to the way in which Germanic speakers pronounced Balto-Finnic in order to model their own pronunciation of Balto-Finnic on it. In other words, Balto-Finns conversed with bilingual speakers of Germanic and Balto-Finnic whose pronunciation of both was essentially Germanic. But access to the Germanic language itself was not sufficient to allow Balto-Finns to become bilingual themselves, either because social segregation prevented this or because contact with Germanic was severed before widespread bilingualism set in. This limited access to Germanic would allow us to understand why Balto-Finnic did not go the way of the vernacular languages that came in contact with Latin in the Roman Empire, where access to Latin was open to almost everybody and massive language shift in favour of Latin ensued.

Before we become too enthralled by this scenario, let us take a closer look at the linguistic data on which it is based.

3. CONVERGENCE TO WHAT?

The idea that Finnic speakers shifted to Germanic may be very different historically from the alternative idea that Finnic speakers imported a Germanic accent, and the former scenario would certainly leave a very different genetic footprint from the latter, but it is difficult to distinguish the two on the basis of the linguistic traces they leave. What both have in common is that the sound structures of Finnic and Germanic, which started from very different beginnings, apparently came to resemble one another significantly. If that is what we observe, we must conclude that both languages converged as a result of contact. That would be an important first conclusion, on which an argument can then be built that allows a choice between the option that Finnic speakers shifted to Germanic and the option that they borrowed a Germanic pronunciation. Success in taking this first step is based on our ability to establish, first, whether both languages converged at a certain stage of their prehistories and, second, whether convergence was so significant that it points to contact with one another.

3.1. Consonants

During the approximately five to six millennia that separate Proto-Uralic from Modern Finnish, there was only one episode during which the consonantal system underwent a dramatic overhaul. This episode separates the Finno-Saamic protolanguage, which is phonologically extremely conservative, from the Balto-Finnic protolanguage, which is very innovative. The initial state is the Finno-Saamic consonantal system, which can be reconstructed as follows:[6]

Finno-Saamic consonants

labials	dentals	alveolars	palatals	velars
p	t	č	ć	k
pp	tt	čč	ćć	kk
	s	š	ś	
	ð		ð′	γ
m	n		ń	ŋ
	l		l′	
	r			
ʋ			j	

(Pronunciations: č is pronounced as in <u>ch</u>ur<u>ch</u>, and čč is its long counterpart; š is pronounced as in <u>sh</u>irt, and ð as in <u>th</u>at. The whole palatal series marked with ′ is formed by pronouncing the corresponding consonant together with j [as in <u>y</u>oung]: ń as in <u>n</u>ew, l′ as in <u>l</u>ewd. The consonants ć, ćć, ś, and ð′ do not exist in English: ć approximates <u>t</u>une, but be sure to insert an [s] between the [t] and [j]-parts, so [tsjun], but avoid pronouncing this as *tshoon*, or [tšun]; and ćć is the long counterpart of ć. The consonant ś can be formed on the basis of <u>t</u>une, pronounced [tsjun], but omitting the [t]. ð′ is the voiced counterpart of *Mat<u>th</u>ew*. The voiced velar fricative γ does not exist in English: it is the voiced counterpart of Scots *lo<u>ch</u>*. The consonant ŋ is pronounced as in *ha<u>ng</u>*.)

By the time Finno-Saamic developed into Balto-Finnic, the consonant system was very different:

Balto-Finnic consonants

labials	dentals	alveolars	palatals	velars
p	t	–	–	k
pp	tt	–	–	kk
	c, cc			
	s, ss	–	–	h
	–		–	–
m, mm	n, nn		–	–
	l, ll		–	
	r			
ʋ			j	

In Balto-Finnic, the entire palatal series has been lost, apart from *j*, and the contrast between dentals and alveolars has disappeared: out of three different *s*-sounds only one remains. The fricatives ð and γ have been lost, and so has the velar nasal *ŋ*. The only increase has been in the number of long (geminate) consonants by the appearance of *ss*, *mm*, *nn*, and *ll*.

The loss of separate alveolar and palatal series and the disappearance of *ŋ* could be conceived as convergences towards Proto-Germanic, which lacked such consonants. This is not obvious for the loss of the voiced fricatives γ, ð, which Proto-Germanic did possess. However, this way of comparing Balto-Finnic and Germanic is flawed in an important respect: what we are doing is assessing convergence by comparing the dynamic development from Finno-Saamic to Balto-Finnic to the static system of Proto-Germanic, as if Proto-Germanic is not itself the result of a set of changes to the ancestral Pre-Germanic consonantal system. If we wish to find out whether there was convergence and which language converged on which, what we should do, therefore, is to compare the dynamic development of Finno-Saamic to Balto-Finnic to the dynamic development of Pre-Germanic to Proto-Germanic, because only that procedure will allow us to state whether Balto-Finnic moved towards Proto-Germanic, or Proto-Germanic moved towards Balto-Finnic, or both moved towards a third language.

The Pre-Germanic consonantal system can be reconstructed as follows:[7]

labials	dentals	palatals	velars	labiovelars
p	t	k'	k	k^w
b/p'	d/t'	g'/k'	g/k'	g^w/k'^w
b^h/p^h	d^h/t^h	g^h/k'^h	g^h/k^h	g^{wh}/k^{wh}
	s			
m	n			
w		j		
	l			
	r			

The slashes in the second and third rows indicate the uncertainty about the Proto-Indo-European nature of the sounds involved. The first row is relatively uncontroversial: they are the voiceless unaspirated plosives, whose English equivalents can be found in *spam*, *stand*, *skew* (i.e. *k* pronounced simultaneously with [j]), *scan*, and *squeek*, respectively.[8]

According to classical Indo-Europeanists' reconstruction, the second row contains the voiced plosives, as in English *burp*, *dot*, *gift* (but make sure to pronounce *g* with a simultaneous [j], as in *eggyolk*), *game*, and *Gwen*. The so-called glottalic theory, however, states that these were glottalic consonants; that is, they resemble *p*, *t*, *k'*, *k*, *k^w* pronounced with a glottal stop immediately before (so-called preglottalized) or after them (so-called ejective; a glottal stop is the sound heard in the middle of the Cockney pronunciation of e.g. *water* [wɔʔɐ], and a preglottalized *t* is present in the Queen's English pronunciation of the same word, [wɔːˈtə]). This glottalization is marked by the symbol [']. Finally, the third row contains plosives which according to the traditional reconstruction were voiced and aspirated (aspirated *bʰ* pronounced approximately as in *clubhouse*), but according to the glottalic theory, these were either voiceless aspirated plosives (as in English *park, tent*, etc.) or simple voiced plosives (as in *burp, dot*, etc.). The majority of Indo-Europeanists adhere to the traditional reconstructions (the first sound of each pair in the diagram), which indeed effortlessly account for the data in most Indo-European languages. A few others, however, stress the importance of the glottalic theory for explaining the data of a small number of Indo-European languages, of which the Germanic branch is one. This is not the place to go into the pros and cons of the glottalic theory. The controversy is mentioned here only to illustrate how difficult it is to give a relatively accurate phonetic reconstruction of the difference between the three rows of plosives. In what follows, I shall stick to the traditional symbolism for the sake of convenience (hence *p, b, bʰ* rather than *p, p', pʰ*), but this is not intended to prejudice the reader against the glottalic theory.

On its way to Proto-Germanic, the Pre-Germanic consonantal system changed considerably as a result of six sound changes:

(1) the merger of the palatals and velars into velar *k, g, g^h
(2) the rule known as Verner's law, which turned voiceless *p, t, k, s into *b^h, d^h, g^h, z if they were preceded by an unstressed syllable: *$wurt$-ónos > *$wurd^h$-ónoz > (by no. 4 and the rule that turned each *o into *a) *$wurdanaz$ > Old English *worden* (past participle 'become')[9]
(3) the rule known as Kluge's law, which turned voiced plosives followed by *n* into double plosives: *$stub^h$-n- > *$stubb$- > (by no. 4) *$stupp$- > Old English *stoppian* 'to stop' (compare Sanskrit *stubhnåti* 'stops, stupefies')[10]
(4) the so-called Germanic consonant shift, also named Grimm's law, which affected all plosives (so the first three rows in the Pre-Germanic diagram):
 – voiceless *p, t, k, k^w became the voiceless fricatives *$f, θ, h, hw$
 – voiced *b, d, g, g^w became voiceless aspirated *p^h, t^h, k^h, k^{wh}
 – voiced *bb, dd, gg (see no. 3) became voiceless aspirated *pp^h, tt^h, kk^h
 – *b^h, d^h, g^h became voiced *b, d, g (after vowels: *$v, ð, γ$); the fate of *g^{wh} is disputed
(5) the development of *t + t* to *ss*[11]
(6) various developments that produced *nn, rr, ll, ww*, and *jj*.

What resulted was the following Proto-Germanic consonant system:

labials	dentals	velars	palatals	labiovelars
p	*t*	*k*		*kʷ*
pp	*tt*	*kk*		*kkʷ*
b/v	*d/ð*	*g/γ*		
(bb	*dd*	*gg)*		
f	*θ*	*h*		*hʷ*
	s, z			
	ss			
m (mm)	*n, nn*			
	l, ll			
	r, rr			
w, ww			*j, jj*	

The third row (*b/v, d/ð, g/γ*) consists of pairs of sounds: by and large, the second member of each pair occurs after vowels, while the first member occurs in other positions. Since their distribution is therefore complementary (i.e. automatically determined by the phonetic environment), each pair represents a single phoneme.

All Germanic languages possess long voiced plosives (*bb, dd, gg*), but it is unclear to what extent these already existed in Proto-Germanic. Therefore, they have been put between parentheses. The same goes for *mm*.

We are now in a better position to answer the question whether Proto-Germanic and Balto-Finnic have converged. Three striking developments affected both languages:

- Both languages lost the palatalized series of consonants (apart from *j*), which in both languages became non-palatalized.
- Both languages developed an extensive set of long (geminate) consonants; Pre-Germanic had none, while Finno-Saamic already had a few.
- Both languages developed an *h*.

These similarities between the languages are considerable. Since both have innovated, it is impossible to decide which language converged on which. If more was known about the chronologies of the developments, a decision might have been possible: if, for instance, Proto-Germanic had undergone all three developments before Balto-Finnic did, we might conclude that Balto-Finnic adapted itself to Proto-Germanic. But for all we know the developments in Balto-Finnic could have preceded those in Germanic, in which case Germanic adapted itself to Balto-Finnic. Either way, we would be at a loss trying to understand what caused the developments to occur in the language that underwent them first. The idea that perhaps both languages moved towards a lost third language, whose speakers may have been assimilated to both Balto-Finnic and Germanic, provides a fuller explanation but suffers from the drawback that it shifts the full burden of the explanation to a mysterious 'language X' that is called upon only in order to explain the developments in Proto-Germanic and Balto-Finnic. That comes dangerously close to circular reasoning.

Perhaps it is useful to concentrate for a moment on the differences between developments in Balto-Finnic and Germanic. Balto-Finnic lost the fricatives ð and γ, which it had no business losing if Germanic had been at the helm, an impression that is strengthened by the fact that in both languages ð and γ occurred only after vowels. Balto-Finnic lost the opposition between the three s-sounds it inherited from Finno-Saamic (*s, š, ś*) and ended up with the same single *s* that Germanic inherited from Proto-Indo-European. This looks like Balto-Finnic modelling itself on Germanic, but since Germanic had not inherited any oppositions in this department that it could lose, appearances may deceive. In fact, Balto-Finnic stubbornly held on to its *c* and *cc*, which were alien to Germanic. All in all, the case for Balto-Finnic being the result of convergence upon Germanic is rather weak.

The case for Germanic being the result of a convergence upon Balto-Finnic is even weaker, it seems: Germanic inherited and remodelled but did not give up a distinction between voiceless and voiced consonants (*p-b, t-d, k-g, s-z*), which Balto-Finnic did not possess. If Germanic had acquired a Balto-Finnic pronunciation, which would happen if speakers of Balto-Finnic switched to Germanic, one might expect that Germanic would have lost the opposition between voiced and voiceless plosives because this opposition was foreign to Balto-Finnic. This is in fact how a strong Modern Finnish accent in, say, English manifests itself.

But this could also be a case of deceiving appearances: a closer look at this particular problem unexpectedly reveals a striking similarity between both languages, which has been flying under the radar so far in this chapter: Balto-Finnic consonant gradation and Verner's law in Germanic.

3.2. Consonant Gradation and Verner's Law

As we have seen in the preceding section, Verner's law is a sound change that affected originally voiceless consonants, so *p, t, k, ḱ, kʷ, s* of the Pre-Germanic system. These normally became the Proto-Germanic voiceless fricatives *f, θ, h, h, hw, s*, respectively. But if *p, t, k* etc. were preceded by an originally unstressed syllable, Verner's law intervened and they were turned into voiced consonants. Those voiced consonants merged with the series *bʰ, dʰ, gʰ* of the Pre-Germanic system and therefore subsequently underwent all changes that the latter did, turning out as *b/v, d/ð, g/γ* in the Proto-Germanic system (that is, *v, ð, γ* after a vowel and *b, d, g* in all other environments in the word). When *s was affected by Verner's Law, a new phoneme *z arose. In a diagram:

Pre-Germanic	Proto-Germanic after originally unstressed syllable (Verner's law)	Proto-Germanic in other environments
*p	> *b/v	> *f
*t	> *d/ð	> *θ
*k, *ḱ	> *g/γ	> *h
*kʷ	no clear examples	> *hw
*s	> *z	> *s

So the development was governed by the position of the stress in the word. Stress did not yet fall in the later, Proto-Germanic position, which almost invariably was on the first syllable, but in the older, Indo-European stress position. In Proto-Indo-European, stress could fall on any syllable and often moved within paradigms, e.g. *breh₂tér, genitive singular *breh₂trós 'brother' contrasting with *méh₂tēr, genitive singular *méh₂trs 'mother'. Verner's law fossilized this old movable stress indirectly, by turning it into an alternation of consonants. This alternation was preserved best in the oldest Germanic languages. Such fossils were preserved predominantly in the strong verbs. Here are a few examples:[12]

Pre-Germanic		Proto-Germanic	
*doúke '(s)he pulled, led'	>	*tauhe	> Old English *tēah*
*dukúnd 'they pulled, led'	>	*tuγunt	> Old English *tugon*
*wórte '(s)he turned'	>	*warθe	> Old English *wearð*
*wurtúnd 'they turned'	>	*wurdunt	> Old English *wurdon*
*wóse '(s)he stayed, was'	>	*wase	> Old English *was*
*wēsúnd 'they stayed, were'	>	*wēzunt	> Old English *wæron*

In the third person singular of each form, Verner's law did not apply because the syllable preceding the middle consonant was stressed in Pre-Germanic, so the Proto-Germanic outcomes are -h/θ/s-. By contrast, in the third person plural forms, the first syllable was originally unstressed, and therefore Verner's law affected the middle consonant, which was turned into -γ/ð/z-. This stress alternation within the paradigm was the general rule in the Pre-Germanic past tense of strong verbs, which goes back to the Proto-Indo-European perfect. The perfect along with its movable stress is preserved in Vedic Sanskrit, which has e.g. third singular perfect *véda* '(s)he has found out, (s)he knows', third plural perfect *vidúr* 'they have found out, they know'. Modern English has completely lost the effects of Verner's law in the past tense of strong verbs, with the exception of *(s)he was, they were*.

While it is very common in the history of European languages for stress to influence the development of vowels, it only very rarely affected consonants in this part of the world. Verner's law is a striking exception. It resembles a development which, on a much larger scale, affected Finno-Saamic: consonant gradation.

Consonant gradation is a complex process. There are two kinds of gradation. One is called rhythmic gradation, the other syllable gradation.[13] Rhythmic gradation affects consonants depending on whether they stand after a stressed or an unstressed syllable. Stress (indicated as ´) is generally on the first syllable, and there is a secondary stress (indicated as `) on each following uneven syllable. After each uneven (= stressed) syllable, a consonant appears in the so-called strong grade, while after each even (= unstressed) syllable the consonant assumes the so-called weak grade. In the Finno-Saamic word *óiketàta*, therefore, the *k and the second *t are in the strong grade, while the first *t is in the weak grade. Whether a consonant is in the strong or weak grade determines its precise outcome in the various Finno-Saamic languages: each language has its own outcomes, but the rule governing them is the same. In Finnish, for instance, strong grades are unchanged, while weak grades change. So in *óiketàta* the k and the second t are strong grades and remain the same, while the first t is a weak grade and changes via *d > ð to zero. The result is Finnish *oikeata*. This is the partitive case (ending in -ta) of the adjective *oikea* 'right'. If we form the partitive case from the word *kukka* 'flower', however, the ending -ta changes its form because now t is in the weak grade, following as it does an even, unstressed syllable: Finno-Saamic *kúkkata* becomes Finnish *kukkaa*. In all Finno-Saamic languages, rhythmic gradation has become phonemic and fossilized. The connection between rhythmic gradation and Verner's law is relatively straightforward: both processes involve changing a voiceless consonant after an unstressed syllable.

The other type of gradation is syllabic gradation. This affects consonants that are not already in the weak grade as a result of rhythmic gradation (so consonants between an uneven and an even syllable, such as the k and second t in Finno-Saamic *oiketata*, as well as the long consonants pp, tt, kk after an even syllable). Syllabic gradation of consonants depends on whether the following syllable ends in a vowel (an open syllable) or in a consonant (a closed syllable). A consonant before an open syllable assumes the strong grade, while it takes on the weak grade before a closed syllable. So in the reconstructed Finno-Saamic word *oiketata*, rhythmic gradation had already put the first t in the weak grade (*oikedàta*), so only k and the second t are free to undergo syllabic gradation. Both consonants appear in the strong grade because both begin an open syllable (ke and ta). This entails that in Finnish they remain unchanged: *oiketata* becomes *oikedata* > Finnish *oikeata*. Similarly, Finno-Saamic *leipä* 'bread' has a genitive *leipän*. In both forms, the *p is left in the strong grade by rhythmic gradation (p follows an uneven = stressed syllable). When syllabic gradation ensues, the *p in *leipä is in the strong grade (the syllable ends in -ä, so is open), while the *p in *leipän is weak grade (the syllable ends in -än, so is closed). In Finnish, the strong grade remains the same, while the weak grade changes: the Modern Finnish forms are *leipä*, genitive *leivän*. Syllabic gradation affects every word that has one of the consonants *p, pp, t, tt, k, kk*, or *s*, in other words, all voiceless obstruents. Here follow a few Finnish examples which show the effects of syllabic gradation and its dependence on whether the following syllable is closed or open:

Syllabic gradation in Finnish

nominative	genitive ('of . . .')	inessive ('in . . .')
kylpy 'bath'	*kylvyn*	*kylvyssä*
loppu 'end'	*lopun*	*lopussa*
koti 'home'	*kodin*	*kodissa*
katto 'roof'	*katon*	*katossa*
joki 'river'	*joen*	*joessa*
viikko 'week'	*viikon*	*viikossa*
mies 'man'	*miehen*	*miehessä*
hammas 'tooth'	*hampaan* (< *hampahan)	*hampaassa* (<*hampahassa*)
kuningas 'king'	*kuninkaan* (< *-ahan)	*kuninkaassa* (<*-ahassa*)
vapaa 'free'	*vapaan*	*vapaassa*

As the last three examples show, syllabic gradation in Finnish is no longer entirely predictable on the basis of whether the following syllable is open or closed: *hampaan* has a strong-grade -p- in front of a closed syllable -aan. This problem was caused by the loss of *h in the earlier form *hampahan, with an open second syllable (the form with -h- still exists in Karelian).

As we saw earlier, rhythmic gradation is connected to stress. Syllabic gradation has less to do with stress than with articulatory energy: given two syllables and an equal amount of energy spent on the production of each of them, a consonant that starts a long (closed) syllable, such as *p in *leipän, is allotted less energy than a consonant that starts a short (open) syllable, as in *leipä*. Hence *p in *leipän has the tendency to lose articulatory force and become weakened to *b > *v, whence the attested Finnish form *leivän*.

Those who have remarked upon the close similarity of gradation to Verner's law have tended to compare Verner's law to both forms of gradation because on a deeper level stress and articulatory energy are related phenomena (e.g. Koivulehto and Vennemann 1996, with references). Yet Germanic in no way shows a counterpart to syllabic gradation, while it does show a counterpart to rhythmic gradation: Verner's law.

The origin and age of gradation in the Finno-Saamic languages have been a bone of contention for a very long time. All Finno-Saamic languages either preserve gradation (Saami, Finnish, Vote, Estonian) or have lost it recently (Veps and Livonian), so there is much to say for reconstructing it back to the Finno-Saamic protolanguage. However, the details of the application of especially syllabic gradation differ from language to language to such an extent that many linguists have doubted the idea of a common inheritance.[14] The deepest differences are between Balto-Finnic on the one hand and Saami on the other:

- In Balto-Finnic, only voiceless obstruents (*p, pp, t, tt, k, kk*, s) are affected, while in Saami almost all consonants and consonant groups are affected. For instance, Finno-Saamic *kala*, genitive *kalan* 'fish' turns up unchanged in Finnish *kala, kalan*, so without gradation of the *-l-*. In Saami, however, *-l-* did undergo gradation, and *kala, kalan* have become northern Saami *guolle, guole*, respectively, with an alternation of long and short *-l-* and loss of the final *-n* of the genitive that originally triggered the weak grade.
- In Balto-Finnic, strong-grade consonants remain the same, while weak-grade consonants are weakened: they become voiced, and in some languages spirantized, and some drop out altogether. In Saami, the situation is normally reversed: strong grades change, while weak grades either remain the same or are weakened. Contrast the development of Finno-Saamic *appi* 'father-in-law', genitive *appin*, which in Finnish became *appi, apin* (weakening of the weak grade of *pp*), while in northern Saami it surfaces as *vuohppá, vuohpá* (where the strong-grade *pp* became *ppp* before turning into *hhp* [written <hpp>], while the weak-grade *pp* remained and later became *hp* [written <hp>]).

These different ways in which gradation affects consonants in the individual languages are very real, but they should not be overemphasized: underlying them is a basic unity consisting of the two gradation rules (rhythmic and syllabic) and their ordering (rhythmic gradation precedes syllabic gradation). This unity is so detailed and specific, and similar phenomena are so rare in the languages of the world, that it is most unlikely that gradation arose independently in Saami and Balto-Finnic (Helimski 1995). Gradation, therefore, was inherited from the Finno-Saamic protolanguage. In fact, the origin of gradation probably goes back all the way to the Uralic protolanguage. Eugene Helimski (1995) has shown convincingly that the same gradation rules can be found in a part of the Uralic family that is as distant from Finno-Saamic as it can possibly be: the Samoyed language Nganasan. This language, spoken by a few hundred people on the Tajmyr Peninsula, the northernmost part of central Siberia, shows both rhythmic and syllabic gradation, as in the following examples:

Proto-North Samoyed	>	Nganasan
*putətə 'trunk'	>	hütəðə
*putətə-tə-ta 'trunk for him'	>	hütəðətəðu

In these forms, the second and fourth *t* of the Proto-North Samoyed reconstructions are in the weak grade because of rhythmic gradation (weak grade
after an even syllable),[15] while the first and third *t* are in the strong grade
(strong grade after an uneven syllable). Then syllabic gradation kicks in,
which affects the first and third *t* (syllabic gradation affects only consonants that have been left in the strong grade by rhythmic gradation): since
both *t*'s head an open syllable, they are in the strong grade, which means
they remain unchanged in Nganasan. Other examples of Nganasan syllabic
gradation (SG = strong grade; WG = weak grade; *d'* is pronounced as in
duke, ð as in *this*, ʔ as in Cockney *water* [wɑʔɐ]):

nominative singular	nominative plural
kuhu 'skin' (SG)	*kubuʔ* (WG)
basa 'metal, money' (SG)	*bad'aʔ* (WG)
kəntə 'sledge' (SG)	*kəndəʔ* (WG)
kaðar 'light' (WG)	*katarəʔ* (SG)

The interplay of rhythmic and syllabic gradation with other developments
in Nganasan has reached an exquisite degree of complexity that even goes
beyond the spectacular effects of gradation in Saami. One single underlying
suffix, *-famfu-*, which expresses that what one says is hearsay, assumes
twelve different forms, which can be as different from one another as *-baŋhu-*
and *-hʲahi-* (Helimski 1995: 50). But behind all this complexity are the same
gradation rules as found in Finno-Saamic. We can therefore repeat for Proto-
Uralic the argument that persuaded us earlier that gradation in Saami and
Balto-Finnic must go back to the common Finno-Saamic protolanguage: the
similarity of the gradation rules in Nganasan to those in Finno-Saamic is
so specific and so detailed, and the phenomenon of gradation so rare in the
languages of the world, that gradation must be reconstructed for the Uralic
protolanguage.

These Nganasan data complement the toolkit that we need to form an
opinion on the relation between Finno-Saamic gradation and Verner's law
in Germanic. The prevailing opinion among scholars of Finnic is (a) that
Verner's law is so remarkably like gradation that there must be a causal
connection between the two, and (b) that Germanic influence on Finnic is so
pervasive that this must be another example: Finnic gradation is the result
of a Germanic accent in Finnic.[16]

It is possible to share the former conviction: Verner's law turns all voiceless obstruents (Pre-Germanic *$p, t, k, \acute{k}, k^w$, s*) into voiced obstruents
(ultimately Proto-Germanic *$b/v, d/ð, g/\gamma, g/\gamma, gw$, z*) after a Pre-Germanic
unstressed syllable. Rhythmic gradation turns all voiceless obstruents after
an unstressed syllable into weak-grade consonants, which means that *p, t,
k, s* become Finnic *$b/v, d/ð, g/\gamma$, z*. This is striking. Given the geographical
proximity of Balto-Finnic and Germanic and given the rare occurrence of

stress-related consonant changes in European languages, it would be unreasonable to think that Verner's law and rhythmic gradation have nothing to do with one another.

It is very hard to accept, however, that gradation is the result of copying Verner's law into Finnic. First of all, Verner's law, which might account for rhythmic gradation, in no way accounts for syllabic gradation in Finnic. And, second, gradation can be shown to be an inherited feature of Finnic which goes all the way back to Proto-Uralic. Once one acknowledges that Verner's law and gradation are causally linked and that gradation cannot be explained as a result of copying Verner's law into Finnic, there remains only one possibility: Verner's law is a copy of Finnic rhythmic gradation into Germanic. That means that we have finally managed to find what we were looking for all along: a Finnic sound feature in Germanic that betrays that Finnic speakers shifted to Germanic and spoke Germanic with a Finnic accent. The consequence of this idea is dramatic: since Verner's law affected all of Germanic, all of Germanic has a Finnic accent.

On the basis of this evidence for Finnic speakers shifting to Germanic, it is possible to ascribe other, less specifically Finnic traits in Germanic to the same source. The most obvious trait is the fixation of the main stress on the initial syllable of the word. Initial stress is inherited in Finno-Saamic but was adopted in Germanic only after the operation of Verner's law, quite probably under Finnic influence. The consonantal changes described in section V.3.1 can be attributed to Finnic with less confidence. The best case can be made for the development of geminate (double) consonants in Germanic, which did not inherit any of them, while Finno-Saamic inherited *pp, tt, kk, cc and took their presence as a cue to develop other geminates such as *nn and *ll. Possibly geminates developed so easily in Proto-Germanic because Finnic speakers (who switched to Germanic) were familiar with them.

Other consonantal changes, such as the loss of the palatalized series in both Germanic and Balto-Finnic and the elimination of the different s- and c-phonemes, might have occurred for the same reason: if Balto-Finnic had undergone them earlier than Germanic, which we do not know, they could have constituted part of the Balto-Finnic accent in Germanic. An alternative take on those changes starts from the observation that they all constitute simplifications of an older, richer system of consonants. While simplifications can be and often are caused by language shift if the new speakers lacked certain phonemes in their original language, simplifications do not require an explanation by shift: languages are capable of simplifying a complex system all by themselves. Yet the similarities between the simplifications in Germanic and in Balto-Finnic are so obvious that one would not want to ascribe their co-occurrence to accidental circumstances.

It is possible that the spread of a language among new groups of speakers can by itself lead to simplifications of the kind observed, even if the language at the expense of which the new language is spreading does not inspire the simplifications directly. The extreme simplification of Latin morphology when it spread amongst the inhabitants of the Western Roman Empire, for instance, was not inspired by the native languages of those inhabitants but by the mere fact of Latin's rapid spread. Accordingly, the Germanic consonantal system may well have been simplified because of its spread amongst a large population of new speakers, who happened to be Balto-Finns. And the Balto-Finnic consonantal system may have been simplified because contact with Germanic was so intense that not only its lexicon but also its sound structure converged.

Finally, we may briefly consider Germanic's iconic sound development, the Germanic consonant shift. Let us remind ourselves of the details, which were presented in V.3.1:

> The so-called Germanic consonant shift, also named Grimm's law, affected all plosives:
> - voiceless $*p, t, k, k^w$ became voiceless fricatives $*f, \theta, h, hw$
> - voiced $*b, d, g, g^w$ became voiceless aspirated $*p^h, t^h, k^h, k^{wh}$
> - voiced $*bb, dd, gg$ became voiceless aspirated $*pp^h, tt^h, kk^h$
> - $*b^h, d^h, g^h$ became voiced $*b, d, g$ (after vowels: $*v, ð, \gamma$); the fate of $*g^{wh}$ is disputed

It has been observed frequently that the last rule of the shift, whereby $*b^h$, d^h, g^h became voiced $*b, d, g$ (after vowels: $*v, ð, \gamma$) may not be altogether correctly formulated because it is doubtful whether truly voiced $*b, d, g$ ensued or rather so-called voiceless lenis $*\d{b}, \d{d}, \d{g}$. A voiceless lenis is produced with reduced muscular tension in the vocal tract (like voiced b, d, g) but without the swinging of the vocal cords that produces voiced consonants (so like voiceless p, t, k). To the average ear they sound halfway between b, d, g and p, t, k. Voiceless lenis pronunciation of b, d, g is typical of the majority of German and Scandinavian dialects, so may well have been inherited from Proto-Germanic. Voiceless lenis is also the pronunciation that has been assumed to underlie the weak grades of Finno-Saamic single $*p, t, k$. If Proto-Germanic $*b, d, g$ were indeed voiceless lenis, the single most striking result of the Germanic consonant shift is that it eliminated the phonological difference between voiced and voiceless consonants that Germanic had inherited from Proto-Indo-European (according to the classical reconstruction of Proto-Indo-European at least: see V.3.1, the Pre-Germanic diagram of consonants). Since neither Finno-Saamic nor Balto-Finnic possessed a phonological difference between voiced and voiceless obstruents, its loss in Proto-Germanic can be regarded as yet another example of a Finnic feature in Germanic.

As a counterweight against this idea that the Germanic consonant shift was inspired by the Finnic sound system, one may argue that the Germanic shift resulted in consonants that look decidedly un-Finnic: the fricatives $*f$ and θ and the aspirated $*p^h, t^h, k^h$. The observation is correct, but the question is what un-Finnic means precisely. We have seen that Finno-Saamic inherited *p, t, k* and *pp, tt, kk*, and that both series were affected by gradation:

Finno-Saamic gradation

strong grade:	*pp	*tt	*kk
weak grade:	*p̆p	*t̆t	*k̆k
strong grade:	*p	*t	*k
weak grade:	*ƀ	*đ	*g̊

The symbol [˘] in *p̆p, *t̆t, *k̆k denotes a shortened, more lenis version of *pp, *tt, *kk. It is interesting to observe how differently various Finno-Saamic languages dealt with this fourfold opposition. Here are the data for *pp and *p (*tt, *t, *kk, *k behave similarly):

	Finno-Saamic	Proto-Saami[17]	Estonian	Finnish	Veps
strong grade:	*pp	*hhp	pp	pp	p
weak grade:	*p̆p	*hp	p	p	p
strong grade:	*p	*p	b	p	b
weak grade:	*ƀ	*ƀ	v	v	b

Proto-Saami, a number of modern Saami languages, and Estonian retained and phonemicized the fourfold opposition, but they did so in very different ways: Saami by retaining and even expanding consonant length and introducing pre-aspiration, and Estonian by retaining consonant length and introducing voice opposition (*p* versus *b*). Finnish reduced the four oppositions to three by merging the weak-grade *p̆p with the strong-grade *p. In Veps, gradation disappeared by the merging of the strong and weak grades of *pp and *p, respectively. What this diagram shows is that the Finno-Saamic languages coped with having four different voiceless *p*-sounds in rather different ways: Finnish lost one, and Veps two of them, while Saami and Estonian preserved the difference between all four but with very different results. We may well speculate that speakers of Balto-Finnic who switched to Germanic exploited the four Balto-Finnic *p*-, *t*-, and *k*- sounds to render their Proto-Germanic counterparts and subsequently modified their pronunciation in much the same way as Saami did, with the difference that Proto-Germanic turned simple *p, t, k* into *f, θ, h*:

	Finno-Saamic	Proto-Saami[18]	Proto-Germanic
strong grade:	*pp	*hhp	*pp^h(< *bb)
weak grade:	*p̆p	*hp	*p^h(< *b)
strong grade:	*p	*p	*p > *f(< *p)
weak grade:	*ƀ	*ƀ	*ƀ/v (< *b^h)

It is clear that this account of the first Germanic consonant shift as yet another example of Finnic influence is to some degree speculative. The point I am making is not that the Germanic consonant shift must be explained on the basis of Finnic influence, like Verner's law and word-initial stress, only that it can be explained in this way, just like other features of the Germanic sound system discussed earlier, such as the loss of palatalized consonants and the rise of geminates.

A consequence of this account of the origins of the Proto-Germanic consonantal system is that the transition from Pre-Germanic to Proto-Germanic was entirely directed by Finnic. Or, to put it in less subtle words: Indo-European consonants became Germanic consonants when they were pronounced by Finnic speakers.

3.3. Balto-Finnic and Germanic Vowels

Since Finnic speakers who turned to Germanic obviously had to cope not only with Germanic consonants but also with Germanic vowels, it is useful to consider whether the vowel systems of Balto-Finnic and Germanic show traces of convergence, too.

While the consonantal systems of Proto-Germanic and Balto-Finnic were the result of considerable changes, the vowel systems of both languages remained relatively stable.

Finno-Saamic vowels

first syllable					other syllables	
short			long		short	
I	*y*	*u*	*ī*	*ū*	*i*	*i*
e		*o*	*ē*	*ō*		
æ		*a*			*æ*	*a*

The symbol *y* denotes phonetic [y], as in German *Brücke*. The symbol *æ* is [æ], as in English *hat*. In non-initial syllables, the appearance of *a* and *i*, on the one hand, and *æ* and *i*, on the other, was determined by which vowel stood in the first syllable: after a front vowel (*i, e, æ, y, ī, ē*), *æ* or *i* appeared; after all other vowels it was *a* or *i*. This phenomenon is called vowel harmony. Vowel harmony survives in Modern Finnish: contrast *kota* 'hut', *olut* 'beer' with *kesä* 'summer', *vävy* 'son-in-law', with *ä* = [æ].

Three changes occurred between Finno-Saamic and Balto-Finnic:

- the rise of *ø* (phonetically [ø], as in German *hören* 'to hear'), from unknown sources
- the addition of long *ȳ, ȫ, ǣ,* and *ā* to the long vowel system, which evenly balanced the long and short vowel systems[19]

- the enlargement of the vowel system in non-initial syllables, so that it exactly matched the set of short vowels occurring in first syllables.[20]

Balto-Finnic vowels

first syllable						other syllables		
short			long			short		
i	*y*	*u*	*ī*	*ȳ*	*ū*	*i*	*y*	*u*
e	*ø*	*o*	*ē*	*ō̇*	*ō*	*e*	*ø*	*o*
æ		*a*	*ǣ*		*ā*	*æ*		*a*

We may now turn to Germanic. The Pre-Germanic vowel system was quite different from that of Finno-Saamic and altogether as unremarkable as vowel systems can be:

Pre-Germanic

short		long	
i	*u*	*ī*	*ū*
e	*o*	*ē*	*ō*
	a		*ā*

By Proto-Germanic times, the short vowel system had been reduced and the long vowel system extended:

Proto-Germanic

short		long[21]	
i	*u*	*ī*	*ū*
e	*a*	*ē*	*ō*
		ǣ	*ā*

It should be immediately evident that the vowel systems of Balto-Finnic and Proto-Germanic are very dissimilar. There is not a trace of one system converging on the other. Interestingly, however, the Proto-Germanic system does show a striking resemblance but to a completely different linguistic group: the Proto-Germanic vowel system is identical to the Proto-Baltic vowel system. Baltic is a subgroup of the Indo-European family whose preserved members are the modern languages Lithuanian and Latvian and extinct Old Prussian. Its closest Indo-European cognate is Slavic. Since Baltic was probably the eastern neighbour of Germanic along the southern coasts of the Baltic Sea, contact between the two Indo-European subgroups may well have been intensive, and consequently convergence is quite plausible.

It would seem that the comparison of the Proto-Germanic and Balto-Finnic vowel systems is much less helpful than the comparison of the consonantal systems, but that would be a prejudiced position: divergences are as informative as convergences in language contact studies. In this particular case, comparison of the vowel systems is of great value because it enables us to decide what the nature of the Balto-Finnic and Proto-Germanic language contact was. Remember that there were two opposing theories about that contact situation. One states that the sound system of Balto-Finnic became adapted to that of Proto-Germanic because speakers of Balto-Finnic adopted a Germanic pronunciation: they abandoned the Finno-Saamic consonants that were lacking in Germanic (e.g. the palatalized series) and introduced others that Germanic did possess (a number of geminates, e.g. *nn*, *ll*). We have already observed that this point of view is highly problematic if we wish to understand consonantal changes as a whole, and we can now see that it is well nigh impossible in light of the vowel systems. The argument proceeds as follows. If changes between Finno-Saamic and Balto-Finnic were indeed propelled by an unconscious desire on the part of Balto-Finnic speakers to adopt a Germanic pronunciation, it would be absurd that Balto-Finnic speakers were quite successful in getting rid of almost all consonants that Germanic speakers could not pronounce but could not find it in their hearts to throw out any of the vowels that were beyond Germanic speakers' competence—and even made things worse by creating more such vowels (ø, ȫ, æ, ȳ). We may conclude that changes between Finno-Saamic and Balto-Finnic were emphatically not propelled by a desire on the part of Balto-Finnic speakers to adopt a Germanic pronunciation (Kallio 2000: 95–96).

The alternative scenario is one according to which a group of speakers of Balto-Finnic were in such intensive contact with speakers of Pre-Germanic that they first became bilingual and then switched to Pre-Germanic, which in the process became Proto-Germanic because those new speakers preserved a Balto-Finnic pronunciation when speaking Pre-Germanic. We have seen that Verner's law in Germanic was a copy of Finnic rhythmic gradation and that the Germanic consonant shift may have been triggered by new speakers' inability to cope with the difference between voiced and voiceless plosives. So the developments in the consonantal system are by and large in favour of Finnic speakers switching to Germanic. Now let us consider the vowel changes from this perspective: was there anything in the Pre-Germanic and Proto-Germanic vowel systems that Balto-Finnic speakers would have difficulty coping with, so that they could leave a Balto-Finnic accent in Germanic? The answer is a clear no: both the Pre-Germanic and the Proto-Germanic vowel systems are subsets of the larger Finno-Saamic and even larger Balto-Finnic vowel systems. On the basis of their own linguistic background, therefore, Balto-Finnic speakers would have no difficulty in pronouncing Germanic vowels more or less correctly as native Germanic speakers did. In other words: if Finnic speakers switched to Germanic, the absence of any noticeable effect on the Germanic vowel system is entirely as expected. This clinches the decision between the two scenarios about the nature of Germanic-Finnic language contact: in all probability, Balto-Finnic speakers switched to Germanic and introduced a Balto-Finnic accent into Germanic. A Balto-Finnic accent is what defines Germanic: there is no Germanic without a Balto-Finnic accent.

3.4. Conclusion on the Origin of Germanic

The Finnic-Germanic contact situation has turned out to be of a canonical type. To Finnic speakers, people who spoke prehistoric Germanic and its ancestor, Pre-Germanic, must have been role models. Why they were remains unclear. In the best traditions of Uralic–Indo-European contacts, Finnic speakers adopted masses of loanwords from (Pre-)Germanic. Some Finnic speakers even went a crucial step further and became bilingual: they spoke Pre-Germanic according to the possibilities offered by the Finnic sound system, which meant they spoke with a strong accent. The accent expressed itself as radical changes in the Pre-Germanic consonantal system and no changes in the Pre-Germanic vowel system. This speech variety became very successful and turned an Indo-European dialect into what we now know as Germanic. Bilingual speakers became monolingual speakers of Germanic.

What we do not know is for how long Finnic-Germanic bilingualism persisted. It is possible that it lasted for some time because both partners grew more alike even with respect to features whose origin we cannot assign to either of them (loss of palatalized consonants): this suggests, perhaps, that both languages became more similar because generally they were housed in the same brain. What we can say with more confidence is that the bilingual situation ultimately favoured Germanic over Finnic: loanwords continued to flow in one direction only, from Germanic to Finnic, hence it is clear that Germanic speakers remained role models.

This is as far as the linguistic evidence can take us for the moment. It is almost certain that the social context in which bilingualism became widespread and Germanic arose is intimately tied up with the life of farming communities in the northeastern European forest zone: there is general agreement that that was the mode of life shared by early Germanic and Balto-Finnic speakers. By contrast, the closest cognate of Balto-Finnic, Saami, adopted Germanic loanwords but shows no trace of its speakers having gone through a bilingual stage on anything near the scale that Balto-Finnic speakers did; also, prehistoric Saami speakers were hunter-gatherers, not farmers.

Yet this is not the last that is to be said about Saami, for it seems that Saami was involved in an extraordinary way with the earliest stages of the break-up of the Germanic languages, approximately during the first centuries AD. This is the theme of the next section.

4. SAAMI AND THE BREAK-UP OF GERMANIC

Once Germanic had arisen in a northeastern European zone of contact between Indo-European and Balto-Finnic, probably in the course of the first millennium BC, it began to spread. This spread was tremendously successful and lasted throughout the first millennium AD, bringing Germanic languages from Poland to the British Isles and from northern Scandinavia to Spain, North Africa, and the Balkans. As a result of this spectacular increase in territory and numbers of speakers, Germanic inevitably began to fragment into dialects as distances between speakers grew and contacts with different languages became prominent, as we have seen in earlier chapters. This section deals with the earliest stages of that fragmentation and with the way in which the history of the Saami languages is implicated in the break-up.

4.1. Proto-Germanic Retains the Difference between $*\bar{a}$ and $*\bar{o}$

For centuries, the Proto-Germanic system of consonants remained relatively stable throughout the Germanic-speaking world. It is in the vowel system that the first cracks began to manifest themselves. The inherited Proto-Germanic vowel system was as follows:

Proto-Germanic

short		long	
i	u	$\bar{\imath}$	$\bar{u}$
e	a	$\bar{e}$	$\bar{o}$
		$\bar{æ}$	$\bar{a}$

The only controversial item in this reconstruction is $*\bar{a}$: it is usually assumed that $*\bar{a}$ had merged with $*\bar{o}$ in Proto-Germanic. That is definitely correct in stressed syllables, which are usually the first syllable of the word because the stress almost always falls on the first syllable. The merger can be seen in the following examples:

Pre-Germanic	Proto-Germanic	Old Norse	English
$*b^h r\dot{a}t\bar{e}r$	$*br\bar{o}\theta\bar{æ}r$	bróðir	brother
$*m\bar{a}t\acute{e}r$	$*m\bar{o}d\bar{æ}r$	móðir	mother
$*b^h l\bar{o}m\bar{o}n$	$*bl\bar{o}m\bar{o}$	blómi	bloom
$*pl\bar{o}t\acute{u}s$	$*fl\bar{o}duz$	flóð	flood

However, outside of the first, stressed syllable the situation is different. This is not immediately obvious: the Germanic languages are notorious for the complicated developments that vowels have undergone in middle and final syllables. Each Germanic language has its individual set of rules that govern the behaviour of vowels in unstressed syllables. Those rules are so difficult to uncover that linguists have been quarrelling about some of them for over a century.

In the oldest stages of the West Germanic languages (this is the group that comprises English, Frisian, Dutch, Saxon, and High German), Proto-Germanic $*\bar{o}$ and $*\bar{a}$ remained distinct in one specific phonetic context: in a final syllable originally closed by a consonant. The difference can be observed in the following examples:

(1) Pre-Germanic long $*\bar{o}$ occurs in a number of final syllables:

	Old English	Old Saxon	Old High German
$*b^h l\bar{o}m\text{-}\bar{o}n$ 'flower'	*blōm-a*	*blōm-o*	*bluom-o*
$*g^h ut\text{-}\bar{o}m$ 'of gods'	*god-a*	*god-o*	*got-o*
$*d^h og^h\text{-}\bar{o}ses$ 'days'	*dag-as*	*dag-os*	–

(2) Pre-Germanic long $*\bar{a}$ occurs in case forms of $\bar{a}$-stem nouns, such as $*teut\text{-}\bar{a}$ 'people':

	Old English	Old Saxon	Old High German
$*teut\text{-}\bar{a}m$ (accusative)	*þēod-e*	*thiod-æ*	*diot-a*
$*teut\text{-}\bar{a}s$ (genitive)	*þēod-e*	*thiod-æ*	*diot-a*
$*teut\text{-}\bar{a}s$ (nominative plural)	*þēod-e*	*thiod-æ*	–

The examples illustrate that $*\bar{o}$ and $*\bar{a}$ before a consonant in final syllables became -*a* and -*e*, respectively, in Old English. In Old Saxon, they became -*o* and -*æ*, respectively, and in Old High German -*o* and -*a*. In other words, $*\bar{o}$ and $*\bar{a}$ both changed in West Germanic, but they did not merge. If they were still kept different in West Germanic, $*\bar{o}$ and $*\bar{a}$ must inevitably have been different vowels in its parent language, Proto-Germanic. We can apply that conclusion to the Proto-Germanic reconstructions of the above-mentioned words (please ignore the consonantal changes, which are irrelevant here):

Pre-Germanic		Proto-Germanic
$*b^h l\bar{o}m\text{-}\bar{o}n$ 'flower'	>	$*bl\bar{o}m\text{-}\bar{o}n$
$*g^h ut\text{-}\bar{o}m$ 'of gods'	>	$*gud\text{-}\bar{o}n$
$*d^h og^h\text{-}\bar{o}ses$ 'days'	>	$*dag\text{-}\bar{o}sz$
$*teut\text{-}\bar{a}m$ 'people'	>	$*þeud\text{-}\bar{a}n$ (not $*þeud\text{-}\bar{o}n$)
$*teut\text{-}\bar{a}s$	>	$*þeud\text{-}\bar{a}z$ (not $*þeud\text{-}\bar{o}z$)
$*teut\text{-}\bar{a}s$	>	$*þeud\text{-}\bar{a}z$ (not $*þeud\text{-}\bar{o}z$)

The idea that $*\bar{o}$ and $*\bar{a}$ were still different vowels in Proto-Germanic and that this difference solves many of the difficulties which would otherwise be encountered if one wishes to find the sound laws governing the behaviour of word-final syllables in Germanic languages is called the Qualitative Theory. The theory dates back to Hermann Möller (1880) and was refined by Jellinek (1891) and Van Wijk (1907–1908). Van Wijk already complained that the Qualitative Theory was at risk of being dismissed improperly, and in spite of his eloquent defence it did indeed disappear from the handbooks and from most Germanicists' memory soon after.[22] The Qualitative Theory is one of many examples in the history of Germanic linguistics in which major advances made by nineteenth-century scholars require careful excavation from under the pressing and sometimes confusing weight of subsequent literature on the subject.

The inherited difference between $*\bar{a}$ and $*\bar{o}$ was preserved in one other phonetic context: in stressed syllables before a word-final nasal (*n* or *m*). Old $*\bar{a}$ is attested in the accusative feminine singular of the pronoun 'that', which was Pre-Germanic $*t\bar{a}\text{-}m$ (here as elsewhere, $*\text{-}m$ is the ending of the accusative singular). This developed into Proto-Germanic $*\theta\bar{a}\text{-}n$ and subsequently into Old Norse *þá* and Old English *þā* (both [θaː]) 'that, her'. This can be contrasted with the Germanic reflexes of the Indo-European word for 'cow', $*g^w ou\text{-}s$, accusative singular $*g^w \bar{o}\text{-}m$. All Germanic forms, including English *cow* and German *Kuh*, are based on $*g^w \bar{o}\text{-}m$, which became Proto-Germanic $*k^w \bar{o}\text{-}n$: Old Norse *kýr*, Old English *cū*, and Old High German *chuo* all go back to a Proto-Germanic paradigm consisting of an innovated nominative $*k^w \bar{o}$ and an inherited accusative $*k^w \bar{o}\text{-}n$. The crucial point is that the pair $*t\bar{a}\text{-}m$ > Proto-Germanic $*\theta\bar{a}\text{-}n$ and $*g^w \bar{o}\text{-}m$ > Proto-Germanic $*k^w \bar{o}\text{-}n$ shows that inherited $*\bar{o}$ and $*\bar{a}$ had remained distinct in Proto-Germanic because if they had merged it would be impossible to explain the distinct vowels in the North and West Germanic languages.[23]

4.2. Early Germanic Differentiation: Long Vowels in Unstressed Syllables

The upshot is, therefore, that Proto-Germanic, the common ancestor of all Germanic languages, still possessed six different long vowel phonemes:

$\bar{\imath}$	$\bar{u}$
$\bar{e}$	$\bar{o}$
$\bar{æ}$	$\bar{a}$

All long vowels occurred in stressed (i.e. initial) and unstressed syllables alike, with the probable exception of $*\bar{e}$, which seems to have occurred only in stressed syllables. That symmetrical state of affairs was going to change dramatically during the earliest stages of the fragmentation of Germanic, when the foundations of the later differentiation into North, West, and East Germanic were laid.

North Germanic is the dialectal group to which Icelandic, Faeroese, Norwegian, Swedish, and Danish belong. Its earliest textual representatives are a very patchy record of inscriptions in the Runic alphabet, which span most of the first millennium AD, and the fully attested Old Norse (or Old Icelandic) literary language, which appears from the eleventh century onwards. To all intents and purposes, the earliest stage of Old Norse can be regarded as equivalent to the ancestor of all North Germanic languages, Proto-North Germanic. Therefore, and also because of its full attestation, Old Norse is an ideal pivot from which to trace back the earliest developments that separated North Germanic from Proto-Germanic.

The changes on which we will concentrate here involve the mutual relationship between the vowels $*\bar{æ}$, $*\bar{a}$, and $*\bar{o}$. What is remarkable is that this threesome undergoes different developments in stressed and unstressed syllables. In stressed syllables, $*\bar{a}$ and $*\bar{o}$ merge as $*\bar{o}$, while $*\bar{æ}$ becomes new $*\bar{a}$:[24]

Proto-Germanic *brāθēr	> Old Norse *bróðir* 'brother'
Proto-Germanic *flōduz	> Old Norse *flóð* 'flood'
Proto-Germanic *sēdan	> Old Norse *sáð* 'seed'

In unstressed syllables, the development was different, but this cannot be observed directly because unstressed syllables underwent many subsequent changes on their way to Old Norse. Two different treatments can be distinguished:

(1) At the absolute end of the word (i.e. without any consonant following), $*-\bar{a}$ and $*-\bar{o}$ merged as $*-\bar{u}$. Examples:

Proto-Germanic *sagā 'saw' > *sagū (> Old Norse *sǫg*)
Proto-Germanic *kʷō 'cow' > *kū (> Old Norse *kýr*)

There are no secure examples that illustrate the behaviour of $*-\bar{æ}$ at the end of the word.

(2) In all other unstressed phonetic environments, developments were different.

(2a) It seems that $*\bar{æ}$ was split into $*\bar{e}$ and $*\bar{æ}$ before other developments ensued:

$*\bar{æ} > *\bar{e}$ Proto-Germanic *brāθēr > *brōθēr (> Old Norse *bróðir* 'brother')	
Proto-Germanic *baridǣz > *baridēz (> Old Norse *barðir* 'you struck')	
Proto-Germanic *wakēdǣt > *wakēdēt (> Old Norse *vakði* '(s)he was awake')[25]	
$\bar{æ} > *\bar{æ}$ Proto-Germanic *wakēdaz > *wakǣdaz (> Old Norse *vakaðr* 'been awake')	

It is unclear what governed this split. Possibly the low vowel $*a$ in the final syllable of *wakǣdaz was responsible for $*\bar{æ}$ remaining unchanged, just as the non-low vowel in the final syllable of *wakēdēt may have caused medial $*\bar{æ}$ to have become non-low $*\bar{e}$.[26]

(2b) Unstressed *ō merged with unstressed *ā, but the resulting vowel was split in two: *ɔ and *ō:

*ō > *ɔ	Proto-Germanic *spak-ōz-æn > *spakɔzē (> Old Norse *spakari* 'more sensible')
	Proto-Germanic *baridōn > *baridɔ (> Old Norse *barða* 'I struck')[27]
*ā > *ɔ	Proto-Germanic *kallādaz > *kallɔdaz (> Old Norse *kallaðr* 'called', masculine)
	Proto-Germanic *kallādæz > *kallɔdēz (> Old Norse *kallaðir* 'you called')
*ō > *ō	Proto-Germanic *hertōnā > *hertōnū (> Old Norse *hjǫrtu* 'hearts')
*ā > *ō	Proto-Germanic *sagānun > *sagōnu (> Old Norse *sǫgu* 'story', accusative)
	Proto-Germanic *kallādā > *kallōdū (> Old Norse *kǫlluð* 'called', feminine)

Here, too, it is not altogether clear what caused the split, but the material seems to suggest that a *u in the third syllable caused long *ā and *ō to have become *ō.

The following chart may be a helpful summary of the North Germanic developments:

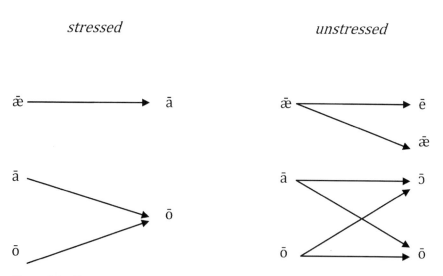

Figure 5.2   From Proto-Germanic to North Germanic

The development of Proto-Germanic *$\bar{æ}$, *$\bar{a}$, and *$\bar{o}$ in **West Germanic** was similar but not entirely identical. West Germanic is the dialectal group that includes English, Frisian, Dutch, Low German (or Saxon), and High German. Its earliest written sources are a very sparse record of short texts written in the Runic alphabet and spanning the best part of the first millennium. After about 700, Old English, Old Saxon, Old Low Franconian (Dutch), and Old High German begin to appear, followed only in the later medieval period by Old Frisian. These languages have passed through numerous sound developments when they first see the light of day in medieval manuscripts, and many of those developments affect the vowels of unstressed syllables.

West Germanic shows a different development of long vowels in stressed and unstressed syllables. In stressed syllables, developments were identical to those observed in North Germanic: *$\bar{a}$ and *$\bar{o}$ merged as *$\bar{o}$, which in Old High German (OHG) became *uo*. Proto-Germanic *$\bar{æ}$ became *$\bar{a}$. The exception to the latter development is that the so-called Ingwaeonic dialects (Old English and Old Frisian) show $\bar{æ}$. This is either preserved Proto-Germanic *$\bar{æ}$ or a local innovation which can be ascribed to contact with Celtic dialects (Schrijver 1999). Examples:

Proto-Germanic *$br\bar{a}\theta\bar{e}r$	> OHG *bruoder* 'brother'
Proto-Germanic *$fl\bar{o}duz$	> OHG *fluot* 'flood'
Proto-Germanic *$s\bar{æ}dan$	> OHG *sāt* 'seed'

In unstressed syllables, the development was different, but as in the case of North Germanic this cannot be observed directly because unstressed syllables underwent many subsequent changes on their way to the attested languages. Two different treatments can be distinguished:

(1) At the absolute end of the word (i.e. without any consonant following), *$-\bar{a}$ and *$-\bar{o}$ merged as *$-\bar{u}$. Examples:

Proto-Germanic *$sag\bar{a}$ 'saw' > *$sag\bar{u}$ (> Old English *sagu*)
Proto-Germanic *$ber\bar{o}$ 'I carry' > *$bir\bar{u}$ (> OHG *biru*)

This development was shared with North Germanic.

(2a) In all other phonetic environments, it seems that *$\bar{æ}$ never became *$\bar{a}$, as in stressed syllables, but was split into West Germanic *$\bar{æ}$ and *$\bar{e}$ before other developments ensued. West Germanic *$\bar{æ}$ subsequently became $æ$ (spelled <e, a>) in Old Saxon (OS) and *e* in Old English (OE). In OHG *$\bar{æ}$ became $\bar{e}$ or *e* before a preserved consonant, and *a* at the end of the word.

*ǣ > *ǣ	Proto-Germanic **brāθǣr* > **brōθǣr* (> OS *brōdar*, OHG *bruoder* 'brother')
	Proto-Germanic **nazidǣt* > **nazidǣ* (> OS, OE *nerede*, OHG *nerita* 'cured')
	Proto-Germanic **wakǣdǣī* > **wakǣdǣ* (> OHG *wahhēta* 'was awake')
	Proto-Germanic **wakǣdaz* > **wakǣdaz* (> OHG *giwahhēt* 'been awake')
*ǣ > *ē	Proto-Germanic **awǣdian* > **awēdia* (> OHG *ewit* 'flock of sheep')

In West Germanic, the split of **ǣ* into **ǣ* and **ē* occurred along different lines than in North Germanic: in North Germanic, the normal reflex was **ē*, while exceptional **ǣ* was probably conditioned by a low vowel **a* in the following syllable. In West Germanic, by contrast, the normal reflex was **ǣ*, and the single example of **ē* was conditioned by a high vowel **i* in the third syllable.[28] What both branches have in common is that the split occurred at all, that it occurred only in unstressed syllables, and that a vowel in the third syllable seems to determine the split.

(2b) In West Germanic, the development of unstressed **ā* and **ō* is complicated by the fact that two forces exerted their influence:

(i) **ā* and **ō* remained distinct in old final syllables if the consonant that originally followed them was lost: **gebān* 'gift' (accusative), **gebāz* 'gift' (genitive) both became OHG *geba*; **gumōn* 'man', on the other hand, became OHG *gumo*. This is the Qualitative Theory of final syllables in Germanic, which was discussed in V.4.1.

(ii) **ā* and **ō* merged in unstressed syllables before a preserved consonant. The resulting vowel split again into **ɔ* (> OHG *ō*) and **ō* (> OHG *ū*), in a way that is strongly reminiscent of North Germanic:

*ō > *ɔ	Proto-Germanic **leub-ōz-ōn* > **leubɔzɔ* (> OHG *liobōro* 'dearer')
*ā > *ɔ	Proto-Germanic **salbādaz* > **salbɔdaz* (> OHG *salbōt* 'anointed')
	Proto-Germanic **salbādōz* > **salbɔdɔz* (> OHG *salbōtō-s* 'you anointed')
*ō > *ō	Proto-Germanic **hertōnā* > **hertōnū* (> OHG *herzun* 'hearts')
*ā > *ō	Proto-Germanic **tungānun* > **tungōnu* (> OHG *zungūn* 'tongue', accusative)

As in North Germanic, the reflex *ō seems to have been determined by the presence of the vowel *u in the following syllable.

The upshot of this dizzying array of developments is presented in the following diagram:

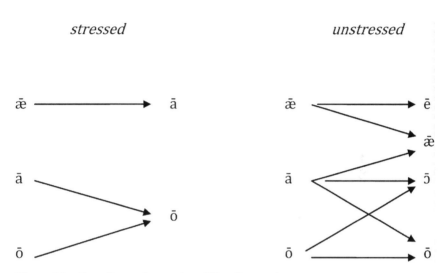

Figure 5.3 From Proto-Germanic to West Germanic

The similarity of West Germanic developments to those in North Germanic is striking. The diagram is identical to that for North Germanic, with one exception: the line connecting unstressed *ā to *ǣ (reflecting the Qualitative Theory) is missing in North Germanic. The vowel system that emerges in West Germanic is identical to the vowel system emerging in North Germanic, but the ways leading to those vowel systems are slightly different: the splits of unstressed *ǣ, *ā, and *ō are triggered by vowels in the following syllable in both West and North Germanic, but they differ in the sense that the North Germanic splits are partly caused by different vowels than the splits in West Germanic.

That developments could have moved in an entirely different direction is shown by Gothic, the only well-known representative of the **East Germanic** subgroup. Gothic hived off from the core of Germanic at a very early date and ended up in southern Europe by the fourth century. The sources of that early period indicate the following developments:

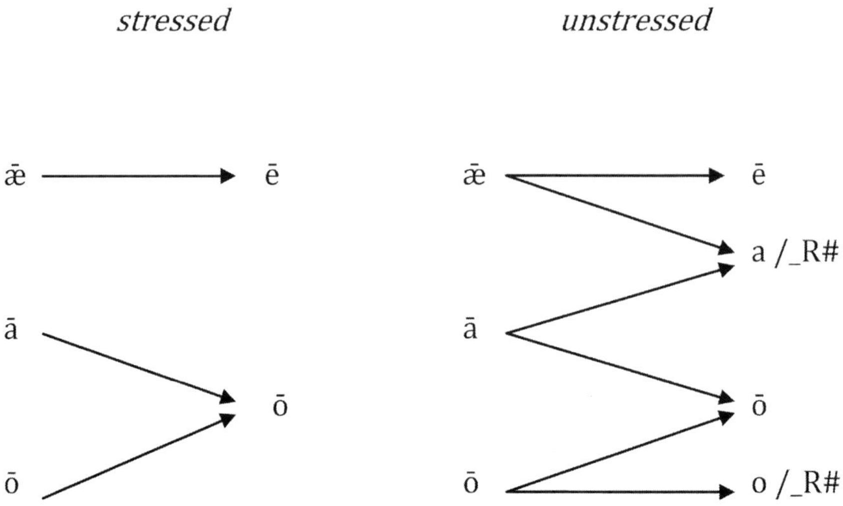

Figure 5.4   From Proto-Germanic to Gothic

In Gothic, long vowels in stressed syllables developed in essentially the same way as in unstressed syllables, with the exception that in unstressed syllables long vowels were shortened before a resonant (*n, *r, *j, or *w, symbolized by R) at the end of the word (the symbols /_R# mean: 'before a resonant at the end of the word').[29] In West and North Germanic, by contrast, long vowels in unstressed syllables developed quite differently from those in stressed syllables. Hence Gothic differs considerably from North and West Germanic in this respect. We have also seen that the obvious similarities between North and West Germanic cannot disguise differences of detail. Therefore, all these developments of the unstressed long vowels cannot have occurred in the common ancestor of all of Germanic, Proto-Germanic, but belong to the early histories of the separate branches.

4.3. Early Germanic Dialectal Vowel Systems

Now that the complex developments of the long vowels in unstressed syllables have been disentangled, it is possible to compare the overall vowel systems of the earliest stages of North Germanic, West Germanic, and Gothic. They are compared at the stage when the split of the long unstressed vowels had already occurred, as explained in V.4.2, but not yet the many early medieval vowel changes such as *i*-umlaut, syncope, apocope, etc., which follow rules that are different for each individual language. This chronology is reasonable: the split of unstressed long vowels must have preceded those later developments for two reasons:

• The unstressed long vowel split is identical in all West Germanic languages, unlike *i*-umlaut, etc., so it belongs to an early period at which West Germanic was not yet differentiated.
• The unstressed long vowel split was governed by the presence of particular vowels in Proto-Germanic third syllables; the loss of short vowels in third syllables is generally assumed to have occurred very early in the history of the Germanic languages.[30]

The starting point of the comparison is the Proto-Germanic vowel system:

long		short	
$\bar{\imath}$	$\bar{u}$	i	u
$\bar{e}$	$\bar{o}$	e	a
$\bar{æ}$	$\bar{a}$		

In early North Germanic and West Germanic, through slightly different developments in each, this had become the following more complex system:

Stressed syllables			
$\bar{\imath}$	$\bar{u}$	i	u
$\bar{e}$	$\bar{o}$	e	$[o]$
	$\bar{a}$		a

Unstressed syllables				
$\bar{\imath}$		$\bar{u}$	i	u
$\bar{e}$ }	result of	{ $\bar{o}$		
$\bar{æ}$ }	split	{ $ɔ̄$		a

In Gothic, however, the system was just a simplification of the Proto-Germanic system:

Stressed and unstressed syllables			
$\bar{\imath}$	$\bar{u}$	i	u
$\bar{e}$	$\bar{o}$		
	$\bar{a}$		a

There are two theoretical and therefore non-compelling reasons to suppose that developments in North and West Germanic were not motivated by internal mechanisms of change but rather by language contact. One reason is that the North and West Germanic systems are considerably more complex and asymmetrical than the Proto-Germanic system, which is something that languages normally avoid if left to their own devices. The second reason is that North and West Germanic were pulled into the same, unexpected direction but the sound laws underlying that direction were rather different, as if developments unfolded independently in North and West Germanic but according to the same invisible master plan. This is typically what would happen in a language contact scenario, if a population switched to Germanic and in the process introduced sound features of its first language into Germanic.

By a stroke of good fortune, this theoretical scenario receives confirmation from the fact that there is another language in geographical proximity that underwent very similar changes to its vowel system: Saami.

4.4. Saami Vowels

The Saami languages are straightforward members of the Uralic language family and form a group that is closely related to the Balto-Finnic languages, which we met in section V.2. The modern Saami languages stem from a common ancestor, Proto-Saami, which can be dated approximately to the beginning of the Common Era. Proto-Saami itself is the sister of Balto-Finnic, and their common ancestor is Finno-Saamic, of unknown date. Proto-Saami differed considerably from Finno-Saamic. In fact, Proto-Saami is the result of the most drastic changes in the entire Uralic language family. Most of those changes involve the sound system.[31] The Finno-Saamic vowel system was introduced in section V.3.3:

Finno-Saamic vowels

first syllable					other syllables		
short			long		short		
i	*y*	*u*	*ī*	*ū*	*i*	~	*i*
e		*o*	*ē*	*ō*			
æ		*a*			*æ*	~	*a*

The main developments that ensued are as follows:

(1) The Saami branch lost *y* (pronounced as in French *pur*), turning it into *i*. It gained a vowel *ɔ* in the second syllable, which developed from a vowel + **w*.

(2) Then it lost vowel harmony, whereby the quality of the vowel of the first syllable determined whether other syllables showed *i*, *æ* (which they did if the first syllable contained one of the front vowels: *i*, *e*, *æ*, *ī*, *ē*) or *i*, *a* (which they did if the first syllable contained one of the back vowels: *u*, *o*, *a*, *ū*, *ō*). Vowel harmony is preserved in Finnish (e.g. *kylässä* 'in the village', *kalassa* 'in the fish'). As a result of the loss of vowel harmony, the difference between **i* and **i* and between **æ* and **a* disappeared: only **i* and **a* remained.

Instead of vowel harmony, Saami adopted its opposite counterpart, umlaut, which means that the quality of a vowel in a non-initial syllable determines the quality of the initial syllable. Examples comprise Finno-Saamic **kolmi* > **kulmi* 'three' (> North Saami *golbma*) and Finno-Saamic **kota* > **kɔta* 'hut' (> North Saami *goahti*): the close vowel *i* in the second syllable of **kolmi* causes the mid vowel *o* in the first syllable to become close *u*; and the open vowel *a* in the second syllable of **kota* causes the mid vowel *o* to become the open vowel *ɔ*.

(3) The low vowels **æ*, **a*, and **ɔ* became long **ǣ*, **ā*, and **ɔ̄*.

By now, Proto-Saami had arrived at the following vowel system, which can be called Proto-Saami 1:

first syllable				other syllables
short		long		short
i	*u*	*ī*	*ū*	*i*
e	*o*	*ē*	*ō*	*ɔ̄*
		ǣ	*ā*	*ā*

This system is practically identical to the Proto-Germanic vowel system, from which it differs in two respects:

- the system in non-first syllables is much reduced
- where Proto-Germanic has short *a*, Proto-Saami 1 has short *o*.

The following developments take Proto-Saami on a course which is strikingly like North and West Germanic (Proto-Saami 2).

(4) In first syllables only, **ā* became **ō*, and **ǣ* became **ā*. This is identical to what happened to those vowels in North and West Germanic first syllables.

(5) In other syllables, the long vowels *ā and *ɔ̄ split into two (Sammal-
     lahti 1998: 184–185):

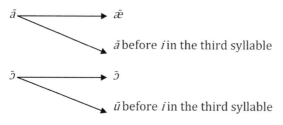

Figure 5.5

Both the split and the conditioning factor of a vowel in the third syllable
are strongly reminiscent of the splits of *ǣ and *ō in non-initial syllables in
North and West Germanic.

This is as far as the striking similarities in the early developments of
Proto-Saami and North and West Germanic go.[32] At some later stage, Proto-
Saami loses the distinctions in vowel length: all close vowels become short,
and all mid and open vowels become long. Quality differences take the place
of quantity differences: the old distinction between ī and i becomes one
between i (as in *beef*) and ɪ (as in *hit*), for instance. This development fore-
shadows vowel changes that affect medieval Germanic but precedes them
by many centuries.

All those Proto-Saami developments have a strikingly Germanic ring to
them.

(1) The loss of y could be motivated by the absence of that sound in
     Germanic.
(2) The loss of vowel harmony and its replacement by umlaut introduces
     a Germanic feature into Saamic.
(3) The lengthening of *æ, *a, and *ɔ to *ǣ, *ā, and *ɔ̄ brings the Saamic
     vowel system closer to that of Proto-Germanic.
(4) The development of *ā and *ǣ in stressed syllables matches Ger-
     manic changes.
(5) So does the split of *ā and *ɔ̄ in unstressed syllables.

Yet it is impossible to ascribe those changes to Germanic influence. Umlaut
is indeed widespread in Germanic, as in *gastiz > Old Norse *gestr* and *han-
duz* > Old Norse *hǫnd*. But Proto-Saami umlaut is much earlier than the
medieval umlaut of Germanic, and it is of a different nature as well, affecting
only vowel height and not frontness/backness as in Germanic, so Proto-
Saami umlaut is unlikely to have been caused by contact with Germanic.

And, most important of all, just as umlaut is an innovation in Proto-Saami it is an innovation in Germanic. Similarly, the vowel changes in points (3)–(5) are innovations in both Germanic and Saami.

This state of affairs is key to understanding its origin: what we are witnessing is neither Saamic converging on Germanic, nor Germanic converging on Saamic. Rather, both languages seem to converge on something else that underlies them. What can that something else be?

4.5. A Lost Substratum

Important recent research by Ante Aikio[33] has revealed that the presence of Saami languages in middle and northern Scandinavia, northern Finland, and the Kola Peninsula is the result of an expansion that can be dated as recently as the Common Era. This expansion started from a Saami homeland in southern Finland and adjacent regions of northwestern Russia, probably under the pressure of the northward spread of farming communities that spoke Finnish. The particularly early borrowing of loanwords from Germanic into Proto-Saami suggests that Proto-Saami was in contact with Germanic when it was still in its southern Finnish homeland. That suggests a Germanic presence in southeastern Sweden and perhaps southwestern Finland as well, which fits in with ideas about the prehistoric expansion of Germanic. Since we have seen in section V.2 that Germanic arose in close contact with Balto-Finnic and since we now know that Balto-Finnic was intrusive in Finland, that particular contact zone probably lay on the southern shores of the Baltic Sea. So the Germanic that came into contact with Proto-Saami in Finland was probably itself the result of a northward expansion from the Germanic homeland.

For reasons unknown, Saami was very successful in spreading northwards and westwards among Scandinavian subarctic hunter-gatherer communities during the first millennium. When it did so, it replaced languages that were spoken there earlier. Those languages contributed massively to the Saami lexicon: Lehtiranta (1989) estimated that about 40 to 50 percent of the earliest Saami lexical stock lacks an etymology.[34]

Similar figures have been proposed for the earliest Germanic lexicon, suggesting contact with an unknown donor language on the southern shores of the Baltic, at the expense of which Germanic spread westwards and northwards. No attempts have as yet been made to systematically study the early borrowed layers in Germanic and Saami, let alone compare them with one another, which is unfortunate. My impression is that there is very little overlap between the two, so that for the time being it is reasonable to suggest that we are dealing with at least two different contact languages, which, given the vast geographical area involved (Poland to Finnmark) and the nature of the terrain, is no surprise. Against this background, the challenge is to make sense of the convergence between Proto-Saami, on the one hand, and North and West Germanic, on the other.

What seems clear is that the peculiar treatment of long vowels in stressed syllables and unstressed syllables, which marks the convergence of Saami and Germanic, is not Proto-Germanic (Gothic escaped it) but dialectal Germanic, so it is a feature associated with the spread of Germanic into new territory, approximately during the first centuries AD. The same developments in Saami, by contrast, are common to all of Saami, so they occurred in the Saami protolanguage, i.e. probably when it was still in southern Finland. Proto-Saami differed so tremendously from its ancestor, Finno-Saamic, that one could say it had changed its phonological type altogether. That by itself is indicative of a language shift; that is, Proto-Saami probably arose when a population speaking a language with a completely different sound system switched to Finno-Saamic, in the process giving rise to Proto-Saamic. So we conclude that North and West Germanic spread and Saami arose at the expense of a language or languages that shared a peculiar vowel system, whose features were impressed upon North and West Germanic as well as Saami. That 'language X' was probably spoken around the beginning of the Common Era on the northern and southern shores of the western Baltic Sea. It may have extended further, but information about this is lacking.

Apart from these very specific features of the vowel system of language X, Saami and Germanic share other early features whose roots may be ascribed to language X:

(1) The rise of umlaut (i.e. unstressed vowels influencing the quality of the stressed vowel in the first syllable), which has already been discussed.

(2) The development of complex consonant alternations in the position straddling the first and second syllable of the word. The root of these alternations lies in Finno-Saamic gradation (see V.3.2), as in Finno-Saamic *kota, genitive *kođan 'hut'. In Saami, this developed into goahti, genitive goađi. Typically for Saamic, the final -n of the genitive was lost, but its effect on gradation remained. So the consonantal alternation between first and second syllables has taken on morphological significance: the difference between a nominative and a genitive case in Saami is marked not by a case ending but by the type of consonant between the first and second syllable. Originally, gradation affected only *p,*t, *k, *pp, *tt, *kk, a situation that is preserved in Finnish. Saami extended gradation to all consonants and introduced phonological complications, such as pre-aspiration (ht < t in goahti) and loss of nasals. It also introduced a third degree of consonantal length, one of the features for which Saami is famous amongst linguists: North Saami, for instance, differentiates between three different lengths of l: čálit 'make (him/her) write!', čállit 'to write', and čál'lit 'writers', where l'l indicates overlong l.[35]

Finno-Saamic gradation is responsible for Verner's law in Germanic (V.3.2). Apart from that, Germanic has used other means to create excessively complex alternations of consonants between the first and second syllable. Compare the following series of related words:

dūb-	Old Norse *dúfa* 'to immerse'
dubb-	Norwegian *dubba* 'to stoop', Middle Dutch *dubben* 'to immerse'
dūp-	Dutch *duipen* 'to hang one's head'
dupp-	High German *düppen*, Norwegian *duppa* 'to nod'
duff-	Faeroese *duffa* 'to bob up and down (of a ship)'
dump-	Norwegian, English, Danish *dump* 'hole, pit, pond'
	East Frisian *dumpen* 'to dive'[36]

It is possible to account for all these derivatives of Indo-European *d^hub^h-* 'deep' on the basis of a small number of Germanic sound laws and analogies, as has been shown by Kroonen (2009: 61), just as it is possible to account for the extreme complexity of Saami gradation on the basis of Saami sound laws. Yet it is impossible to understand based on Saami and Germanic themselves why those languages have bothered to create this type of complexity at all and why they have put it to use to express morphological and semantic differences. It may well be that this is yet another feature that Saami and Germanic introduced when the population that spoke language X was assimilated.

Because of its remarkable consonantal features, I have called language X the 'language of geminates'.[37] This is just a convenient label: it is unclear whether one or more languages are involved, or whether it is a phonological and morphological profile of a number of languages that happen to have been spoken in northern Europe, irrespective of their mutual affiliations. On a more abstract level, the rise of umlaut and the introduction of consonantal alternations at the end of the first syllable fall under a common heading: both involve a tendency to express morphological distinctions (such as case and number in nouns, and tense, mood, person, and number in verbs) in or around the first syllable rather than by suffixes and endings. This tendency distinguishes Saami from Balto-Finnic, North and West Germanic from Proto-Germanic, and, further to the west, Irish from Continental Celtic. Consider the following nominal paradigms, which illustrate this northern European syndrome:

	Old Irish	Old Icelandic		Saami
nominative	*f'er* 'man'	*fjǫrðr* 'fjord'	nom.	*giehta* 'hand'
accusative	*f'er*	*fjǫrð*	gen.-acc.	*gieđa*
genitive	*f'ir'*	*fjarðar*	illative	*gīhtii*
dative	*f'iur*	*firði*	locative	*gieđas*

It is remarkable that the northern European syndrome cuts right across three language families. It seems that any language that happened to venture into northern Europe during the first millennium fell victim to this syndrome, irrespective of its affiliation. What this suggests is that the languages spoken in the vast area between Finland and Ireland shared a common phonological basis that was alien to Indo-European and Uralic but left its imprint on those languages as soon as northern European populations switched to them.

This is where the story of Germanic must end—not because we have reached the boundaries of what can be known about the origins of Germanic, but because our present state of knowledge does not allow us to drive away the mists that engulf Germanic beyond the point we have reached so far. Future clarity can be expected in two directions.

There is much more information about the 'language of geminates' that can be gleaned from the languages that replaced it. Loanword studies have only just started to yield results, and systematic investigations have yet to be undertaken. If the language of geminates has left phonological traces, it probably also left its mark on the syntax of northern European languages, but nobody knows what to look for because nobody has ever tried. The other direction in which progress can be made is one that traces Pre-Germanic further back in time, across the two to three millennia that separate it from Proto-Indo-European. This inevitably means raking up the old question of the exact nature of the relationship between Germanic and Balto-Slavic, and it also means reassessing the most ancient loanwords that Uralic languages have adopted from the ancestor of Germanic. These are big questions, and at every new step of the way the number of languages that the traveller is supposed to master in order to answer them increases, while at the same time the chances of finding evidence of language contact become more remote.

VI. Conclusions

This book has tried to answer the question whether language contact has been involved in the rise of the Germanic language family as a whole and of the individual Germanic languages that developed from Proto-Germanic in late Antiquity and the early medieval period. The answer is yes in the following instances:

- Germanic as a separate branch of Indo-European arose as a result of contact with Balto-Finnic (more particularly, probably as a result of Indo-European–Finno-Saamic bilingualism and a subsequent switch to Indo-European, which as a result became Germanic; chapter V.2–3).
- The early break-up of Proto-Germanic into West and North- Germanic was probably engineered when speakers of a lost northern European language (or languages) with a peculiar vowel and consonant system came into contact with Germanic, to which they ultimately switched. A lost language with a sound system with very similar properties was probably involved in turning Finno-Saamic into Proto-Saami. The absorption of this group of languages accompanied the spread of Finno-Saamic in Finland and in central and northern Sweden and Norway, and the spread of Germanic in southern Scandinavia and presumably the northern German plain, including the northern part of the Netherlands (chapter V.4).
- The Old English language as it is known from approximately AD 700 onwards resulted from intensive contact with British Celtic. The signature of this contact is the phonetics underlying Old English *i*-umlaut, *a/u*-umlaut, and breaking, which agrees strikingly, not so much with other Germanic languages, or with surviving British Celtic (Welsh, Cornish, and Breton phonetics and phonology were heavily influenced by Late Spoken Latin), but with Irish (which can be shown to be a recent newcomer from Britain into Ireland: see II.8; it preserves pre-Roman British Celtic phonetics). This contact probably took the form of a rapid shift of a population speaking Celtic and/or Latin with a broad Celtic accent to the language of the Anglo-Saxon settlers. From this merger resulted the early Anglo-Saxon cultures of eastern England,

which spread westwards in largely hostile fashion at the expense of a sub-Roman population of speakers of British Latin and British Celtic. In as far as the linguistic evidence can tell us, it was predominantly the socially lower-ranking population of sub-Roman eastern Britain (which spoke Celtic or Latin with a strong Celtic accent) that threw in its lot with the Anglo-Saxon immigrants. We can identify a socially higher-ranking population which consisted of fluent speakers of western European Late Spoken Latin living in western Britain. This Latin-speaking population gradually switched to speaking western British Celtic. It is tempting to regard these upper-class Latin speakers of the west as fugitives from the Lowland Zone (chapter II).

- High German differs from Low German and Dutch predominantly by having undergone the High German consonant shift (HGCS). In its simplest form, the HGCS turns aspirated plosives (e.g. [tʰ]) into affricates (e.g. [tˢ]), which in the position after vowels may continue to develop into fricatives (e.g. [s(s)]). The most complex form of the HGCS occurred in the Middle German Rhineland and in northern Italy, in the lost dialect of Langobardian. In both areas, contact with Late Spoken Latin was intense, and it is possible to explain the complex form of the HGCS by assuming that fifth- to sixth-century Latin speakers who also spoke Germanic replaced the Germanic aspirated plosives, which were alien to Latin, with Late Latin affricates, which came phonetically close. Crucially, those Latin speakers replaced aspirated plosives with affricates only in those positions in the word in which affricates occurred in Late Latin. In early medieval Langobardian Italy and the Franconian Rhineland, new cultures were welded which prided themselves on their barbarian Germanic roots as well as on being heir to Roman civilization. It was in this culturally self-confident environment that Germanic with a Late Latin accent (i.e. the HGCS) flourished and spread at the expense of other varieties of Germanic (chapter III).

- Where Germanic met Late Latin along the Lower Rhine, Lower Maas, and Schelt, Dutch arose. Between Coastal Dutch in the west, which is identical to prehistoric Frisian, and Eastern Dutch, which to all intents and purposes is identical to northern German, curious Germanic dialects originated that are unique within the family in that they were hardly affected by *i*-umlaut. Instead, they show spontaneous fronting of back vowels in complex geographical patterns. This is Western Dutch, a group of dialects ancestral to the medieval and modern Dutch written language. The Western Dutch area links up intricately with the Old French (Picardian and Walloon) area to its south. Dialectal boundaries within Old French continue northwards into Western Dutch, according to a pattern that strongly suggests that the entire area used to be largely Old French–speaking (or at least bilingual in Old French and Germanic) in the earliest medieval period. Subsequently, Old French retreated southwards, leaving the Western Dutch area speaking

Germanic with a strong Old French accent by the Carolingian period (in approximately the eighth to ninth centuries; chapter IV).

It turns out that language contact, and more particularly language shift, played a pivotal role in the rise of Germanic and three of its modern representatives. This idea is not new. In the words of Antoine Meillet (1917: 74):

> Just as the Consonant Shift and the profound transformation of the vowel system, this fact [i.e. the replacement of a free tonal accent by word-initial intensity stress] indicates external influence. This is a type of pronunciation that is alien to Indo-European; it was introduced by the population that had learned to speak the dialect which has become Germanic.[1]

What is new is that what to Meillet was a single act of language shift has now become a sequence of contact situations involving bilingualism and shift as Germanic arose and subsequently spread gradually across north-western Europe.

This book follows in Meillet's footsteps by highlighting the importance of sound change in tracking down prehistoric language contact. This is because, together with syntactic change, sound change is capable of revealing language shift more clearly than morphological or lexical change. Due to the nature of the comparative method, sound change is much more informative about the prehistory of languages than syntactic change, which is why I have restricted myself to arguing for prehistoric language contact exclusively on the basis of sound change (I.1).

One of the main reasons why Meillet's idea that Germanic resulted from language shift became unfashionable was the rise of structural linguistics, according to which a language is considered to be an integrated system of interconnected elements (sounds, morphemes, lexemes, syntactic rules) which strives towards equilibrium and in which one change provokes others. Structuralism was the greatest breakthrough in twentieth-century linguistics, and all modern linguistic theories are derived from it. Most structuralist approaches account for sound change in terms of the sound system in which the changes take place. Many theories focus on accounting for sound change in terms of general human linguistic faculties, whether those be formulated as the Universal Grammar supposedly underlying all languages or as otherwise hard-wired in the human brain. Such approaches have strongly favoured language-internal explanations of sound change as being somehow simpler and more elegant than explanations on the basis of language contact. Fortunately, as evidence for the pervasive role of language contact in language change is mounting, those approaches are becoming outdated. In some cases, language-internal and language-external explanations are complementary. In others, either the language-internal or the language-external explanation is evidently false.

In the context of this theoretical discussion, it is important to weigh internal and external explanations against one another, which is what I have attempted to do. This entails arguing as explicitly as possible. In sections II.6 and more particularly in II.6.2, a methodology was developed that is capable of singling out sound changes that were probably caused by external factors (contact), even if we happen to know nothing about the contact situation involved. However, a confirmation of the involvement of language contact can be gained only if we have enough knowledge about the contact language that caused the change. What this confirmation invariably boils down to is establishing significant convergence of the languages in contact and identifying which language converged on which. If language A converges on language B, this is an indication that speakers of B have switched to A and in the process retained a B-type accent.

In the case of British Celtic and English, convergence lies in the strikingly similar phonetic basis underlying Old English and the Old Irish type of Celtic. Since Old English moved towards Celtic, this indicates that speakers of Celtic with Old Irish phonetics switched to Old English.

In the case of the HGCS, convergence takes the form of a precise correspondence of the Rhineland German system of the HGCS with the early Romance distribution of affricates across different positions in the word, suggesting a causal relationship between the two. Since Rhineland German was moving towards early Romance, speakers of early Romance apparently switched to German, introducing the HGCS as a Romance accent.

Similarly, making sense of the excessively complex Western Dutch vowel changes involves comparing Western Dutch with neighbouring French dialects of the early medieval period, and realizing that they converge extremely closely. Since Dutch converged on French rather than vice versa, speakers of Old French must have switched to Dutch and whilst doing so introduced an Old French accent, which is responsible for making Dutch the odd one out amongst the Germanic languages.

The running thread is always: convergence is so detailed and so precise that it cannot be due to accident, and one of the two languages involved can be shown to have converged on the other. If that can be established, the correct explanation of the sound changes involved must be based on language contact.

A consequence of reintroducing language contact into historical linguistics is that it stresses the role of speakers in language change. The ubiquity of language change caused by language contact is a reminder that the structure of a language is to a large extent determined by the vagaries of human history rather than by the innate tendencies of the language beast that inhabits our brains. Old English is the product of contact between the Germanic dialects of Anglo-Saxon immigrants and a British Celtic sound system, which means that without British Celtic Old English would not have existed, and consequently neither would Modern English. High German and Dutch would not have existed if Latin had not been their neighbour and if socio-political relations between speakers of Latin, speakers of Germanic, and bilinguals had been slightly different than they were along the Rhine in late Antiquity and the early medieval period. Their ancestor, Proto-Germanic, would not have existed if it were not for the influence of Balto-Finnic and for the highly specific relationship between speakers of Indo-European, of Balto-Finnic, and of both languages in the Baltic Sea region during the first millennium BC. Once it is realized that the direction in which languages change is at the mercy of the arbitrary events that shake the lives of their speakers, the futility of searching for natural or even universal tendencies in language change becomes evident. This is a sobering thought.

Perhaps even more sobering, especially for those who suffer from the misconception that languages should be kept free from external influence, is the conclusion that there is no such thing as a pure language, at least in the Germanic-speaking world. English, Dutch, and German all arose from early medieval counterparts of modern Hispanic English and Turkish German, whereas their presumably unadulterated sister dialects have been dead and buried since time immemorial.

Notes

NOTES TO CHAPTER 1

1. Many important original publications, including the Neogrammarian manifesto, have been made accessible in English by Lehmann (1967). Jespersen (1922: 19–99) and Pedersen (1962) remain invaluable works about nineteenth-century historical linguistics.
2. Durie and Ross (1996) assess the value of the comparative method more than a century after its discovery.
3. Such exceptions do indeed occur. Breton *ebeul*, *eubeul* 'pony' has *eu* in a non-initial syllable, but this is accounted for by a special rule that states that **e* in a final syllable becomes *eu* if the preceding syllable originally contained **eu* (this, again, is a sound law without exceptions). Welsh *nawfed* 'ninth' contains *aw* in a non-final syllable, which can be explained by analogy: a usual way of forming an ordinal from a cardinal number is by adding *-fed* to the cardinal, e.g., *wyth* 'eight', *wythfed* 'eighth'. The word for 'nine' is *naw*, and the word for ninth should have been **nofed according to the sound laws, but the latter was replaced by *nawfed* because that corresponds better to the regular pattern of deriving ordinals from cardinals. The double star ** indicates an incorrect form or a form that never existed.

NOTES TO CHAPTER 2

1. Hines (1990: 19–20).
2. Higham (2007: 6), with his footnote 34.
3. Glossary: *gestern* 'yesterday', *sah* 'saw', *einen* 'a(n)', *Frosch* 'frog', *ich* 'I', *nehme an* 'presume'.
4. Coates (2007: 177–181).
5. Padel (2007: 228–229); his opinion essentially agrees with that of Coates (2007).
6. Pelteret (1995: 43, 319–328); Lutz (2009: 239–243).
7. See Grimmer (2007); Woolf (2007).
8. See especially the various articles in Filppula et al. (2002), in particular David White's forceful article 'Explaining the Innovations of Middle English: What, Where and Why', pp. 153–174; see also the series *The Celtic Englishes*, edited by Hildegard Tristram. Volume 13/2 of the journal *English Language and Linguistics*, July 2009, is dedicated entirely to the presumed Celtic influence on the English of England. Miller (2012), who deals with external influences on English, reports on the possible Celtic contribution to English on pp. 35–40.

9. Rivet and Smith (1979).
10. Collingwood et al. (1990–1995).
11. McWhorter (2009: 172–178).
12. E.g. Würzburg glosses 17c20 *is burbe dom cía do-gnéo móidim* 'it is foolishness to me that I should do boasting (i.e. that I did boast)'.
13. A corpus of inscriptions and an important discussion on how to use them for dating purposes is Sims-Williams (2003). Inscriptions are referred to by their number in Macalister (1945–1949): *Corpus Inscriptionum Celticarum Insularum* (CIIC).
14. Sargent (2002); Woolf (2003).
15. On Latin influence on Highland British Celtic, see Schrijver (2002, 2007: 166–168); Russell (2011).
16. On British Latin, see Adams (2007: 577–623); Smith (1983). The Latinization of Highland British Celtic is extensively discussed in Schrijver (2002: 100–102).
17. All this goes back to Parsons (2011: 127), who is more circumspect, however: he keeps open the possibility that these Latin terms were borrowed into Anglo-Saxon previously, on the Continent, so that they tell us nothing about the linguistic situation in Britain. Since the main bulk of Anglo-Saxon settlers set out from areas that were at a considerable distance from the late Antique Roman Empire, the plausibility of that scenario is remote.
18. Editions: CIIC (Macalister 1945–1949); *Early Christian Monuments of Wales* (ECMW; Nash-Williams 1950); Okasha (1993); Redknap et al. (2007); Edwards (2007); Thomas (1991–1992). Inscriptions are cited from Sims-Williams (2003: 369–387), with reference to CIIC and ECMW. See especially Charles-Edwards (2012), which appeared too late for me to take full stock of it.
19. Thus already Williams (1943: 209–210). Jackson (1953: 622–623) suggests the possibility that the genitive is triggered by an omitted noun such as *corpus*: (*corpus*) *Figulini hic iacit* 'the body of Figulinus lies here', attributing this to Ogam Irish influence, but a comparable construction does not exist in Ogam Irish.
20. Jackson (1953: 623) dates this type of confusion as late as the late sixth century or early seventh century (but see Sims-Williams [2003: 272] on the *Tegernacus* inscription).
21. /ə/ is pronounced as received pronunciation *-er* in *mother*.
22. Characters in brackets [ ] are in phonetic script: [tʲ] = English *ch* in *chip*; [ɪ] = English *i* in *chip*; [j] = *y* in *young*; [ā] = long a. ['] denotes that the stress is on the following vowel. So ['jātʲɪt] is pronounced approximately as (English) *jahtchit*.
23. Grandgent (1907: 103–104); Bonnet (1890: 123–124).
24. Other examples of Celtic Latin inscriptions that contain *ic* are CIIC 344/ ECMW 73, CIIC 324/ECMW 34, CIIC 327/ECMW 43, and CIIC 395/ECMW 102.
25. Grandgent (1907: 106–107); Stotz (1996–2004: III:158–162).
26. Meyer-Lübke (1895: 29). The obscure and damaged inscription CIIC 372/ ECMW 160 DE[. . .]BARBALOM FI[L]IVS BROCAGNI, whose Ogam Irish counterpart is almost completely illegible (cf. Sims-Williams 2003: 114, 218, 371), may perhaps be another instance: *de* [ ]*barbalom* 'of [?]barbalus', where in the fashion of Late Spoken Latin the preposition *de* + accusative replaces the Classical Latin genitive case.
27. The confusion reflects a merger of Classical Latin short *ŭ* and long *ō*. Other examples in the medieval British Latin corpus comprise CIIC 499/Ok 77 NEPVS 'grandson' (*nepōs*) and CIIC 408/ECMW 229 PRONEPVS 'great-grandson'

(*pronepōs*); cf. also CIIC 505 (Isle of Man) MONOMENTI 'grave monument' for Classical Latin *monumenti* and all instances cited below as examples of *-us* being spelled as *-o*.

28. The latter is a decidedly un-Celtic development: in British Celtic, **gn* became **γn > *jn*, whose **j* merged with a preceding vowel; cf. the Latin loanwords *signum* and *lignum* 'wood', which became *swyn* and *llwyn* in Welsh.

29. *ae > e*: all examples are genitives in *-ae* of *a*-stems, e.g. CIIC 320/ECMW 26 ORVVITE MVLIERI '(his) wife Orfita' (*Orfitae mulieris*), CIIC 401/ECMW 183 CAVNE (*Caunae*), and CIIC 451/ECMW 401 TVNCCETACE (*Tuncetacae*); *ē* is spelled as <i> in CIIC 461/Ok 66 TRIS FILI ERCILINGI 'the three sons of Ercilingus' (*trēs fīlī Ercilingi*).

30. Bourciez (1946: 51).

31. Grandgent (1907: 126); cf. Adams (2007: 636).

32. On the hypothesis that the Latin case system of these inscriptions was hopelessly confused, one might propose that genitives in *-i* instead of the expected *-is* do not represent phonological loss of *-s* but rather the generalization of the *o*-stem genitive *-ī*. That would not explain the nominatives in *-i*, *-e*, however, nor the forms in *-o* from *-us*.

33. This observation that British Latin survived as a spoken language because it developed in tandem with Late Spoken Latin on the Continent has also been made by Charles-Edwards (2012: 110), who adds the argument that Latin loanwords in Irish presuppose a Late Spoken Latin in western Britain.

34. For the names in this inscription, see Sims-Williams (2003: 46–47, 343, 38–39, 318).

35. As in *iacit = iacet* and *cive(s) = civi(s)*, discussed earlier, and *nomena = nomina* 'names' in CIIC 448/ECMW 370.

36. In all of Late Spoken Latin, the Classical Latin vowels *ĕ*, *ĭ*, and *ae* have merged in final syllables (Meyer-Lübke 1890: 259, 262), so it would not be surprising if the same had happened in British Latin.

37. The alternative of taking *Onerati* to be a genitive masculine and filling the following gap with [VXSOR] 'Honoratus' wife' is unlikely because it would place *uxsor* after the husband's name rather than in its usual British Latin position before it.

38. For an extensive discussion of the attested and reconstructable forms, see Coates in Coates and Breeze (2000: 15–32); see also section II.5.3.3 below.

39. Schrijver (1995a: 259–264).

40. Schrijver (1995a: 30–44).

41. For details of vowel changes in final syllables in Late Spoken Latin, cf. Meyer-Lübke (1890: 259, 262–264, 272–277, 565–567).

42. I have omitted the Latin *u*-stems, which on the evidence of the genitive *magistrati* (CIIC 394/ECMW 103) instead of *magistratus* had apparently merged with the type *hortus*. For that reason, bilingual Irish-Latin inscriptions treat Irish *u*-stem names as Latin names with a genitive ending *-i* (CIIC 500/Manx AMMECATI, ROCATI; CIIC 327/ECMW 43 and CIIC 457/Ok 18 DVNOCATI; Jackson 1953: 187–188). The type *faciēs* has also been omitted because of the small number of its members.

43. For this information I am indebted to Henry Hurst, University of Cambridge.

44. Editions: Lambert (2002: 304–306); Tomlin (1988: 133). Interpretations: Tomlin (1987); Schrijver (2005a: 57–60); Mullen (2007). There is limited uncertainty about the reading of the second (*deiana?*), third (*deieda?*), and sixth (*cuamunai?*) words.

45. Close vowels are produced with the tongue close the palate (such as in English *keen* and *do*); open vowels are produced with the tongue and lower jaw down

(such as in English *hat* and *jar*); mid vowels are in between (such as in English *jay* and *goat*).

46. [ˇ] indicates nasalization: [ṽ] is pronounced by simultaneously pronouncing English *v* and having air escape from the nostrils as if pronouncing *n*. This is a very rare sound in the languages of the world. It occurs in modern Scots Gaelic.

47. By Hubert Petersmann, during a lecture in Munich (December 2000); cf. Petronius 117.5. He also interpreted the endings in *devina deveda* as late Latin datives, but Mullen (2007: 39) more plausibly takes them as vocatives (the corresponding Celtic dative is found in *cuamiinai*). *Devina* is late Latin and also a well-known Latin loan into Celtic (*dīvīnus* > Welsh *dewin* 'divine'), and *Deveda* could be the Celtic divinity of betrothal (Welsh *dyweddi* 'betrothal'). For similar Latin-Gaulish hybrids, see Meid (1980).

48. <cua> can theoretically be read as /kwa/, but this is problematic in view of the fact that British Celtic, like Gaulish, generally turns *kw into *p*; the alternative is /kua/, with a diphthong /ua/ that until Châteaubleau lacked a parallel elsewhere in the early Celtic corpus.

49. That also means, incidentally, that the names in *-defer* cannot be used to show that speakers of British Celtic rather than Latin had lingered on in Hampshire until the Anglo-Saxon conquest (*pace* Parsons 2011: 113).

50. See Richard Coates in Coates and Breeze (2000: 15–17) for a synopsis of the sources and pp. 17–31 of the same for an admirable discussion of many aspects of etymology and transmission. Coates's views on both issues differ from those presented here.

51. The shortening of long vowels before resonants (*r*, *l*, *m*, *n*) and plosives, which occurred in many Indo-European languages, is known as Osthoff's law (cf. Schrijver 1995a: 29n1 on Celtic).

52. To be more precise, borrowing must have occurred after the rule *nd* > *nn* had ceased to be productive and after the development of pretonic *u to *$ə$ had eliminated the possibility of borrowing *$Lund$- as anything other than Welsh *Llund-* (where <u> is phonetically [ʉ]). This suggests a date of borrowing around 600 at the earliest.

53. Schrijver (1995b).

54. Rix et al. (2001: 412–413).

55. What remains unexplained is the medieval Latin form *Londonium*, with second syllable -*o*-. Perhaps it represents an artificial Latinization based on examples such as Old English *Wreocen* < *Viroconium* (Wroxeter), *Canonium* (Kelvedon, Essex), *Ariconium* (Weston, Herefordshire), and *Dumnonii* (Devon and Scotland).

56. /θ/ and /ð/ are the sounds spelled <th> in English words like *think* and *there*, respectively.

57. For a detailed discussion with references to secondary literature, see Schrijver (2009: 197–198).

58. This is the usual way of presenting vowel systems: the top row contains close vowels (produced with the tongue close to the palate, and the mouth only slightly opened), and the following rows contain vowels that are step by step more open (produced with the tongue one or more degrees lower, away from the palate, and with the mouth gradually more open). The left column contains front vowels (produced with the tongue moved forward), the following column contains central vowels (produced with the tongue in the rest position), and the third column has the back vowels (produced with a retracted tongue). One can get a sense of what those terms mean in practice by pronouncing in sequence the vowels of English *mane*, *hurt*, and *boat*: the tongue moves horizontally from front to central to back position: e - ɜ - o, but in all three stays in

the same vertical plane (mid); in English, back vowels are automatically also pronounced with rounded lips, which affects o.

59. *Rounded* means pronounced with rounded lips. [y] is the vowel of French *pur*, and [ø] occurs in French *peur* (at least as a frequent variant besides the more open [œ]). The sounds do not exist in standard English. Consequently, English native speakers who have a stab at speaking French usually replace them with their closest English equivalents, the vowels in standard English *good* [ʊ] and *hurt* [ɜ], respectively.

60. Languages such as North Welsh, Estonian, and Russian do have unrounded close and mid back vowels: try to pronounce the vowel of English *rude* and strain yourself to keep your tongue in place whilst holding your lips in the unrounded position (as if pronouncing the vowel in *keep*); avoid unnecessary convulsions (use a mirror or consult an honest friend), and you are close to pronouncing correctly the vowel in Russian *byk* 'bull' and North Welsh *tŷ* 'house'.

61. Consonants can be back and front, too, which means they share specific movements of the tongue with [u] and [i], respectively.

62. Typically non-gradual are some forms of dissimilation and assimilation (like that of *r* to *l* in Latin *peregrīnus* 'foreigner' > *pelegrīnus*, whence English *pilgrim*) and contact-induced change.

63. Or at least translatability, by offering speakers a few simple rules that turn the sounds of one dialect into another.

64. Schrijver (2002: 106–107), with slight adaptations of symbols.

65. Schrijver (2002: 104), with slight adaptations of symbols.

66. Mallory (2013: 243–286) argues in favour of two windows of opportunity: c. 1000 BC and during the second or first century BC. The former is almost impossibly early for linguistic reasons, while the latter is close enough to the first century AD date suggested in this chapter.

67. Oppenheimer (2007) and Sykes (2007) are well-publicized examples of a fast-growing literature on the genetic 'origin of the British'; both offer good introductions to methodology. A very sound survey on Irish genetic origins is Mallory (2013: 215–242).

68. Isaac (2009) argued convincingly that the original Welsh name for Ireland was *Ywerddon* and that the Modern Welsh name *Iwerddon* (fourteenth century onwards) stems from a confusion with a very similar-looking but etymologically different word meaning 'fertile land', Proto-Celtic *$\bar{\imath}$werjū*, which is also found in Old Irish *íriu* 'land' and ultimately stems from Proto-Indo-European *$piHwer\text{-}ih_2$* 'fat, fertile'.

69. Stüber (1998: 96).

70. O'Rahilly (1943: 8–9) reconstructed Old Irish nominative *Éïrn*, genitive *Éärn*, accusative *Érnu*, dative *Érnaib*, which regularly became Middle Irish *Érainn, Érann, Érnu, Érnaib*; for the phonological development cf. Old Irish *íarn, íairn* > Middle Irish *íarann, íarainn* 'iron'. See further Uhlich (1995: 15–16) for the impossibility of reconstructing *i-* or *ī-*. As the regularly expected Middle Irish forms would have been *Éirinn, Érann, Éirniu*, non-palatal -*r*- must have spread from the genitive *Érann*.

71. O'Rahilly (1957: 88n3, 188, 190n2) on Iar mac Dedad.

72. Pokorny (1916: 236) accounts for the forms with *ī-* by assuming that this is a Greek rendering of Celtic *$\bar{e}$-* or *ei-*, which is unlikely because Ionic Greek possessed both close *$\bar{e}$* and the diphthong *ei* and therefore had no need to replace the Celtic sound with anything else. O'Rahilly's desperate attempt (1943: 26) to connect both forms on the basis of a deep Indo-European root etymology is obsolete.

73. Bergin (1946: 152–153); Vennemann (1998) on Semitic *'y-wr'(m)* 'Copper Island'.
74. De Bernardo Stempel (2000: 96–107) provides Celtic etymologies for almost all names. The majority are mere possibilities.
75. Jackson (1953: 328–329).
76. McManus (1991); Ziegler (1994).
77. McManus (1991: 175n35), *pace* Harvey (1985).
78. Schrijver (2000); Isaac (2003); Schrijver (2005b).
79. Raftery (1994: 200–203).
80. The Brigantian uprising coincided with the Batavian revolt on the other side of the North Sea (AD 69–70). Both were tied up with Roman power struggles that ensued after the death of Nero. On the Roman side, the commander Petillius Cerialis was involved in quenching both revolts. We know very little about how Rome's adversaries were organized and whether they were in contact with one another, but it seems conceivable that the defeat of the Batavian confederacy inspired some of the skilled seafaring peoples along the coast of the Low Countries who had been involved in the Batavian revolt to sail across the North Sea and join the Brigantes. When in AD 74 Brigantia was crushed, those exiles may have joined Brigantian exiles moving into Ireland. This scenario would explain why Ptolemy has the tribes of the *Manapoi* and *Kaukoi* along Ireland's east coast (compare the *Menapii* and *Chauci* along the coast in the Low Countries). Needless to say, this is just speculation.
81. Charles-Edwards (2000: 151–152).
82. See the special volume of the journal *Emania*, volume 11 (1993).
83. Charles-Edwards (2000: 155–158).
84. A palatalized consonant is formed by pronouncing a consonant and a [j] (as in English *yes* [jɛs]) at the same time, so that they merge. In English the *c* in *cute*, the *d* in *duke*, the *p* in *puke*, and the *tth* in *Matthew* are palatalized [kʲ], [dʲ], [pʲ], and [θʲ], respectively.
85. The fronted pronunciation of the vowels is not directly attested in Old Irish. However, since all Modern Irish and Scots Gaelic dialects agree on this point and since it is virtually impossible to pronounce these forms without recourse to such phonetics, their subphonemic presence in Old Irish is guaranteed.
86. In Old Irish, *au* is spelled consistently, while *iu* interchanges with *i*. This is understandable because there is no phonological opposition between /iuCʲ/ and /iCʲ/, while there is between /auCʲ/ and /aCʲ/.
87. Campbell (1977: 82–83).
88. Greene (1973: 134).
89. Schumacher (2007: 185–195). Lutz (2009) argues for a development of the Old English double paradigm on British soil, taking insufficient account of Schumacher's argument.
90. Parsons (1997), with references.

NOTES TO CHAPTER 3

1. See in general Pohl (2002).
2. Neumann (1998: 5–6).
3. Schrijver (2003b).
4. Koller and Laitenberger (1998); see pp. ix–x on the name.
5. A different point of view is expressed by Seebold (1998: 15): 'Im ganzen sieht es so aus, dass *Sweben* einer umfassenden Selbstbezeichnung der kontinentalen Germanen (wenigstens im Osten) sehr nahekommt'.

6. Note that what is relevant is the position of *p, *t, and *k at the time when the HGCS operated, sometime during the early medieval period. Later changes to that position are irrelevant.

7. For a detailed account of the reflexes of the HGCS in German dialects, see Goblirsch (2005: 182–199), with plentiful references to the secondary literature.

8. The failure of the HGCS to affect these words is usually explained differently. See Schrijver (2011a: 225–231) for a detailed discussion of the fate of word-final *t. Another rule that has hitherto remained unrecognized is the development of shifted *t > *ts to t if it came into contact with *d by the loss of an intervening vowel, e.g. pre–Old High German *lāted 'ye let' > *lātsed > *lātsd > *lātt > type V lōt (Schrijver 2011a: 233–236).

9. Davis (2005); Goblirsch (2005: 197); Iverson and Salmons (2006). Davis (2011) discusses the history of the vowel system, which is relevant for determining the relation between vowel length and the HGCS in this dialect.

10. Remacle (1948, development 32).

11. Crompvoets (1988: 103–105).

12. Haubrichs (1987: 1354–1355); Wagner (1977).

13. Schwan and Behrens (1963: 115–119); Rheinfelder (1953: 197–211); Richter (1934: 83); Schrijver (2011a: 240–242).

14. The only French dialect that did not turn pj into ch is Walloon: the dialect of Liège has sèpe instead of standard French sache (Remacle 1948, development 38).

15. Iverson and Salmons (2006); Davis (2008a, 2008b).

16. See Pohl (1997; 2002: 186–212); see also Landschaftsverband Rheinland 2008).

17. Pohl (2002: 196–197).

18. Rolf Bergmann *referred to by* Vennemann (2008: 240 including footnote 65, 241); see also Schrijver (2011a: 243–245).

19. The analysis is that of Schrijver (2011a: 244–245), based on Rohlfs (1949).

20. Whether it was *ts or *tʃ depended on the subdialect within northern Italian Latin.

21. German in present-day northern Italy is the result of a later expansion, based on type I dialects.

22. See especially Wormald (2003).

23. Translation: Wormald (2003: 34).

24. Translation: Wormald (2003: 28).

25. Wormald (2003: 34–35).

26. Wormald (2003: 35).

27. Wormald (2003: 32).

28. The historical analysis of type II that was suggested in section III.3 above bears out that type II started out as type I but had other sound developments interfering with its effects.

29. Franconian actually did so in the case of i-umlaut. Vennemann (2008) proposed that the HGCS was originally characteristic of almost all of Germany but was undone by the influence of the Franks, whose language originally had not experienced the HGCS. According to this view, the extent to which the HGCS has been ousted corresponds to the intensity of Franconian influence, and hence the HGCS was preserved better in the south than in the north. One of his cues was the HGCS in Langobardian; he assumes the HGCS had already affected Langobardian in its first-century AD *Urheimat* along the Lower Elbe. That idea is irreconcilable with the ideas expressed in the present chapter.

NOTES TO CHAPTER 4

1. Durrell (1990: 73), with references.
2. Data from Boutkan and Kossmann (1996: 20–25).
3. [ɜ] is pronounced approximately as *u* in English *curse* but with simultaneous rounding of the lips.
4. The [y] and German *ü* are pronounced as in French *nuque* [nyk], which approaches the Glasgow English pronunciation of the vowel in *good*.
5. Van Bavel (2010): 142–145), with references.
6. Howell (2006).
7. Goossens (1980).
8. A more common name is Ingwaeonic, but since that refers to a hotchpotch of old and recent features in a number of languages, it has outlived its usefulness.
9. Schrijver (1999: 18–19), with references.
10. The same Coastal Dutch development is found in the place name *Swieten* (South Holland) < *Swōti- < *Swŏti- (compare English *sweet*, standard Dutch *zoet* [zut]). Other examples are those where *ō developed from *an in typically Coastal Dutch, English, and Frisian fashion, as in Middle Dutch *hiele* 'heel' < *hōhila- < *hanhila; Modern Dutch (Zeeland) *smieë* 'soft, smooth' < *smōdi- < *smōθi- < *smanθi-.
11. Other examples are Middle Dutch *clāvere* 'clover' < *klaibra- (Old English *clāfre*) as opposed to non-Coastal Dutch *klēver* and the place name *Haamstede* < *haima-* 'home' (Old English *hām*) as opposed to non-Coastal Dutch *heem*. Cf. De Vaan (2011).
12. Mostert (2009: 83–162).
13. Schrijver (1999, 2002: 102–108).
14. The different treatment of this *y depends on phonetic context: if *y stood before a single consonant at the end of the word or before a double consonant (this is what is called a closed syllable), it became ɜ, spelled <u>. If *y was followed by a single consonant and a vowel (in a so-called open syllable), it became ŏ, spelled <eu>.
15. See Weijnen (1991: 4–5) on modern dialects; Franck (1910: 64) and Goossens (1980: 195) on Middle Dutch.
16. It could also be spelled <oe>, <o>, but these are ambiguous because they can also be used to spell back vowels. Eastern spellings of <u, ue> may denote [u].
17. Map 113 shows similar results for *behoef, behuef* 'need'.
18. See Goossens (1980: 166–167); see Goossens (1962: 320–321) on the possibility that [bryr] reflects a form with regular *i*-umlaut, which is problematic by itself (analogical introduction from the plural or a diminutive in *-kīn?) as well as unnecessary in view of other instances of spontaneous fronting of *ō.
19. Weijnen (1991: 81).
20. Weijnen (1991: 38); almost all these dialectal forms belong to the Western Dutch area, so cannot be explained by *i*-umlaut because that did not affect Western Dutch. Modern Dutch [muder] is an artificial archaism because regular sound change should have deleted the *-d-*; the source of the archaism may be the language of the church (Mary as *moeder Gods* 'mother of God').
21. Van Loey (1976: 73).
22. Kloeke (1936). A complication is the fact that modern English *Wednesday* and Frisian *weensdei* (but not Old English *wōdnesdæg*, Old Frisian *wōnsdei*, or any other Germanic form) seem to show *i*-umlaut. A corresponding Coastal Dutch form is attested in Middle Dutch *dies wenesdaghes* (AD 1260). On the basis of these forms, the detailed investigation by Pijnenburg (1980: 144–176, particularly 154–157) comes out in favour of *i*-umlaut in *weunsdag*. This cannot be correct, however: either *weunsdag*, with its predominantly western

distribution, is Western Dutch, in which case it could not undergo *i*-umlaut because Western Dutch did not; or it is Coastal Dutch, but that turned *$\bar{o}$ into *$\bar{e}$ > *ie* rather than into *$\ddot{o}$ by *i*-umlaut.

23. Goossens (1980: 183).
24. Taeldeman (1978: 9–10) dates this diphthongization, which affected all long vowels except *$\bar{a}$ in Flanders and Brabant, very early, before the spontaneous fronting. His chronology is based on structural considerations inspired by transformational-generative phonology rather than on medieval sources and is probably incorrect for some vowels, such as *$\bar{o}$, which in medieval Flanders became *ou* (see main text above).
25. Schönfeld and Van Loey (1970: 80) point to Dutch *roer* 'reed' < *$*rauza-$ and *op-doemen* 'to loom' < Middle Dutch *dōmen* 'to steam' < *$*daumjan$, which may have originated from Flanders.
26. Daan and Francken (1972: 33–38); Van Loon (1986: 66–70); Weijnen (1991: 11, 21); Franck (1910: 69).
27. Nielsen (1985: 129–130, 206); Van Loon (1986: 68–69).
28. For instance by Schrijver (1999: 12–13).
29. The split of English *u* into [ʊ] (*full*) and [ʌ] (*cut, son*) is so late (sixteenth century) that it cannot be connected (e.g. Ekwall 1975: 51).
30. Van Loon (1986: 68).
31. Schönfeld (1932).
32. E.g. Gysseling (1961: 51); Weijnen (1964: 12); Van Loon (1986: 80); Daan and Francken (1977: 17); Weijnen (1991: 32). Proponents of an indigenous development point to the link of *$\bar{u}$ > *$\bar{y}$ with the development of *$\bar{o}$ > *$\bar{u}$, in terms of a push or pull chain: dialects that do not show the latter also do not show the former. Both developments are clearly linked, but that is quite compatible with the idea that the vowel system reacted to a fronting whose origin was external. Those who favour an internally Dutch origin of fronting of *$\bar{u}$ must either assume that French fronting was independent and that the French *y*/*u* line links up with the Dutch one purely by chance (which would just be too accidental to accept), or assume that the development started in Dutch and was borrowed into French as a Germanic substratum feature (which such linguists never do because they regard an internal explanation as a superior alternative to an explanation based on language contact).
33. The latter option is preferred by Goossens (1980: 193–194, following Tavernier-Vereecken).
34. [ɝ] is pronounced as in English *curse* but with extra lip rounding, [y] as in French *pur*.
35. Gysseling (1960: 78); Schrijver (1999: 4).
36. One important aspect of Buccini's account that cannot easily be dismissed are hyper-Franconianisms such as Modern Dutch *roop* 'rope' and *oot* 'oats' instead of expected *$*reep$, *$*eet$. The background is that the Proto-Germanic diphthongs *$*ai$ and *$*au$ regularly merged as *$\bar{a}$ in Coastal Dutch (as they did in Old English and Frisian) but became *$\bar{e}$ and *$\bar{o}$, respectively, in Franconian Dutch. Examples are *$*raip-$ and *$*slaut-$, which regularly became Coastal Dutch *$*r\bar{a}p-$ 'rope' and *$*sl\bar{a}t-$ 'ditch', as opposed to *$*r\bar{e}p-$ and *$*sl\bar{o}t-$ in Franconian Dutch. Speakers of Coastal Dutch who wished to speak Franconian Dutch were aware that where they said *$\bar{a}$, Franconian speakers used either *$\bar{e}$ or *$\bar{o}$. By Franconizing *$*r\bar{a}p-$ and *$\bar{a}t-$ as *r\bar{o}p-* and *\bar{o}t-* rather than *$*r\bar{e}p-$ and *$\bar{e}t-$, they selected the incorrect one of the two possible substitutes.
37. See in general Hofman et al. (2000).
38. On seal boxes and the Batavians, see the important article, with plentiful references, by Derks and Roymans (2002).
39. See especially Gysseling (1981: 111–115).

40. Künzel et al. (1988: 379, 380).
41. For quick and easy reference to the reconstruction of Dutch in the first millennium, see Van Loon (1986: 45–70). The only difference with my presentation is that he dates the development of *$\bar{u}$ to *$\bar{y}$ to the Middle Dutch period, so after c. 1100, because he regards fronting as a reaction to the Middle Dutch development of *uo to *$\bar{u}$. But it is just as possible that fronting *created* the opportunity for that shift, in which case fronting precedes *uo > *$\bar{u}$. Orthography is of no help: both [ū] and [ȳ] would have been spelled as <u> in Old Dutch as well as generally in Old French.
42. [i] as in English *heat*, [ɪ] as in English *hit*.
43. For the Celtic etymology see Künzel et al. (1988: 116), who, however, refer to a non-existent Gaulish suffix *-ate* (place names such as *Arelate*, *Condate*, *Carpentorate*, and *Argentorate* do not contain a suffix *-ate* but are compounds with a second member *-late*, *-date*, or *-rate*; see Lambert 1994: 38). What Gaulish does have is a suffix *$-atis$, which can be added to place names and indicates an inhabitant of the place: *Tolosa* 'Toulouse', *Tolosatis*; *Namausus* 'Nîmes', *Namausatis*. The same suffix is found in the Gaulish tribal name *Atrebates*, who gave their name to modern *Arras* (Dutch *Atrecht*), in northwestern France. This is derived from *$attreb\bar{a}$ 'habitation'; cf. Middle Welsh *athref* (Lambert 1994: 35).
44. It should go on record that they did acquire a few Germanic consonants that were alien to Late Latin/Old French: *w (but so did French in general, by acquiring lots of Germanic loans containing /w/), *x (if Late Latin *kx^j< *kj did not have a hand in this) and *h (but so did many northern dialects of French, again under Germanic influence). More significant is that they did adopt Germanic stress: Old French stressed the final syllable of the word, not counting final -ə, whereas Germanic normally stressed the first syllable.

NOTES TO CHAPTER 5

1. E.g. Mallory (1989: 84–87).
2. Riessler (2008); Kusmenko (2011).
3. Collinder (1965); Kortlandt (1989); Koivulehto (1995); Kortlandt (2001), unfortunately without reference to Koivulehto's article.
4. Literature on the subject is extensive. See especially Koivulehto (1999). For older loanwords from Germanic, see Hahmo et al. (1991–2012).
5. See in general Sammallahti (1998).
6. This section is much indebted to Kallio (2007).
7. Pre-Germanic is a stage that has already lost the Proto-Indo-European laryngeals but retains the difference between palatovelar and labiovelar plosives. It may or may not have had a series of pure velar plosives, the phonemic status of which remains unresolved. This Pre-Germanic system is also the system that underlies Balto-Slavic as well as most other Indo-European branches.
8. Note, however, that according to Vennemann (1984) the voiceless plosives were aspirated; in his system, the voiced plosives were glottalized, and the voiced aspirates were plain voiced plosives.
9. Please remember that in this book *b^h, d^h, etc. are just convenient symbols with an ill-described phonetic content. The traditional assumption is that Verner's law (no. 2) postdated Grimm's law (no. 4), hence that Pre-Germanic *p, t, k, k^w first became *f, θ, x, x^w by Grimm's law, which then yielded *v, δ, γ, γ^w; these finally became b, d, g, gw after consonants in most Germanic languages and across the board in High German. In view of the latter complication and

for the sake of the most efficient formulation of Kluge's law, I prefer the reverse order, following Vennemann (1984: 20–22) and particularly Kortlandt (1988, 1991). Readers who prefer the traditional rule order can easily make the necessary permutations.

10. This account of Kluge's law follows the account given by Kortlandt (1991); see also Kroonen (2009: 15–22).
11. Hill (2003: 73–216).
12. Adapted from Meillet (1917: 50–51).
13. The terms are those used in an extremely important article on the history of gradation in the Uralic languages: Helimski (1995). This account of gradation follows Helimski.
14. See the discussion in Helimski (1995: 17–20, 27–28). Sammallahti (1998: 3) formulates it guardedly thus: both branches of Finno-Saamic developed gradation separately, but its roots lie in phonotactic preconditions that were inherited from Proto-Uralic.
15. To be more precise, the unit that Nganasan uses is not the syllable but the mora. The difference is that a long vowel counts as one syllable but two morae. Since long vowels are not of Proto-Uralic date, the syllable coincides with the mora in Proto-Uralic.
16. Thus Posti (1953: 74–86); Koivulehto and Vennemann (1996).
17. Sammallahti (1998: 192–193).
18. Sammallahti (1998: 192–193).
19. Kallio (2007: 232, 239–240).
20. In non-initial syllables, the loss of *w after vowels had created the vowels y, u, o, which did not exist in Finno-Saamic (Kallio 2007: 232; Itkonen 1997: 237–238; Sammallahti 1999: 72–73).
21. On the retained difference between *$\bar{o}$ and *$\bar{a}$, see V.4.1 below.
22. A very useful book on the development of final syllables in Germanic is Boutkan (1995). Boutkan dismissed the Qualitative Theory on improper grounds as well; see Schrijver (2003a: 195–198). A response to my article is Kortlandt (2005), who in an attempt to salvage Boutkan's dismissal of the Qualitative Theory manages not to discuss the Qualitative Theory at all. What he does discuss are a number of details concerning the Old English *$\bar{a}$-stems, which Boutkan himself had done a better job explaining and contextualizing.
23. For a detailed argumentation, see Schrijver (2003a: 201–206). Guus Kroonen (2010) has made an interesting attempt to undermine the argument by eliminating the relevance of *$t\bar{a}m$ > Old Norse *þá*. He revives the older notion that *$t\bar{a}m$ became Proto-Germanic *$\theta\bar{o}n$ (so with merger of *$\bar{a}$ with *$\bar{o}$) and was subsequently shortened to *$\theta a(n)$ when this pronoun was used in unstressed position (short *o did not exist in the language at the time, so shortening did not yield that vowel). At a later date, the unstressed variant *θa ousted the stressed variant *$\theta\bar{o}$, and newly stressed *θa was lengthened to *$\theta\bar{a}$, whence the Old Norse form *þá*. This convoluted explanation with its ad hoc shortening in unstressed position (which for some reason did not affect any other form in the paradigm) could be buried for all time if it were not for the Faeroese accusative singular *ta*, which indeed has a short vowel, as Kroonen points out. However, a short vowel in Modern Faeroese does not prove a short vowel in ancestral Proto-Norse of more than a millennium ago. All we know for certain, as Kroonen shows himself beyond doubt, is that in Faeroese Pre-Germanic *$t\bar{a}m$ 'that, her' > Faeroese *ta* did not merge with the Pre-Germanic accusative plural masculine *$tons$ 'those, them' > Faeroese *tá* in spite of the fact that standard Old Norse has the form *þá* for both of them. That is an interesting and possibly archaic feature of Faeroese: Faeroese may have preserved the difference

between eleventh-century *þá 'her' and *þá^n 'them' (with nasalization of the vowel in the latter), which the early Old Norse of the *First Grammatical Treatise* still has but standard Old Norse no longer does. Or Faeroese may have innovated by shortening *þá 'her' but not *þá 'them' in the same way that Kroonen assumes Proto-Germanic *θōn was the only form in its paradigm to be shortened (compare Old Norse svá 'so', which is attested in two forms in Faeroese: long svá and short and contracted so). Either way, the Faeroese evidence cannot show that there must have been a shortened accusative singular *θa(n) 'that, her' in prehistoric Germanic.

24. The only exception is *tām > Old Norse þá 'that, her', which was discussed in V.4.1.
25. Old long vowels in middle syllables were lost by syncope if they were close (as ē is), while they were preserved as a if they were open (as ā is): Heusler (1964: 37).
26. This is also suggested by other forms in the past tense paradigm: *wakǣdōn > *wakēdō > Old Norse vakða 'I was awake'; *wakǣdunt > *wakēdun > vǫkðu 'they were awake'.
27. In Old Runic inscriptions, the suffix of the first singular of the weak past was -do.
28. Hirt (1931: 48); compare Gothic awepi 'flock of sheep'.
29. For details, see Schrijver (2003a: 215–217).
30. On the early loss of *u in the third syllable, see Boutkan (1995: 67–69, 72), and on the dative plural suffix *-muz or *-miz and the forms Vatvims, Aflims in late Antique inscriptions of the Lower Rhine region, see Boutkan (1995: 196–197). In many instances, analogy restored a lost vowel.
31. This account of Saami historical phonology is based on Sammallahti (1998: 181–189).
32. Later developments in Saamic are similar to Germanic developments but less strikingly so (see Schrijver 2003a: 219–220).
33. Aikio (2006: 39–47).
34. Aikio (2004) collected many such substrate terms, analysed their phonology, and added material from place names.
35. Sammallahti (1998: 48).
36. Kuiper (1995).
37. A geminate is a double or long consonant, such as ff, bb, and pp in the words mentioned in the main text. See Schrijver (2001).

NOTE TO CHAPTER 6

1. Meillet (1917: 74), my translation. The original reads: 'Comme la mutation consonantique et comme la transformation profonde du vocalisme, ce fait indique une influence extérieure. Il y a là un type de prononciation étranger à l'indo-européen; il a été introduit par la population qui a appris à parler le dialecte qui est devenu le germanique.'

Bibliography

Adams, J. N. (2007). *The Regional Diversification of Latin 200 BC–AD 600*. Cambridge: Cambridge University Press.

Aikio, A. (2004). An essay on substrate studies and the origin of Saami. In I. Hyvärinen, P. Kallio, J. Korhonen (Eds.), *Etymologie, Entlehnungen und Entwicklungen* (pp. 5–34). Helsinki: Société Néophilologique.

———. (2006). On Germanic-Saami contacts and Saami prehistory. *Suomalais-Ugrilaisen Seuran Aikakauskirja 91*, 9–55.

Bavel, B., van. (2010). *Manors and Markets: Economy and Society in the Low Countries, 500–1600*. Oxford: Oxford University Press.

Bergin, O. (1946). *Ériu* and the ablaut. *Ériu 14*, 147–153.

Berteloot, A. (1984). *Bijdrage tot een Klankatlas van het Dertiende-eeuwse Middelnederlands*. Koninklijke Academie voor Nederlandse Taal- en Letterkunde.

Blok, D. P. (1974). *De Franken in Nederland*. Bussum: Fibula-Van Dishoek.

———. (1981). Hoofdlijnen van de bewoningsgeschiedenis. In *Algemene Geschiedenis der Nederlanden* I (pp. 143–152). Haarlem: Fibula Van Dishoeck.

Bonnet, M. (1890). *Le latin de Grégoire de Tours*. Paris: Hachette.

Bourciez, E. (1946). *Eléments de linguistique romane*. Paris: Klincksieck.

Boutkan, D. (1995). *The Germanic Auslautgesetze*. Amsterdam: Rodopi.

Boutkan, D., Kossmann, M. (1996). *Het stadsdialect van Tilburg* (Cahiers van het P. J. Meertens-Instituut nr. 7). Amsterdam: P. J. Meertens-Instituut.

Buccini, A. (1988). Umlaut alternation, variation, and dialect contact: Reconditioning and deconditioning of umlaut in the prehistory of the Dutch dialects. In T. alsh (Ed.), *Synchronic and Diachronic Approaches to Linguistic Variation and Change* (pp. 63–80). Washington, DC: Georgetown University Press.

———. (2010). Between Pre-German and Pre-English: The origin of Dutch. *Journal of Germanic Linguistics 22*, 301–314.

Campbell, A. (1977). *Old English Grammar*. Oxford: Oxford University Press.

Charles-Edwards, T. M. (2000). *Early Christian Ireland*. Cambridge: Cambridge University Press.

———. (2012). *Wales and the Britons, 350–1064*. Oxford: Oxford University Press.

Coates, R. (2007). Invisible Britons: The view from linguistics. In N. J. Higham (Ed.), *Britons in Anglo-Saxon England* (pp. 172–191). Woodbridge: Boydell Press.

Coates, R., Breeze, A. (2000). *Celtic Voices, English Places: Studies of the Celtic Impact on Place-Names in England*. Stamford: Shaun Tyas.

Collinder, B. (1965). *Hat das Uralische Verwandte? Eine sprachvergleichende Untersuchung* (Acta Societatis Linguisticae Upsaliensis 1.4). Uppsala: Societas Linguistica Upsaliensis.

Collingwood, R. G., et al. (1990–1995). *The Roman Inscriptions of Britain*. 2 vols. Stroud: Sutton.

Crompvoets. H. (1988). De beide Limburgen als dialectologisch slagveld. In J. Goossens (Ed.), *Woeringen en de Oriëntatie van het Maasland* (pp. 89–109) Bijlagen van de Vereniging voor Limburgse Dialect- en Naamkunde, nr. 3.). Hasselt: Vereniging voor Limburgse Dialect- en Naamkunde. Daan, J. H., Francken, M. J. (1972). *Atlas van de Nederlandse Klankontwikkeling*. Vol. 1 Amsterdam: Noord-Hollandse Uitgevers Maatschappij.

Daan, J. H., Francken, M. J. (1977). *Atlas van de Nederlandse Klankontwikkeling*. Vol. 2. Amsterdam: Noord-Hollandse Uitgevers Maatschappij.

Davis, G. (2005). Entstehung und Alter der hochdeutschen Lautverschiebung in Wermelskirchen. *Zeitschrift für Dialektologie und Linguistik 72*, 257–277.

———. (2008a). Analogie, intrinsische Dauer, und Prosodie: Zur postvokalischen Ausbreitung der ahd. Lautverschiebung im Fränkischen. *Beiträge zur Geschichte der deutschen Sprache und Literatur 130*, 1–17.

———. (2008b). Towards a progression theory of the OHG consonant shift. *Journal of Germanic Linguistics 20/3*, 197–241.

———. (2011). The dialect of Wermelskirchen: Three vowel systems in just 40 years? *Zeitschrift für Dialektologie und Linguistik 78/3*, 321–333.

De Bernardo Stempel, P. (2000). Ptolemy's Celtic Italy and Ireland: A linguistic analysis. In D. Parsons, P. Sims-Williams (Eds.), *Ptolemy: Towards a Linguistic Atlas of the Earliest Celtic Place-Names of Europe* (pp. 83–112). Aberystwyth: CMCS Publications.

Derks, T., Roymans, N. (2002). Seal-boxes and the spread of Latin literacy in the Rhine delta. In Alison Cooley (Ed.), *Becoming Roman, Writing Latin? Literacy and Epigraphy in the Roman West* (pp. 87–134). *Journal of Roman Archaeology*, supplementary series number 48.

Durie, M., Ross, M. (Eds.) (1996). *The Comparative Method Reviewed: Regularity and Irregularity in Language Change*. Oxford: Oxford University Press.

Durrell, M. (1990). Westphalian and Eastphalian. In C. V. J. Russ (Ed.), *The Dialects of Modern German: A Linguistic Survey* (pp. 59–90). London: Routledge.

Edwards, N. (2007). *A Corpus of Early Medieval Inscribed Stones and Stone Sculpture*, Vol. 2, *South-West Wales*. Cardiff: University of Wales Press.

Ekwall, E. (1975). *A History of Modern English Sounds and Morphology*. Oxford: Blackwell.

Filppula, M., Klemola, J., Pitkänen, H. (Eds.) (2002). *The Celtic Roots of English* (Studies in Languages 37). Joensuu: University of Joensuu, Faculty of Humanities.

Franck, J. (1910). *Mittelniederländische Grammatik mit Lesestücken und Glossar*. Leipzig: Tauchnitz.

Goblirsch, K. (2005). *Lautverschiebungen in den germanischen Sprachen*. Heidelberg: Winter.

Goossens, J. (1962). Die gerundeten Palatalvokale im niederländischen Sprachraum. *Zeitschrift für Mundartforschung 29*, 312–328.

———. (1980). Middelnederlandse vocaalsystemen. *Verslagen en Mededelingen van de Koninklijke Academie voor Nederlandse Taal- en Letterkunde 1980/2*, 161–251.

Grandgent, C. H. (1907). *An Introduction to Vulgar Latin*. Boston: Heath & Co.

Greene, D. (1973). The growth of palatalisation. *Transactions of the Philological Society 1973*, 127–136.

Grimmer, M. (2007). Britons in early Wessex: The evidence of the law code of Ine. In N. J. Higham (Ed.), *Britons in Anglo-Saxon England* (pp. 102–114). Woodbridge: Boydell Press.

Gusmani, R. (1996). Die hochdeutsche Lautverschiebung in den altdeutschen 'Pariser Gesprächen'. *Historische Sprachforschung 109*, 133–143.

Gysseling, M. (1960). Chronologie van enkele klankverschijnselen in het oudste Fries. In K. Dijkstra (Ed.), *Fryske Studzjes Oanbean oan Prof. dr. J. H. Brouwer* (pp. 77–80). Assen: Van Gorcum.

———. (1961). *Proeve van een Oudnederlandse Grammatica*. Gent: Studia germanica gandensia.

———. (1981). Germanisering en taalgrens. In *Algemene Geschiedenis der Nederlanden I* (pp. 100–115). Haarlem: Fibula Van Dishoeck.

Hahmo, S.-L., Hofstra, T., Kylstra, A. D., Nikkilä, O. (Eds.) (1991–2012). *Lexikon der älteren germanischen Lehnwörter in den ostseefinnischen Sprachen*. Vols. 1–3. Amsterdam: Rodopi.

Harvey, A. (1985). The significance of *Cothraige*. *Ériu 36*, 1–9.

Hasenclever, M. (1905). *Der Dialekt der Gemeinde Wermelskirchen*. Marburg: Elwert.

Haubrichs, W. (1987). Lautverschiebung in Lothringen. In R. Bergmann et al. (Eds.), *Althochdeutsch*, Vol. 2, *Wörter und Namen, Forschungsgeschichte* (pp. 1350–1400). Heidelberg: Winter.

Heeroma, K. (1951). Ontspoorde frankiseringen. *Tijdschrift voor Nederlandse Taal en Letterkunde 68*, 81–96.

Helimski, E. (1995). Proto-Uralic gradation: Continuation and traces. In H. Leskinen (Ed.), *Congressus Octavus Internationalis Fenno-Ugristarum 10.–15.8.1995. Pars I Orationes plenariae et conspectus quinquennales* (pp. 17–51). Jyväskylä: Moderatores.

Heusler, A. (1964). *Altisländisches Elementarbuch*. Heidelberg: Winter.

Higham, N. J. (2007). Britons in Anglo-Saxon England: An introduction. In N. J. Higham (Ed.), *Britons in Anglo-Saxon England* (pp. 1–15). Woodbridge: Boydell Press.

Hill, E. (2003). *Untersuchungen zum inneren Sandhi des Indogermanischen* (Münchener Forschungen zur historischen Sprachwissenschaft 1). Bremen: Hempen Verlag.

Hines, J. (1990). Philology, archaeology and the *Adventus Saxonum vel Anglorum*. In A. Bammesberger, A. Wollmann (Eds.), *Britain 400–600: Language and History* (pp. 17–36). Heidelberg: Winter.

Hirt, H. (1931). *Handbuch des Urgermanischen I*. Heidelberg: Winter.

Hofman, R., Smelik, B., Toorians, L. (Eds.) (2000). *Kelten in Nederland*. Utrecht: de Keltische Draak.

Howell, R. B. (2006). Immigration and koineisation: The formation of early modern Dutch urban vernaculars. *Transactions of the Philological Society 104/2*, 207–227.

Isaac, G. (2003). Some Old-Irish etymologies, and some conclusions drawn from them. *Ériu 53*, 151–155.

———. (2009). A note on the name of Ireland in Irish and Welsh. *Ériu 59*, 49–55.

Itkonen, T. (1997). Reflections on Pre-Uralic and the 'Saami-Finnic Protolanguage'. *Finnisch-Ugrische Forschungen 54*, 229–266.

Iverson, G., Salmons, J. (2006). Fundamental regularities in the second consonant shift. *Journal of Germanic Linguistics 18*, 45–70.

Jackson, K. H. (1953). *Language and History in Early Britain*. Edinburgh: Edinburgh University Press.

Jellinek, M. (1891). *Beiträge zur Erklärung der germanischen Flexion*. Berlin: Speyer und Peters.

Jespersen, O. (1922). *Language*. London: Allen and Unwin.

Kager, R. W. J. (2007). Representations of [voice]: Evidence from acquisition. In J. M. van de Weijer, E. J. van der Torre (Eds.), *Voicing in Dutch* (pp. 41–80). Amsterdam: John Benjamins.

Kallio, P. (2000). Posti's superstrate theory at the threshold of a new millennium. In J. Laakso (Ed.), *Facing Finnic: Some Challenges to Historical and Contact Linguistics* (Castrenianumin toimitteita 59, pp. 80–99). Helsinki: Suomalais-Ugrilainen Seura.

———. (2007). Kantasuomen konsonanttihistoriaa. In J. Ylikoski, A. Aikio (Eds.), *Sámit, sánit, sátnehámit. Riepmočála Pekka Sammallahtii miessemánu 21. beaivve 2007* (Suomalais-Ugrilaisen Seuran Toimituksia 253, pp. 229–249). Helsinki: Suomalais-Ugrilainen Seura.

Kloeke, G. G. (1936). Woensdag: met een kaart. *Tijdschrift voor Nederlandse Taal- en Letterkunde 55*, 148–156.

Koch, J. T. (1991). Ériu, Alba, and Letha: When was a language ancestral to Gaelic first spoken in Ireland? *Emania 9*, 17–27.

———. (1994). Windows on the Iron Age: 1964–1994. In J. P. Mallory, G. Stockman (Eds.), *Ulidia: Proceedings of the First International Conference on the Ulster Cycle of Tales* (pp. 229–237). Belfast: December Publications.

Koivulehto, J. (1995). Indogermanisch-Uralisch: Lehnbeziehungen oder(auch) Urverwandtschaft? In R. Sternemann (Ed.), *Bopp-Symposium 1992 der Humboldt-Universität zu Berlin* (pp. 133–148). Heidelberg: Winter.

———. (1999). *Verba Mutuata*. Helsinki: Suomalais-Ugrilainen Seura.

Koivulehto, J., Vennemann, T. (1996). Der finnische Stufenwechsel und das Vernersche Gesetz. *Beiträge zur Geschichte der deutschen Sprache und Literatur 118/2*, 163–182.

Koller, E., Laitenberger, H. (Eds.) (1998). *Suevos-Schwaben: Das Königreich der Sueben auf der iberischen Halbinsel, 411–585*. Tübingen: Günter Narr.

Kortlandt, F. H. H. (1988). Proto-Germanic obstruents. *Amsterdamer Beiträge zur älteren Germanistik 27*, 5–6.

———. (1989). Eight Indo-Uralic verbs? *Münchener Studien zur Sprachwissenschaft 50*, 79–85.

———. (1991). Kluge's law and the rise of Proto-Germanic geminates. *Amsterdamer Beiträge zur älteren Germanistik 34*, 1–4.

———. (2001). *The Indo-Uralic verb*. Leiden: privately published.

———. (2005). The inflexion of the Indo-Germanic -stems in Germanic. *Amsterdamer Beiträge zur älteren Germanistik 60*, 1–4.

Kroonen, G. (2009). *Consonant and Vowel Gradation in the Proto-Germanic n-Stems*. PhD dissertation, University of Leiden.

———. (2010). Faeroese *ta* and its relevance to the Germanic *Auslautgesetze*. *Amsterdamer Beiträge zur älteren Germanistik 66*, 21–28.

Kuiper, F. B. J. (1995). Gothic *bagms* and Old Icelandic *ylgr*. *NOWELE 25*, 72–76.

Künzel, R. E., Blok, D. P., Verhoef, J. M. (1988). *Lexicon van Nederlandse Toponiemen tot 1200*. Amsterdam: P. J. Meertens-Instituut.

Kusmenko, J. (2011). *Der samische Einfluss auf die skandinavischen Sprachen. Ein Beitrag zur skandinavischen Sprachgeschichte*. Berlin: Nordeuropa-Institut.

Lambert, P.-Y. (1994). *La langue gauloise*. Paris: Errance.

———. (2002). *Recueil des inscriptions gauloises II.2. Textes gallo-latins sur instrumentum*. Paris: CNRS Éditions.

Landschaftsverband Rheinland (Ed.) (2008). *Die Langobarden: Das Ende der Völkerwanderung*. Bonn and Darmstadt: Rheinisches Landesmuseum Bonn.

Lehmann, W. P. (1967). *A Reader in Nineteenth-Century Historical Indo-European Linguistics*. Bloomington: Indiana University Press.

Lehtiranta, J. (1989). *Yhteissaamelainen sanasto*. Helsinki: Suomalais-Ugrilainen Seura.

Loey, A., van. (1976). *Middelnederlandse Spraakkunst II. Klankleer.* Groningen: Tjeenk Willink.

Loon, J., van. (1986). *Historische Fonologie van het Nederlands.* Leuven: Acco.

Lutz, A. (2009). Celtic influence of Old English and West Germanic. *English Language and Linguistics 13/2*, 227–249.

Macalister, R. A. S. (1945–1949). *Corpus Inscriptionum Celticarum Insularum I–II.* Dublin: Stationery Office.

Mallory, J. P. (1989). *In Search of the Indo-Europeans: Language, Archaeology and Myth.* London: Thames and Hudson.

———. (2013). *The Origins of the Irish.* London: Thames and Hudson.

McCone, K. (2005). Mögliche nicht-indogermanische Elemente in den keltischen Sprachen und einige frühe Entlehnungen aus indogermanischen Nachbarsprachen. In G. Meiser, O. Hackstein (Eds.), *Sprachkontakt und Sprachwandel* (pp. 395–435). Wiesbaden: Dr. Ludwig Reichert Verlag.

———. (2006). *The Origins and Development of the Insular Celtic Verbal Complex.* Maynooth: Department of Old Irish, National University of Ireland, Maynooth.

McManus, D. (1991). *A Guide to Ogam.* Maynooth: An Sagart.

McWhorter, J. H. (2009). What else happened to English? A brief for the Celtic hypothesis. *English Language and Linguistics 13/2*, 163–191.

Meid, W. (1980). *Gallisch oder Lateinisch? Soziolinguistische und andere Bemerkungen zu populären gallo-lateinischen Inschriften.* Innsbruck: Innsbrucker Beiträge zur Sprachwissenschaft.

Meillet, A. (1917). *Caractères généraux des langues germaniques.* Paris: Hachette.

Meyer-Lübke, W. (1890). *Grammaire des langues romanes I: Phonétique.* Paris: H. Welter.

———. (1895). *Grammaire des langues romanes II: Morphologie.* Paris: H. Welter.

Miller, D. G. (2012). *External Influences on English: From Its Beginnings to the Renaissance.* Oxford: Oxford University Press.

Möller, H. (1880). Zur Declination; germanisch AEO in den Endungen des Nomens und die Entstehung des o (a_2). *Beiträge zur Geschichte der deutschen Sprache und Literatur 7*, 482–547.

Mostert, M. (2009). *In de Marge van de Beschaving: de Geschiedenis van Nederland, 0–1100.* Amsterdam: Bert Bakker.

Mullen, A. (2007). Evidence for written Celtic from Roman Britain: A linguistic analysis of *Tabellae Sulis* 14 and 18. *Studia Celtica 41*, 31–45.

Nash-Williams, V. E. (1950). *The Early Christian Monuments of Wales.* Cardiff: University of Wales Press.

Neumann, G. (1998). Die Bezeichnung der germanischen Völker aus sprachwissenschaftlicher Sicht. In E. Koller, H. Laitenberger (Eds.), *Suevos-Schwaben: Das Königreich der Sueben auf der iberischen Halbinsel, 411–585* (pp. 1–9). Tübingen: Günter Narr.

Nielsen, H. F. (1985). *Old English and the Continental Germanic Languages:* Innsbruck: Innsbrucker Beiträge zur Sprachwissenschaft.

Okasha, E. (1993). *Corpus of Early Christian Inscribed Stones of South-West Britain.* London: Leicester University Press.

Oppenheimer, S. (2007). *The Origins of the British.* 2nd ed. London: Robinson.

O'Rahilly, T. F. (1943). On the origin of the names *Érainn* and *Ériu. Ériu 14*, 7–28.

———. (1957). *Early Irish History and Mythology.* Dublin: Dublin Institute for Advanced Studies.

Osthoff, H., Brugmann, K. (1878). *Morphologische Untersuchungen auf dem Gebiete der indogermanischen Sprachen.* Leipzig: Hirzel.

Padel, O. J. (2007). Place-names and the Saxon conquest of Devon and Cornwall. In N. J. Higham (Ed.), *Britons in Anglo-Saxon England* (pp. 215–230). Woodbridge: Boydell Press.

Parsons, D. N. (1997). British *Caratīcos*, Old English *Cerdic*. *Cambrian Medieval Celtic Studies 33*, 1–8.

———. (2011). Sabrina in the thorns: Place-names as evidence for British and Latin in Roman Britain. *Transactions of the Philological Society 109/2*, 113–137.

Pedersen, H. (1962). *The Discovery of Language*. Translated by J. W. Spargo. Bloomington: Indiana University Press.

Pelteret, D. A. E. (1995). *Slavery in Early Medieval England from the Reign of Alfred until the Twelfth Century*. Woodbridge: Boydell Press.

Pijnenburg, W. J. J. (1980). *Bijdrage tot de Etymologie van het Oudste Nederlands*. PhD dissertation, University of Leiden.

Pohl, W. (1997). The empire and the Lombards: Treaties and negotiations in the sixth century. In W. Pohl (Ed.), *Kingdoms of the Empire: The Integration of Barbarians in Late Antiquity* (pp. 75–134). Leiden: Brill.

———. (2002). *Die Völkerwanderung: Eroberung und Integration*. Stuttgart: Kohlhammer.

Pokorny, J. (1916). Der älteste Name Irlands. *Zeitschrift für vergleichende Sprachforschung 47*, 233–239.

Posti, L. (1953). From Pre-Finnic to Late Proto-Finnic: Studies on the development of the consonant system. *Finnisch-Ugrische Forschungen 31*, 1–91.

Raftery, B. (1994). *Pagan Celtic Ireland*. London: Thames and Hudson.

Raybould, M. E., Sims-Williams, P. (2007). *The Geography of Celtic Personal Names in the Latin Inscriptions of the Roman Empire*. Aberystwyth: CMCS.

Redknap, M., Lewis, J. M., Charles-Edwards, G. (2007). *A Corpus of Early Medieval Inscribed Stones and Stone Sculpture*, Vol. 1, *South-East Wales and the English Border*. Cardiff: University of Wales Press.

Remacle, L. (1948). *Le problème de l'ancien wallon*. Liège: Faculté de Philosophie et Lettres.

Renfrew, C. (1987). *Archaeology and Language: The Puzzle of Indo-European Origins*. London: Jonathan Cape.

Rheinfelder, H. (1953). *Altfranzösische Grammatik I: Lautlehre*. Munich: Hueber.

Richter, E. (1934). *Beiträge zu Geschichte der Romanismen: Chronologische Phonetik des Französischen bis zum Ende des 8. Jahrhunderts*. Halle: Niemeyer.

Riessler, M. (2008). Substratsprachen, Sprachbünde und Arealität in Nordeuropa. *NOWELE 54/55*, 99–130.

Rivet, A. L. F., Smith, C. (1979). *The Place-Names of Roman Britain*. London: Batsford.

Rix, H., et al. (Eds.) (2001). *Lexikon der indogermanischen Verben*. 2nd ed. Wiesbaden: Reichert Verlag.

Rohlfs, G. (1949). *Historische Grammatik der italienischen Sprache*. Vol. 1. Bern: Francke.

Russell, P. (2011). Latin and British in Roman and post-Roman Britain: Methodology and morphology. *Transactions of the Philological Society 109/2*, 138–157.

Sammallahti, P. (1998). *The Saami Languages, an Introduction*. Karasjok: Davvi Girji.

———. (1999). Saamen kielen ja saamelaisten alkuperästä. In P. Fogelberg (Ed.), *Pohjan poluilla: Suomalaisten juuret nykytutkimuksen mukaan* (pp. 70–90). Helsinki: Suomen Tiedeseura.

Sargent, A. (2002). The north-south divide revisited: Thoughts on the character of Roman Britain. *Britannia 33*, 219–226.

Schönfeld, M. (1932). *Oe-relicten in Holland en Zeeland.* Mededelingen van de Koninklijke Academie van Wetenschappen, Afdeeling Letterkunde, Vol. 73. Amsterdam: Koninklijke Academie van Wetenschappen

Schönfeld, M., Van Loey, A. (1970). *Schönfelds Historische Grammatica van het Nederlands.* Zutphen: Thieme.

Schrijver, P. (1995a). *Studies in British Celtic Historical Phonology.* Amsterdam: Rodopi.

———. (1995b). Welsh *heledd, hêl,* Cornish **heyl,* "Latin" *Helinium,* Dutch *zeelt. NOWELE 26,* 31–42.

———. (1999). The Celtic contribution to the development of the North Sea Germanic vowel system, with special reference to Coastal Dutch. *NOWELE 35,* 3–47.

———. (2000). Non-Indo-European surviving in Ireland in the first millennium AD. *Ériu 51,* 95–99.

———. (2001). Lost languages in northern Europe. In C. Carpelan, A. Parpola, P. Koskikallio (Eds.), *Early Contacts between Uralic and Indo-European: Linguistic and Archaeological Considerations* (pp. 417–425). Helsinki: Suomalais-Ugrilainen Seura.

———. (2002). The rise and fall of British Latin: Evidence from English and Brittonic. In M. Filppula, J. Klemola, H. Pitkänen (Eds.), *The Celtic Roots of English* (Studies in Languages 37, pp. 87–110). Joensuu: University of Joensuu, Faculty of Humanities.

———. (2003a). Early developments of the vowel systems of North-West Germanic and Saami. In A. Bammesberger, T. Vennemann (Eds.), *Languages in Prehistoric Europe* (pp. 195–226). Heidelberg: Winter.

———. (2003b). The etymology of Welsh *chwith* and the semantics and morphology of PIE **k(ʷ)sweibʰ-.* In Paul Russell (Ed.), *Yr Hen Iaith: Studies in Early Welsh* (pp. 1–23). Aberystwyth: Celtic Studies Publications.

———. (2005a). Early Celtic diphthongization and the Celtic-Latin interface. In J. de Hoz et al. (Eds.), *New Approaches to Celtic Place-Names in Ptolemys Geography* (pp. 55–67). Madrid: Ediciones Clásicas.

———. (2005b). More on non-Indo-European surviving in Ireland in the first millennium AD. *Ériu 55,* 137–144.

———. (2007). What Britons spoke around 400 AD. In N. J. Higham (Ed.), *Britons in Anglo-Saxon England* (pp. 165–171). Woodbridge: Boydell Press.

———. (2009). Celtic influence on Old English: Phonological and phonetic evidence. *English Language and Linguistics 13/2,* 193–211.

———. (2011a). The High German consonant shift and language contact. In C. Hasselblatt, P. Houtzagers, R. van Pareren (Eds.), *Language Contact in Times of Globalization* (pp. 217–249). Amsterdam: Rodopi.

———. (2011b). Old British. In E. Ternes (Ed.), *Brythonic Celtic-Britannisches Keltisch: From Medieval British to Modern Breton* (pp. 1–84). Bremen: Hempen Verlag.

Schumacher, S. (2007). *Die Deutschen und die Nachbarstämme*: Lexikalische und strukturelle Sprachkontaktphänomene entlang der keltisch-germanischen Übergangszone. *Keltische Forschungen 2,* 167–207.

Schützeichel, R. (1956). Zur ahd. Lautverschiedung am Mittelrhein. *Zeitschrift für Mundartforschung 24,* 112–24.

———. (1960). *Mundart, Urkundensprache und Schriftsprache: Studien zur Sprachgeschichte am Mittelrhein.* Bonn: Röhrscheid.

Schwan, E., Behrens, D. (1963). *Grammatik des Altfranzösischen.* Darmstadt: Wissenschaftliche Buchgesellschaft.

Seebold, E. (1998). Die Sprache(n) der Germanen in der Zeit der Völkerwanderung. In E. Koller, H. Laitenberger (Eds.), *Suevos-Schwaben: Das Königreich der Sueben auf der iberischen Halbinsel, 411–585* (pp. 11–20). Tübingen: Günter Narr.

Sims-Williams, P. (2003). *The Celtic Inscriptions of Britain: Phonology and Chronology, c. 400–1200.* Oxford: The Philological Society.

Smith, C. (1983). Vulgar Latin in Roman Britain: Epigraphic and other evidence. In H. Temporini, W. Haase (Eds.), *Aufstieg und Niedergang der römischen Welt*, Vol. 29/2. (pp. 893–948). Berlin: de Gruyter.

Stotz, P. (1996–2004). *Handbuch der lateinischen Sprache des Mittelalters.* Munich: Beck.

Stüber, K. (1998). *The Historical Morphology of n-Stems in Celtic.* Maynooth: Department of Old Irish, National University of Ireland, Maynooth.

Sykes, B. (2007). *Saxons, Vikings, and Celts: The Genetic Roots of Britain and Ireland.* New York: Norton.

Taeldeman, J. (1978). *De Vokaalstructuur van de 'Oostvlaamse' Dialekten.* Amsterdam: Noord-Hollandse Uitgevers Maatschappij.

Thomas, C. (1991–1992). The early Christian inscriptions of southern Scotland. *Glasgow Archaeological Journal 17*, 1–10.

Thomason, S. (2001). *Language Contact: An Introduction.* Edinburgh: Edinburgh University Press.

Thomason, S., Kaufman, T. (1988). *Language Contact, Creolization, and Genetic Linguistics.* Berkeley: University of California Press.

Tomlin, R. S. O. (1987). Was British Celtic ever a written language? Two texts from Roman Bath. *Bulletin of the Board of Celtic Studies 34*, 18–25.

———. (1988). The Curse Tablets. In B. Cunliffe (Ed.), *The Temple of Sulis Minerva at Bath*, Vol. 2, *The Finds from the Sacred Spring* (pp. 59–277). Oxford: Oxford University Committee for Archaeology.

Tristram, H. (Ed.) (1997). *The Celtic Englishes.* Heidelberg: Winter.

———. (2000). *The Celtic Englishes.* Vol. 2. Heidelberg: Winter.

———. (2003). *The Celtic Englishes.* Vol. 3. Heidelberg: Winter.

———. (2005). *The Celtic Englishes.* Vol. 4. Potsdam: Universitätsverlag Potsdam.

Uhlich, J. (1995). On the fate of intervocalic *-u?- in Old Irish, especially between neutral vowels. *Ériu 46*, 11–48.

Vaan, M., de (2011). West Germanic *ai in Frisian. *Amsterdamer Beiträge zur älteren Germanistik 67*, 301–314.

Vennemann, T. (1984). Hochgermanisch und Niedergermanisch: Die Verzweigungstheorie der germanisch-deutschen Lautverschiebungen. *Beiträge zur Geschichte der deutschen Sprache und Literatur 106*, 1–45.

———. (1998). Zur Etymologie von *Éire*, dem Namen Irlands. *Sprachwissenschaft 23*, 461–469.

———. (2008). Lombards and Lautverschiebung: A unified account of the High Germanic Consonant Shift. *Sprachwissenschaft 33*, 213–256.

Wagner, N. (1977). Butilin und die zweite Lautverschiebung. *Sprachwissenschaft 2*, 338–248.

Weinreich, U. (1953). *Languages in Contact.* The Hague: Mouton.

Weijnen, A. A. (1964). Fonetische en grammatische parallellen aan weerszijden van de taalgrens. *Tijdschrift voor Nederlandse Taal- en Letterkunde 80*, 1–25.

———. (1991). *Vergelijkende Klankleer van de Nederlandse Dialecten.* 's Gravenhage: SDU.

Wijk, N., van. (1907–1908). Germanisches. *Indogermanische Forschungen 22*, 250–266.

Williams, I. (1943). II. The Epigraphy of the Inscription. In C. Fox et al. (Eds.), *The Domnic Inscribed Slab, Llangwyryfon, Cardiganshire* (Archaeologia Cambrensis 97, pp. 205–212).

Woolf, A. (2003). The Britons: From Romans to barbarians. In H.-W. Goetz et al. (Eds.), *Regna and Gentes* (pp. 355–373). Leiden: Brill.

———. (2007). Apartheid and economics in Anglo-Saxon England. In N. J. Higham (Ed.), *Britons in Anglo-Saxon England* (pp. 115–129). Woodbridge: Boydell Press.

Wormald, P. (2003). The *Leges Barbarorum*: Law and ethnicity in the post-Roman West. In H.-W. Goetz, J. Jarnut, W. Pohl (Eds.), *Regna and Gentes* (pp. 21–53). Leiden: Brill.

Ziegler, S. (1994). *Die Sprache der altirischen Ogam-Inschriften*. Göttingen: Vandenhoeck & Ruprecht.

Index

The index comprises three sections: **Symbols** refers to explanations of linguistic symbols. The **Thematic index** refers to topics that are not readily evoked by the table of contents. The **Linguistic index** contains references to words from the languages discussed in the book.

Numbers refer to pages. Superscript numbers refer to endnote numbers.

SYMBOLS

THEMATIC INDEX

affricate 99; in Gallo-Romance 111–12
Afrikaans 18
Alans 115
Alboin 114
Anglo-Norman 14
Anglo-Saxon settlement of Britain 15, 22
Arbogast 143
archaeology and linguistics 73–4
aspiration: associated with Romance palatalization 110–13; loss in Dutch 122, 152; of plosives in German 100–1, 103, 109–10; of plosives in Germanic 109–10, 122; of plosives in South African English 18
Audoin 114
auxiliary 'to do': Celtic 24; English 21–2, 93
Avar 96, 114

Baltic 177
Balto-Finnic 160; convergence with Germanic 162–79
Batavians 141–2, 153; Batavian revolt 208[80]
Bath pendant 49–52
Baudecet: Gaulish inscription of 49, 51
Bauto 143
Benrather Line 104
bilingualism 14
bottleneck: population bottleneck influences language diversity 84
breaking: in Old English 62, 89, in Old Frisian and Old Norse 65; *see also* umlaut
Breton 16; reconstruction of 30–1
Brigantians 86, 208[80]
Britain: number of inhabitants in late Antiquity 16; Roman Britain society in the early Middle Ages 19
British Celtic 30–1; early phonetics well preserved in Irish 87; eastern and western 30–1; Latin affecting 32; linguistic distance between Irish and 79–81; Lowland and Highland 32–3; Lowland British Celtic sources 49–57; vowel system in Highland 72
Burgundians 115

case loss in English 21
Celtic: contact with Germanic on Continent 93; contraction 14; language family 10; in the Low Countries 141; P-Celtic and Q-Celtic 80–1; *see also* British Celtic
Châteaubleau: Gaulish inscription of 49–52
chronology: absolute chronology of sound changes 28–30; relative chronology of sound changes 25–7
Codex Sangallensis 116
Cologne 102
comparative method 5–11
competition between languages 13–14
complementary distribution 166
consonant gradation 167–73
Cornish 16; reconstruction of 30–31

derivation 78
dialect 12; dialect continuum 31
diphthong 10
Dorestad 154
Dutch: basis of Dutch koine 156–7; Coastal Dutch 127–30; Eastern Dutch 125; expansion over Romance territory 97; language shift from French to Dutch 149–52; loss of aspiration 122–3; loss of old vowel quantity 152–3; $\bar{u}$ / $\bar{y}$ isogloss continued into French 135; Western Dutch 126–7, 131–6, 137–41; Western Dutch resulting from contact between Frisian and Franconian 138–41
Duurstede 154

Eburones 141
Edictum Rothari 115
English: Celtic influence on Middle English 21–2; Celtic influence on Old English 87–91; double paradigm of 'to be' 92–3; expansion 12–14; Irish English 59–60; Old English vowel systems 62–3; South African English 18; written standard 21–2

LINGUISTIC INDEX

Saxon (Old)
blōmo 181
brōðar 186
dagos 181
fugl 134
godo 181
nerede 186
settian 124
skāp 128
thiodæ 181

Welsh (Old, Middle, Modern)
afon 33
athref 212[43]
byddaf 92
carawys 30
chwyfu 95
crug 33
dewin 206[47]
diskynn 54
dyn 44
dyn 68
dyweddi 206[47]
ebestyl 44
Emreis, Emrys 43–4
esgyb 44
Gwynnhoedl 28

hunn 26
hwnn 26
Iwerddon 78, 207[68]
keirch 43
kenif 50
kymynn 30
kyrn 43
Llundein 43, 53–7
llwyn 205[28]
llyry 44
Meilyg 44
myfyr 44
nawfed 203[3]
penn 33
pryd 80
pynt 44
Pyr 44
rhos 33
seil 43
Selyf 44
swyn 205[28]
Tudyr 44
wyf 92
wythfed 203[3]
yspeil 43
ystyr 44
Ywerddon 77–8, 207[68]